Navigating Uncertainty

For Jake and Kate, both navigating an uncertain world in their own ways.

Navigating Uncertainty

Radical Rethinking for a Turbulent World

Ian Scoones

polity

First published in 2024 by Polity Press

Polity Press
65 Bridge Street
Cambridge CB2 1UR, UK

Polity Press
111 River Street
Hoboken, NJ 07030, USA

ISBN-13: 978-1-5095-6007-3
ISBN-13: 978-1-5095-6008-0(pb)

A catalogue record for this book is available from the British Library.

Library of Congress Control Number: 2024931431

Typeset in 10.5 on 12pt Sabon
by Fakenham Prepress Solutions, Fakenham, Norfolk NR21 8NL

Printed and bound by CPI Group (UK) Ltd, Croydon, CR0 4YY

The publisher has used its best endeavours to ensure that the URLs for external websites referred to in this book are correct and active at the time of going to press. However, the publisher has no responsibility for the websites and can make no guarantee that a site will remain live or that the content is or will remain appropriate.

Every effort has been made to trace all copyright holders, but if any have been overlooked the publisher will be pleased to include any necessary credits in any subsequent reprint or edition.

For further information on Polity, visit our website:
politybooks.com

Contents

Preface and Acknowledgements

This book has emerged through a long process. The disconnect between accredited science and so the recommendations for management and policy – often steeped in western, colonial assumptions – and what farmers and pastoralists in many parts of the world actually do as they navigate uncertainty has troubled me for a long time.

In the 1980s, I trained as a biologist and for my PhD was expected to use quantitative bioeconomic modelling techniques to look at livestock population dynamics, but the field realities in Zimbabwe just didn't match. Later, I went on to think more broadly about pastoral systems and how, in highly variable environments, mainstream rangeland management approaches are a poor fit. Uncertainty was a central theme, and I even edited a book called *Living with Uncertainty* in 1994, building on research collaborations with Roy Behnke, Camilla Toulmin and others exploring 'non-equilibrium' rangeland ecologies. My post-PhD work in Zimbabwe focused on risk and uncertainty in dryland farming systems and was explored in our 1996 book, *Hazards and Opportunities*.

Through all these experiences, how standard ways of thinking and approaches to planning and management do not match lived realities became increasingly apparent. The existing approaches to development were simply not working in uncertain settings. Subsequent work on environmental policy narratives, sustainable livelihoods and the politics of policy processes all reinforced this. It was through the ESRC STEPS Centre, based at the Institute of Development Studies (IDS) and the Science Policy Research Unit (SPRU) at the University of Sussex from 2006 to 2021, that these themes really came together. In our 2010 book, *Dynamic Sustainabilities*, we explored how pathways to sustainability are always contingent, uncertain and negotiated politically.

My European Research Council (ERC) Advanced Grant that supported the PASTRES programme (Pastoralism, Uncertainty and Resilience: Global Lessons from the Margins, pastres. org) from 2017 to 2023 was the opportunity to examine some of these issues more deeply. Working with six amazing PhD students and other colleagues conducting studies in six countries in Africa, Asia and Europe, we investigated how pastoralists understand and respond to diverse uncertainties. Our collective book published in 2023, *Pastoralism, Uncertainty and Development*, shared some of the findings. Some of our cross-cutting research on uncertainty, which this book draws on, is now illustrated in a series of fantastic cartoons drawn by Dan Locke (pastres.org/uncertainworlds), while photo-stories and documentary photography curated by Roopa Gogineni and Shibaji Bose highlight how uncertainty is perceived across our research sites (seeingpastoralism.org).

In 2019, the PASTRES programme and the STEPS Centre co-hosted an incredibly formative symposium focused on the theme of 'uncertainty'. With contributions on topics ranging from finance to pandemics, migration, crime and religion, we examined how a focus on uncertainty offered important challenges for societal transformation (steps-centre.org/uncertainty). The 2020 book that I co-edited with Andy Stirling, *The Politics of Uncertainty*, offered a huge range of perspectives across twelve great chapters.

This book emerges from all these experiences and more. While the wider intellectual debates about risk and uncertainty have informed and challenged my thinking, it has been the grounded experiences in different places that have brought these to life. In this book, I have tried to combine real-life case studies with broader reflections, linking to debates in the literature. Many of the cases come from my own research work, but there are also others from students and colleagues who have been working on these themes. All informants' quotes have been anonymized, but hopefully these voices help make the arguments more tangible and real. In each of the chapters, I have included examples from both the so-called 'global North' and 'global South' since the uncertain challenges we face are of course universal. Each chapter in this book takes a different theme, most of which I have worked on in one way or other. The chapter on finance connects the experience of the global financial crash with work I have done on informal markets in pastoral areas and connects to the wider challenges of ensuring that economic analysis addresses the epistemic challenge of uncertainty. The next chapter on technology draws on our work on agricultural biotechnology in Brazil, India, southern Africa and the United Kingdom, while the following chapter on critical infrastructure is indebted to conversations with Emery Roe over many years and PASTRES work with pastoralists in Kenya. The chapter on pandemics builds on work by the STEPS Centre and more recent work in Zimbabwe on the COVID-19 pandemic, while the final two thematic chapters on disasters and climate change in many ways cut across work that I have done over a long time on drought responses in dryland farming and pastoral areas in Africa.

This is not a conventional 'academic' book, although I hope it shows rigour and depth, and sources for further reading are provided in the text. Instead, this short book aims to offer a big-picture argument in a reasonably accessible style about how taking uncertainty seriously must reshape our world. The radical rethinking in the subtitle means drawing on diverse sources and inspirations, and making the connections across places, people, disciplines and sectors that only a book covering such a wide range of themes and cases from such diverse settings can do.

Responding to uncertainty requires the skills of navigation, the book argues. This means drawing on multiple knowledges and deep practical wisdom. There is no single path, and destinations must always be negotiated. Under conditions of uncertainty, we cannot predict and plan but must use a range of skills and capabilities to ensure a reliable passage. Such navigation may be challenging, and there can be many obstacles. Political, economic, social or cultural barriers may prevent some people reaching a desired destination, while for others sailing through is easy. Histories of colonization, marginalization and exclusion may affect what uncertainties emerge for whom. Navigating uncertainty – the title of the book – is thus always political, contested and contingent.

Writing this book was made possible by a three-month writing sabbatical from IDS, my first in 28 years at the Institute. Additional thinking and writing time were made possible through my wonderfully flexible ERC Advanced Grant (No. 70432), which also supported the open-access publication of this book. Being able to think, reflect and write over several months during 2023 was an incredible luxury. A big challenge was making the book short and clear, as there was so much to say and inevitably many omissions. I hope, though, that the result is worth reading.

A book of this sort of course emerges from many interactions over many years, and there are far too many people to thank here. As co-directors of the STEPS Centre, Melissa Leach and Andy Stirling have been especially important. Others associated with the Centre have had an enormous influence, too, including, among many others, Dipak Gyawali, Mike Hulme, Sheila Jasanoff, Emery Roe and Brian Wynne. For nearly 40 years, my field-based inspirations have particularly come from Zimbabwe. These are rooted in a long-term collaboration with Felix Murimbarimba and the late B. Z. Mavedzenge and as part of collaborative research with Ben Cousins, Ruth Hall and others at PLAAS in South Africa. In East Africa, research linked to the PASTRES programme with Tahira Mohamed, Hussein Mahmoud, Michele Nori, Masresha Taye, Hussein Wario and others has also been enormously influential. And among all this, the brilliant newsletter, *The Marginalian*, put together by Maria Popova, has been an important weekly encouragement to read more widely and purchase yet more books.

Finally, I must thank my editors at Polity, Karina Jákupsdóttir and Jonathan Skerrett, the three extremely helpful anonymous reviewers and those that kindly read different parts of the manuscript, including Shibaji Bose, Michael Jonik, Hayley McGregor, Lars Otto Naess, Emery Roe, Shilpi Srivastava, Andy Stirling and Masresha Taye, as well as support with copyediting, formatting and reference checking from Ben Jackson and Gail Ferguson.

Ian Scoones, Brighton, December 2023

1

Navigating Uncertainty

Introduction

Uncertainties are everywhere. Whether it's climate change, pandemics, disasters, financial volatility, new technologies or the outbreak of war, we don't know what the future holds. Navigating uncertainties, where we cannot predict what will happen, is essential. But how is this done, and what can we learn about responding to, managing and living with, and indeed from, uncertainty from different experiences?

As Helga Nowotny (2015: 1) argues, uncertainty 'is written into the script of life'. Similarly, Bruno Latour (2007: 245) explains, 'The world is not a solid continent of facts sprinkled by a few lakes of uncertainties, but a vast ocean of uncertainties speckled with a few islands of calibrated and stabilized forms.' This book is concerned with the 'vast ocean of uncertainties' as they appear in different facets of contemporary life. In order to understand this, I have sought to ground the book in a series of themes, each central to getting to grips with how we understand and act on uncertainties, with examples drawn from diverse settings, from both the so-called global North and global South.

In terms of the themes that the book covers, I start in the next chapter with an exploration of financial crises and the challenges of managing financial volatility and the implication of taking uncertainty seriously within economic thinking and practice. I then turn to a discussion of technology and the politics of regulation, asking what is safe and for whom? Next, I move on to exploring 'critical infrastructures' and how reliability is generated by a variety of professionals and their networks, before examining the challenges of disease outbreak preparedness, drawing lessons from the COVID-19 pandemic. After that, I discuss disasters more generally and the way we prepare for and respond to them. The final thematic chapter looks at climate change, perhaps the biggest challenge of all, and how we must all learn to live with high levels of climate variability while continuing to reduce emissions. The book concludes with a discussion of ways forward and the need to transform our perspectives on uncertainty from ones of despair and fear to those of hope and opportunity, creating a new politics of care and responsibility for a turbulent world.

Later, I introduce the concept of uncertainty and distinguish it from risk.[1] All the chapters that follow contrast a control-oriented, risk-based calculative approach, where we assume we know about and can manage the future with a more flexible, practice-based approach that is responsive to uncertain conditions. The book argues that, if uncertainty is to be navigated effectively, new approaches are needed that are more open, inclusive and collective, some reclaimed and adapted from previous times and different cultures.

Uncertainties – where we don't know, or are not confident about, the likelihoods of future outcomes – are not new. While the world has always been uncertain, as the chapters that follow show, it is perhaps our modernist attempts to predict, manage and control that are failing. Today, our collective capacities for navigating uncertainty and dealing with ignorance have declined. Yet, despite the ideological commitments to certainty and control, a hubristic faith in technology, together with controlling forms of economic and political order, can quickly unravel. Providing encouragement for the future, throughout the book we will encounter different people who are incredibly well practised at living with and from uncertainty, and the book argues that we can learn a lot from them to equip us better for today's challenges. The big question for us all today is whether the dominant approach to confronting uncertainty – to reduce everything to calculable risk – is sufficient, or whether we have to re-learn and revive other approaches more attuned to an uncertain world.

Centring uncertainty

As I explore later in this chapter, there are many examples of diverse intellectual and cultural traditions where uncertainty is central. It is perhaps a peculiar anomaly that, for a relatively short period, western visions of modernity have ignored or suppressed uncertainty in the pursuit of a particularly narrow vision of 'innovation' and 'development'. Indeed, as we shall see, even within the core western canons that have framed our ideas of modernist progress, there have been many heterodox, dissenting views where uncertainties are taken seriously.

The physical and natural sciences, seen to be at the heart of modernization and progress, are of course founded on principles of uncertainty and doubt, with ignorance driving the quest for new, but never certain, knowledge (Firestein 2012). Uncertainty is key to an enlightened scientific view, much preferable, some argue, to the unconditional faith of religion.[2] As the Nobel prize-winning physicist Richard Feynman notably said:

> It is imperative in science to doubt; it is absolutely necessary, for progress in science, to have uncertainty as a fundamental part of your inner nature. To make progress in understanding, we must remain modest and allow that we do not know. Nothing is certain or proved beyond all doubt. You investigate for curiosity, because it is unknown, not because you know the answer. (Feynman 2001 [1956]: 247–8)

While Newtonian perspectives dominated with a fixed vision of universal laws, this was disrupted by quantum physics – not least through Heisenberg's 'uncertainty principle' – and more recently by developments in complexity science and chaos theory, where non-linear dynamics of complex systems are explored. Ilya Prigogine, another noted Nobel Laureate and recognized for pioneering work on complexity, dissipative structures and patterns of irreversibility, argues that 'The future is uncertain; this is true for the nature we describe and this is true on the level of our own existence. But this uncertainty is at the very heart of human creativity.'[3] He observes, 'In an unstable world, absolute control and precise forecasting are not possible' (Prigogine 1989: 396). In the celebrated book, *The End of*

Certainty: Time, Chaos, and the New Laws of Nature, written together with philosopher Isabelle Stengers (1997), they note, 'The more we know about our universe, the more difficult it becomes to believe in determinism.'

Economics with its huge influence on contemporary policy has often tried to emulate the assumed certainties of a scientific discipline through 'blackboard proofs' and elaborate equilibrium models, but these have often failed to live up to their claims, providing poor policy tools for increasingly complex and volatile economic systems (Colander and Freedman 2018; Coyle 2021; DeMartino, Grabel and Scoones 2024), just as similarly doctrinaire Soviet-style state planning (Innes 2023). Despite the attempts at developing an 'economics of control' (Lerner 1944) that would guide policy through what Milton Friedman (1953) called a 'positive economics', which was to be based on universal laws and standard models of neoclassical economics, many have argued that the pursuit of such a mechanistic view is pointless.

Prior to the narrowing of the discipline, many leading economists of course recognized the importance of uncertainty. Frank Knight, in particular, highlighted the distinction between risk and uncertainty in his 1921 book *Risk, Uncertainty and Profit*. Similarly, when thinking about future economic trends, John Maynard Keynes observed, 'about these matters there is no scientific basis on which to form any calculable probability whatever. We simply do not know . . .' (Keynes 1937: 213–14). In the same vein, but from a very different political standpoint, Friedrich von Hayek argued in his famous article, *The Use of Knowledge in Society*, that economists must take account of 'unorganized' knowledge, 'the knowledge of the particular circumstances of time and place' (Hayek 1945: 521). In his 1974 Nobel Prize speech, he argued that 'I prefer true but imperfect knowledge, even if it leaves much undetermined and unpredictable, to a pretence of exact knowledge that is likely to be false' (Hayek 1975: 438). Fortunately, such older, foundational debates in economics are being returned to today as economists grapple with our uncertain world (DeMartino, Grabel and Scoones 2024).

Such heterodox perspectives that take uncertainty seriously articulate well with the growth of ideas within other allied disciplines that also influence policy thinking, whether social

psychology, sociology or anthropology. Advances in our understandings of neurobiology and associated developments in
psychology, for example, point to the importance of human
cognition being centrally around 'surfing uncertainty', with the
brain understood as an 'action-oriented engagement machine'
(Clark 2015: 295), which is able to learn from incoming stimuli
on the go with initial guesses adapted in order to respond
to a highly dynamic world. In navigating uncertainty, the
interactions between reason, intuition and emotion become
vitally important (Damasio 2006). Current understandings go
far beyond the earlier perspectives based on risk-based experiments around gambling games and 'risk aversion weightings'
(Kahneman, Slovic and Tversky 1982; Pidgeon and Beattie
1998) to a recognition that engaging with uncertain conditions
requires continuous context-sensitive, intuitive and emotional
responses that are always adaptive, but never optimal.[4]

Within social anthropology, Mary Douglas (1966, 1986,
1992) was a pioneer in arguing that cultural perspectives
on uncertainty are essential to understanding contemporary
life. She observed that, 'Every choice we make is beset by
uncertainty. That is the condition of human knowledge . . .
unwrapping the gifts we receive from randomness, thriving
on the cusp of uncertainty and knowing when is the right
moment to act, delay or forgo action are different ways of
embracing uncertainty' (1986: 42, 172). In discussions of how
cultural practices and religious beliefs intersect with day-to-day
responses to uncertainty, social anthropological perspectives
highlight how in many settings across the world – and certainly
not just confined to some idealized 'traditional', 'pre-modern'
world – uncertainties are key (da Col and Humphrey 2012;
Cooper and Pratten 2014).

Across disciplines and policy domains, therefore, it is increasingly realized that assuming a stable, linear mechanistic view is
inadequate, even dangerous. Disciplinary training and educa-
tional systems that teach 'certain' knowledge through established
models therefore may not be fit for purpose. Take the education of
children at school. Perhaps one of the most important attributes
of a contemporary education must be to navigate uncertainty. It
is something that we all must do, and increasingly so in the face
of climate change, pandemic events, economic shocks and so
on. Yet the didactic, top-down form of education – even when

it embraces themes such as 'sustainability' – too often fails to address the soft skills required to navigate uncertainty, preferring instead to deliver 'facts' from an assumed settled 'science'. The same applies to many areas of education – like training to be a medical doctor, for instance – where in the end it is the practical skills, tacit knowledge and learned wisdom that are crucial when confronting complexity and uncertainty. At all levels, new forms of education and training are therefore required that put uncertainty centre stage (Kirby and Webb 2023).

It is perhaps no surprise that there is now a plethora of pop-psychology manuals, business guides and inspirational self-help books, Instagram feeds, TikTok accounts and YouTube videos available that highlight how individuals can confront their fears, manage risk and embrace uncertainty to become more 'resilient'.[5] This book, you may be glad to hear, is not one of this genre, but it has a similar starting point: uncertainties are very real and are central to today's world, and we need new ways of responding. Despite the dissenting, heterodox voices across disciplines and areas of practice, the very premises of many mainstream policy positions are fundamentally challenged if uncertainty is taken seriously. Whether these are equilibrium versions of neoclassical economics, the need for market-based insurance provision to 'de-risk' society or the requirements of standard risk-based regulatory systems or audit and security regimes to control and manage populations, all fail when uncertainty and ignorance impinge – where we don't know the likelihoods of outcomes or even the array of possible outcomes at all.

The core argument of this book, therefore, is that taking uncertainty seriously means rethinking our world quite fundamentally – from top to bottom, from politics and policy to individual practice. This is, as I have already hinted, not a new argument, but it is definitely an urgent one. Luckily, there are many ideas, frameworks, experiences and practices to draw from, reviving and renewing perspectives from the past and taking inspiration from diverse places and people for new, uncertain challenges. In the chapters that follow, juxtapositions of experiences from very different settings allow for wider lessons to be learned on how we need to transform our worlds of both thinking and practice in order to embrace uncertainty.

A risk society?

In 1986, Ulrich Beck's book, *Risk Society*, was published in Germany. It came on the back of a series of disasters, most notably the nuclear accident in Chernobyl, but also the *Challenger* space shuttle disaster, a massive pollution leak in Basel and so on. Risk seemed to be dominating the world, the inadvertent consequence of technological, capitalist modernity. This, Beck argued, was refashioning politics, requiring a rethinking of expertise and institutions for governance. Rather than class differences, it was the distribution of risks that had become the salient political category, he suggested (Beck 1992). The new 'sub-politics' that emerges among publics responding to the diverse risks of modernity becomes part of a period of 'reflexive modernization', he argued, leading in turn to a more 'cosmopolitan society' of engaged citizens confronting diverse risks (see Beck, Giddens and Lash 1994; Giddens 1999; Adam, Beck and van Loon 2000; Beck and Levy 2013).

Not surprisingly, these debates about 'risk' (actually in most cases referring to uncertainty and ignorance in the terms of this book; see below) generated a fevered reaction among sociologists, political scientists and public commentators. Was this really a new period in world history, one set apart by the consequences of technological risks? Or was there in fact much more continuity, with the experiences of the mid-1980s a peculiar and particular set of circumstances (Curran 2018)? Was this a phenomenon of capitalism in (mostly) northern Europe, which didn't translate into other settings? Were there in fact other forms of 'risk society' in other places and cultures (Caplan 2000; Leach, Scoones and Thompson 2002)? And has 'risk' really displaced class or other dimensions of social difference as the driver of politics, or is it actually the intersections between risk and uncertainty and class, race, gender and other dimensions of difference that are of interest (Mythen, Burgess and Wardman 2018)?

Other theorists have captured the contemporary moment in other ways. Niklas Luhmann (1993) argued that the notion of risk emerges in modern societies to replace concepts of 'danger' and more predetermined futures. Zygmunt Bauman (2013) talks of our 'liquid times', where the certainties of the past no longer apply. 'Nomadism', he suggests, is an important trait of 'liquid modern humans' as we move between networks, identities and occupations. 'Nomadic subjects' are those, Rosi Braidotti (1994) argues, who must continuously negotiate a fluid, hybrid, globalized world with new sensibilities and identities. Life is therefore necessarily shifting and mobile, improvised and adaptive, rather than fixed, sedentary and static. Societies centred on networks emerge through the accelerated processes of globalization and mobility, as well as technological connectivity (Castells 1996; Negri 2008) and, within societies, relationships are connected 'rhizomatically', creating a new form of politics constituted by uncertainty (Deleuze and Guattari 1988).

Many of these ideas continue to resonate,[6] especially in the context of the wider environmental crisis. A particularly influential strand highlights the 'systemic risks' to the planet and human survival of crossing what are termed 'planetary boundaries' (Rockström et al. 2009; Rees 2021), with 'tipping points', potentially pushing the system over the edge (Lenton et al. 2019). There are, many argue, multiple, systemic, compounding and cascading risks that are a major danger to life on Earth, combining climate change, biodiversity loss, pollution, pandemic threats and a host of other threats.

However, too often apocalyptic, dystopian visions result in calls for a control-oriented response, creating 'Earth system stability', for instance, through strong, centralized risk-based intervention, rather than imagining an alternative politics of uncertainty and sustainability. The image is of a 'cockpit' controlling the Earth, with science at the centre (Hajer et al. 2015). A strange combination of doomsday-style hype and technocratic solutionism dominates, whether around artificial intelligence or climate policy (Hulme 2023). Sadly, such a view is promoted by many who are completely sanguine about the failures of top-down technocratic approaches of the past, yet are somehow drawn to such solutions with often fantastical imaginaries of ecomodernist technology, rigid approaches to 'risk management' and a strong system of centralized environmental global governance saving the day (e.g., Asafu-Adjaye et al. 2015).

This tension around appropriate political responses to systemic risks and complex crises is being played out too around the fashionable idea of the 'polycrisis'. Popularized by economic historian Adam Tooze[7] and derived from older ideas of French sociologists Edgar Morin and Anne Brigitte Kern,[8] the term has been widely discussed by everyone from Larry Summers to the World Economic Forum in Davos.[9] That there are intersecting crises that have a combined effect is fairly obvious, and too often the discussion follows the line that the polycrisis simply needs to be managed, returning to assumed normality and stability through techno-managerial intervention. As so often happens, the term then becomes depoliticized and anodyne. Yet the idea of the polycrisis, Tooze argues, suggests that it is the systemic consequences of combined, simultaneous crises that are important – where the emergent whole is more than the sum of its parts. The polycrisis is thus new, strange, weird, something that is not ordinary or easily tamed through standard approaches.[10] This perspective draws on long-established ideas about complex systems, where non-linear interactions and deep uncertainties intertwine. In this sense, ideas around uncertainty – rather than simple risk management and control – become important.

The polycrisis is, however, not a single, time-limited event, but one located in a long history of recurrent crises of capitalism, accelerating in the 'neoliberal' era (Harvey 2007). As Giovanni Arrighi (1994) points out, centres of power are always shifting and, with a 'long view', instability is normal as contestations are continuous. Similarly, Mike Savage (2021) argues that today's world is guided by what he calls an 'imperial modernity', one constituted through actually quite predictable long-term political-economic processes centred on capitalist accumulation, colonial expansion and class, gender and racial discrimination.[11]

However, such long-run patterns, even if in some senses predictable, give rise to ongoing uncertainties about the future. The assumed stability of an international 'world order', for example, no longer applies, as power, politics and international relations reconfigure. In contrast to the conventional risk-based 'control' view, this gives rise to what Peter Katzenstein and Lucia Seybert (2018) describe as a 'protean' view of power. Taking uncertainty and complexity seriously, they argue, radically overturns standard views of global politics and international relations. Crises in capitalism – or state socialism for that matter – provoked by changing configurations of capital, land, labour, social reproduction, technology and power, and increasingly through the effects of environmental and climate change, thus give rise to new uncertainties and so new challenges for society, policy and governance, locally, nationally and globally.

Crises, like uncertainties, are constructions of knowledge, narratives that are told about both the past and the future; they are not simply 'out there' in nature. Depending on where you are situated, crises look very different – for some horrifying and scary, for others nothing out of the ordinary, just part of everyday life. As Janet Roitman (2013) argues, the idea of 'crisis' must be seen as a narrative device used to explain critical junctures, periods of contingency and fluidity, moments when truths are revealed and choices about the future are made. Crises in turn may be invoked – or actively manufactured – to support particular, powerful positions and claims, very often as routes to bringing things back to a desired 'normal'. Crises are therefore normatively defined, both in relation to what went before and what is desired for the future (Koselleck 2000).

As Antonio Gramsci (1971: 276) famously observed, 'the crisis consists precisely in the fact that the old is dying and the new cannot be born; in the interregnum a great variety of morbid symptoms appear'. Such 'morbid symptoms' may be used to argue for a return to the status quo or may be the basis for imagining alternatives at moments when things are uncertain and in flux. Who gets to define and frame a crisis is therefore extremely important. Economic, environmental, food, energy or health crises – and their many intersections in the form of the polycrisis – are constructed in this way. This is why a focus on navigating uncertainties – the product of incomplete, unsettled, indeterminate knowledges – rather than focusing on crises as ontologically defined tangible 'things' to be managed and controlled becomes so important.

As in previous periods of massive upheaval – whether the European uprisings of 1848 (Clark 2023) or the creating of a new global order in the interwar years (Tooze 2014) – what is clear today is that there is no possibility of returning to a stable 'normal': accommodating instability and navigating uncertainty are at the core of contemporary policy challenges. The process is always contingent, contested and often conflictual: there are multiple pathways and no single goal. The abiding myth of linear progress towards a singular modernity is well and truly shattered.

One default response to an acknowledgement of the centrality of uncertainty and the rejection of a planned, linear approach is to argue that an individualized, market-based response must follow, centred on a (neo)liberal, open-ended vision of modernity, where technology and the market come to the rescue. However, periods of crisis and associated uncertainty can also suggest alternative paths. As stable, linear views are challenged, multiple visions of progress and modernity open up, redefining what we mean by 'development' or 'innovation', for example. As this book argues, the challenges of navigating uncertainty can instead reveal more effective, often collective, collaborative responses. And in the process, diverse forms of what might be called a 'risk society', located in different contexts, are revealed, conditioned by a new politics of uncertainty.

Locating uncertainties

Uncertainties – and the traversing of planetary boundaries, the polycrisis and the rest – therefore do not come from nowhere. As all the chapters discuss, they are the result of long-run processes of change that generate vulnerabilities that are distributed unevenly, both across the globe and within societies, according to class, race, age, gender and so on. There are, as Amitav Ghosh (2021) explains so powerfully in *The Nutmeg's Curse*, always colonial imprints in crises. Experiences of empire and conquest help explain current crises and the responses that follow.[12]

Crises of course look different to different people in different places and must be understood as 'context' (Vigh 2008), just as uncertainty must be understood in relation to how people appreciate, accommodate and respond to variability. As Brian Wynne showed for sheep farmers in Cumbria in the United Kingdom in the wake of the Chernobyl radiation release, they understood risks in very different ways to scientists:

> Much of [the] conflict between expert and lay epistemologies centred on the clash between the taken for granted scientific culture of prediction and control, and the farmers' culture in which lack of control was taken for granted . . . The farmers assumed predictability to be intrinsically unreliable as an assumption, and therefore valued adaptability and flexibility, as a key part of their cultural identity and practical knowledge. (Wynne 1996a: 67)

In the same way, other herders – this time in Amdo Tibet in China – see uncertainties in relation to their own Buddhist worldviews. As one mentioned, 'What happened is already in the past, and what is going to happen is unpredictable; all we can depend on is the present, we deal with what is happening now.' In an impermanent world, herders have to 'embrace the ongoing, perpetual and contingent flow of processes and relations' (Tsering 2023: 53). Uncertainties are therefore not 'out there' in the world but emerge from 'the relationships between what is known and who is doing the knowing' (Scoones and Stirling 2020: 11).

This grounded, contextual perspective on uncertainty of course chimes with ideas of situated knowledges and plural and partial perspectives highlighted in feminist epistemology (Haraway 1988; Harding 1991). As with 'actor network theory' (Latour 2007), the emphasis is therefore on knowledge relations 'all the way down', as uncertainties and their implications have to be understood from different 'standpoints' and in relation to the hybrid networks that form our ideas and their effects. This may be in respect of gender, race, class or indeed emerge from the entanglements of human and non-human worlds.[13]

Risk, uncertainty and ignorance: what do we mean?

In this book, I do not use the terms 'risk', 'uncertainty' and 'ignorance' interchangeably. There are quite distinct meanings of each, with very different implications. As Andy Stirling explains (1999, 2010: Fig. 1.1), a simple matrix comparison can be drawn that contrasts knowledge about outcomes and knowledge about likelihoods of them happening, suggesting four dimensions of incertitude.

- *Risk* is when we know and are confident about the likelihoods of known outcomes, so we can predict, plan, calculate and control. This is the dominant technocratic vision, which works well in some circumstances and remains important – like when engineering a bridge, for example. But in many circumstances these conditions do not apply.

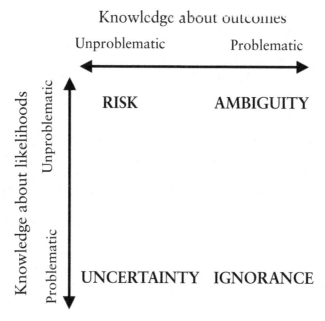

Figure 1.1 Dimensions of incertitude. *Source*: Based on Stirling (1999, 2010)

- *Uncertainty* is when we know the range of possible outcomes, but we don't know – or are not confident about – the likelihoods of them happening. This is very common. High levels of variability, non-linear interactions and complex systems all give rise to uncertainties – think any ecological, economic or political system. This of course represents quite a lot of the world's challenges.
- *Ignorance* is the condition when we don't know the outcomes nor their likelihoods when, in the famous words of Donald Rumsfeld, former US Defense Secretary, we need to address the 'unknown unknowns – the ones we don't know we don't know'.[14] Ignorance can be dangerous, whether it's the emergence of what the World Health Organization refers to as 'disease X' that emerges totally out of the blue or the surprise that arises from a 'black swan' event in a complex financial system (Taleb 2007). These are real possibilities, meaning ignorance, or non-knowledge, has to be thought about.

- *Ambiguity* is where there is dispute about the outcomes and their importance, even if we are confident about the likelihoods. Here contestation of what is important in a complex system comes to the fore, with different views expressed from different standpoints. The key issues are therefore about meanings, values and alternative views, rather than about probabilities.

Note that all these dimensions refer to *knowledge* about outcomes and their likelihoods – uncertainty (and incertitude more broadly) is not a description of the world but is about our (inevitably differentiated) understanding of it (Wynne 1992). To repeat, uncertainty is a state of knowledge, not a state of nature.[15] As this book argues across a number of cases, a variable, volatile, turbulent world gives rise to multiple forms of uncertainty, which in turn create a new politics, one that is radically different to our stable, linear, modernist view.

How, then, are uncertainties responded to? As already noted, modernist social and technical imaginaries offer an illusion of control, often based on the paraphernalia of risk management – managing according to assumptions of risk when the reality is uncertainty, even ignorance (Beck et al. 2021). Yet, as Michael Power (2004) argues, the 'risk management of everything' that has emerged as a solution as part of the 'audit culture' of the neoliberal era too often fails. Standard forms of risk assessment, management and communication – what some call risk governance (Renn 2008) – are designed to provide for the regulation of technology and the assurance of safety in the face of identified risks. However, even with greater participation in the process, including via public consultations, most such processes resort to instrumental, mechanistic routines. These fail to open up to diverse knowledges and framings, offering instead narrow, definitive pronouncements on risk, rather than plural and conditional advice that is required under conditions of uncertainty and ignorance (Stirling 2008). In the context of systemic risk – or the polycrisis, if you like – such risk management approaches are frequently applied, aiming to give a sense of authority and control.

In some ways, despite the mainstream obsession of closing down to risk and holding on to control, approaches that enable uncertainties to be navigated are becoming increasingly mainstream. The military have long recognized that volatility, uncertainty, complexity and ambiguity (VUCA) are essential features of any operation, and military strategy and organization must take these features seriously.[16] Major business consultancies, such as the RAND Corporation, have similarly developed approaches to robust decision making under deep uncertainty (Marchau et al. 2019), while large corporations, notably the oil company Shell, have long made use of flexible scenarios to think about uncertain futures as part of business planning.[17] In the international aid and humanitarian sector as well as environmental management, 'operating at the edge of chaos' (Ramalingam 2013) and 'adaptive management' (Allen and Garmestani 2015) have become increasingly influential in challenging complex, often conflict-prone places where conventional planning will not do.

These are all good starting points but do not always deal with the more radical epistemic challenges of uncertainty. Here a useful entry point is the idea of 'post-normal science', first suggested by Silvio Funtowicz and Jerry Ravetz in 1990, and extensively developed since. In conditions where uncertainties are everywhere, values clash, stakes are high and the issue is urgent (which is the case for all the themes discussed in this book, most of the time), a different type of science is needed, they argue. This requires both different sources of evidence – from multiple different origins involving different types of knowledge – and different styles of assessment – involving a wider 'extended peer community' to assess what is going on. Such an approach has many methodological as well as practical implications, not least how to deal with what John Law (2004) calls 'mess', the indeterminate, mobile, messy complexity of uncertain realities. Since most of the settings we work in can be characterized in these terms, then asking, again following Andy Stirling (2008), about how to 'open up' to uncertainty rather than 'close down' to risk is a central challenge for all of us.

Diverse perspectives

Uncertainty is therefore vital for how we navigate the world. But how is uncertainty understood more broadly? As hinted at earlier, uncertainty has been central to debates in physics, ecology, economics, social psychology, anthropology and many other disciplines, but it sometimes becomes shrouded by false certainties and hubristic visions of control as disciplines narrow. If we are to open up to uncertainty once more, given the challenges we all face, then what inspirations can we draw from? Fortunately, there are many – from diverse places and voices.

Perhaps each era is claimed as an 'age of uncertainty', as J. K. Galbraith argued for in his 1977 television series on economic and political thinking, as in each period we must face new unknowns.[18] In the sixteenth century, during the first Elizabethan era in England, none other than William Shakespeare wrote convincingly about uncertainty, reflecting on the religious conflicts of the time. Religion had once provided the absolute certainty – only God knew what the future would hold – but now a challenging, more secular world had to be confronted. While René Descartes thought that certainties could emerge through a logical science, Shakespeare used drama to explore uncertainty and how we all must navigate doubt.[19]

The Enlightenment period in Europe from the late seventeenth to early nineteenth century saw people escaping the certainties of religion as they grasped new forms of scientific rationality and reason. Probabilistic thinking emerged as a guide to negotiating this new world, inspired by the work of Thomas Bayes, Daniel Bernoulli and Pierre-Simon Laplace, among others (Hacking 1975; Stigler 1986; Daston 1988). However, for many, this was also a time of extreme precarity, making navigating uncertainties about the future central to people's lives. Literary works by the likes of Daniel Defoe and Henry Fielding emphasized the challenges of adventure and the allure of gambling as routes to escaping immiseration. The themes of luck, chance and providence repeatedly appear in the literature of the time, with the tensions between secular reason, imagination and spirituality frequently explored (Molesworth 2010; Hoydis 2019). With the emergence of Darwinian evolutionary theory and the expansion of scientific and industrial endeavour during the nineteenth century, all underpinned with contemporary ideas of statistics, many European and North American authors – such as Mary Shelley, Henry James, James Conrad and Gustave Flaubert – examined the themes of hazard, fortune, speculation and risk

through a relational exploration of an uncertain world. As
Michael Jonik argues:

Many questioned the prevailing models of determinism and causal
necessity and unsettled the bases of religious belief and scientific knowledge. Probabilistic methods spread across evolutionary
biology, demographics, health, politics, economics, urban planning,
insurance, meteorology, and military strategy, inscribing risk
and uncertainty into every aspect of life. Concomitantly, many
nineteenth-century novelists dramatized the risks individuals and
communities faced. (Jonik 2014: 21)

Responding to historical contexts over the past centuries,
therefore, many artists – and not only in Europe and North
America of course – have engaged with the unknown as a source
of inspiration and a way of engaging with the human condition.
In a letter written in 1817, the poet John Keats described how
creativity emerges from a humble, open sense of 'negative
capability' as 'when a man is capable of being in uncertainties,
mysteries, doubts, without any irritable reaching after fact and
reason.'[20]
Not surprisingly, the theme of uncertainty has also been central
to debates in philosophy and ethics. The field of virtue ethics ever
since Aristotle highlights the importance of 'practical wisdom'
(*phronesis*) when confronting uncertainty, especially when
values conflict. This complements other forms of knowledge,
either technical (*techne*) or scientific (*episteme*). As many have
argued, it is practical wisdom – often combined with technical
and scientific inputs – that becomes important when grappling
with uncertain, contested issues such as sustainability (Caniglia
et al. 2023). Such virtues emerge from learning-by-doing and
practical experience and reflection, just as happens among the
'reliability professionals' discussed in later chapters in this book.
The Greek and Roman Stoic philosophers understood clearly
that human suffering arises from attempting to control things that
are not in our control, most notably the future. The right answer
to how to respond under uncertainty is always 'it depends'; and
it depends on context, requiring the sort of practical wisdom that
virtue ethics argues for. Avoiding the imposition of top-down
plans and galvanizing individual commitments is seen as the way
forward although, as critics point out, this may avoid the wider

politics of uncertainty through locating solutions in individual behaviour.[21]

There are similarities, of course, with how world religions address uncertainty. Buddhism, with its notions of imperma-nence and unfolding change, embraces uncertainty centrally. Negotiating the relationships between humans and the world – including balancing apocalyptic threat, hope and sanctuary – are central to Christian religious beliefs (Skrimshire 2014; Oxley 2020). Islamic scriptures prohibit speculation, greed and gambling, and so Islamic finance is governed in particular ways, balancing risk and justice. In ancient Samkhya Hindu philosophy, a plural perspective on understanding, influenced by consciousness, perception and experience, equally presents ways of encountering uncertainties in the world.[22]

African religious and cultural perspectives similarly engage with uncertainties (Mawere and Mubaya 2016). As Jane Guyer (2002) explains, Yoruba identity in Nigeria is not related to a fixed substance but is more about unfolding practices, reflecting what Achille Mbembe and Sarah Nuttall (2004: 349) describe as 'the power of the unforeseen and of the unfolding . . . [and] people's relentless determination to negotiate conditions of turbulence to introduce order and predictability into their lives' (Mbembe and Nuttall 2004: 349). Among Andean peoples of South America, ideas of 'Mother Earth' (*pachamama*) offer a more holistic version of understanding the connections between people and the environment, where ambitions of external control are resisted (Velásquez 2022). An experiential, affective stance on uncertainty – whether refracted through a religious or spiritual sensibility or not – is therefore widespread among diverse cultures.

Across the world, ways of confronting uncertainty are offered by astrologers, prophets, soothsayers, clairvoyants, shamans, oracles, monks, imams, priests and their equivalents (Geschiere 1997). Ideas of fortune and luck, contingency and anticipation are wrapped up in people's experience and are central to how day-to-day practices confront uncertainties (Whyte 1997; da Col and Humphrey 2012), while rituals, performative storytelling, rumour and gossip are all ways of grappling with uncertainties, both as individuals and collectives (Graeber 2012; Newhouse 2017).

These reflections are, of course, not confined to 'pre-modern', 'traditional' societies, unhelpfully exoticized by anthropologists over the years, but are relevant everywhere. The bankers and financiers who we will meet in the next chapter were engaged continuously in ritual performance, gossip and informal discussion when confronted with market volatility; the reliability professionals governing the vagaries of the electricity system in California discussed in chapter 4 draw on deep, experiential, often tacit, practical wisdom, while the pastoralists of northern Kenya, discussed in chapter 6, when confronting drought disasters, draw on diverse knowledges – from local astronomers and the traditional forecasters, as well as satellite-informed meteorological information.

Making do in difficult circumstances, and so living for the moment in order to survive, is often an important response to a highly variable and so uncertain world. This suggests a different view of time, changing the relationship between now and the future (Johnson-Hanks 2002). Culturally embedded concepts of time affect how we view the future and our ability to predict, anticipate and control outcomes. Departing from a view of time as linear, ordered and unidimensional, this means accepting collapsed, multi-layered time (Guyer 2007; Bear 2016). As Barbara Adam argues, this implies seeing 'multiple processes simultaneously, embrac[ing] contradictions and paradoxes, the unknowable and unknown' (1996: 110).

In sum, navigating uncertainty is always located in a cultural milieu, where notions of time, the future and the role of people within a wider universe are defined. These perspectives, varying across places and people, very much condition how responses to an uncertain world are fashioned. But what are the implications for politics and for how societies can respond collectively to an uncertain world?

What about politics?

As the chapters in this book show, uncertainties in knowledge about the world are generated from a range of sources – from globalized, financialized capitalism; from the rapid development and deployment of technologies; from pandemics and other disease outbreaks; from natural hazards; and of course from climate change. And, most importantly, from the combination of all of the above – and more. Uncertainties as conditions of knowing are always the outcome of underlying structural material conditions and political economies. Some argue that a focus on uncertainty depoliticizes and ignores the structural forces that influence our world. I would argue the opposite: a focus on uncertainty centres these concerns but also highlights the knowledge politics that are crucial to addressing contemporary challenges.

At this historical juncture, it is the intersection of a particular style of globalized capitalism and a range of environmental processes, most notably climate change, that presents the greatest challenge and generates the most acute uncertainties, whether from pandemic risks or climate-related disasters (Borras et al. 2022). It is in turn the structural and historical conditions – of class, gender, race, colonialism and marginalization – that together create the circumstances that give rise to a host of uncertainties in today's world, presenting many challenges for individuals, communities and public policy alike. It is this confluence of factors that makes the argument for opening up to uncertainty so crucial, and why this book, I would argue, is important for recasting the way we think about innovation, development and public policy more generally, in both the global North and global South (Leach et al. 2021, 2024).

Ways of knowing structure political responses. The privileged, white, liberal, 'colonial' vision of modernity, with its open-ended view of the future, for example, contrasts dramatically with the experiences of much of the majority world, and indeed those especially vulnerable and exposed to uncertainties everywhere (Grove et al. 2022). A perspective that takes uncertainty seriously must, this book argues, emerge from engagement with such contexts, north and south. Natasha Lennard (2022) argues that 'The uncertainties we face today are a problem precisely because they are hinged on violent certainties – commitments held fast, which discipline the very shape of how and what it is considered reasonable to doubt.' Certainties, as representations of the world frequently linked to ideological positions, are thus 'ways of ordering the world as we live in it'. Challenging such world-ordering certainties through opening up to doubt and uncertainty is therefore imperative. In the chapters that follow, we learn how too often 'violent certainties' – imposed through models, plans and technocratic policies – structure and inform much policy and practice across domains, yet through understanding how people actually navigate uncertainties in practice, alternatives can emerge.

The way we think about 'risk' and 'uncertainty' is therefore inevitably political, and it is this knowledge politics, structured by wider political economies, which is the major focus of this book. For some, a focus on 'risk' is a route to control and management, central to the achievement of progress and modernity. An individualized approach to risk management is thus often part of the neoliberal toolbox where the market takes charge through 'de-risking'. In this way, 'seeing like a state' (Scott 1998) involves imposing order through the techniques of risk assessment and management. It is no surprise therefore that the bureaucratic state emerged from a concern with risk, statistics and probability (Hacking 1990). 'Trust in numbers' and a modernist pursuit of scientific 'objectivity' are seen as important to the ordering of public and political life and the creation of a particular style of policy (Porter 1996) centred on a 'biopolitical' imagination (Collier 2009).

Yet this is not the only way. Embracing uncertainty can result in an alternative, more hopeful, emancipatory politics. For example, James Scott (2017) contrasts the history of the ordered, regimented, controlled nature of small agrarian city-states with the pastoral 'barbarians' who made use of the extensive rangelands. They were the ones that could 'live with uncertainty' and were highly successful as a result. That our modernist model has become based on the settled agrarian vision rather than the mobile pastoral alternative is telling. Perhaps our collective failures to navigate today's uncertainties are rooted in such historical contingencies. How then can we encourage a new politics of uncertainty appropriate to contemporary societies?

As in science, acknowledging uncertainty is central to democratic, inclusive, deliberative forms of debate that can give rise to collaboration and cooperation (Dryzek 2002; Hajer and Wagenaar 2003). Centring uncertainty in democratic processes therefore means challenging singular and narrow notions of modernity and progress, which are single-tracked and hardwired. Accepting that there is no single endpoint, no uniform pathway for development and no one version of progress can be liberatory (Scoones and Stirling 2020). It requires a continuous negotiation about the direction of innovation and development and open debate about the diversity of options and the distribution of the risks and benefits that arise. And it means navigation along multiple pathways, potentially discovering new and hidden ones along the way (Leach, Stirling and Scoones 2010). Open, progressive approaches that embrace uncertainty thus must rely on informed and engaged citizens who are able to embrace uncertainty and participate in solving problems collectively using hands-on practical reasoning, as John Dewey described in his 1929 classic, *The Quest for Certainty*. Diverse perspectives are vital resources for progress, not threats to the stable order.

Once again, such perspectives are not new. Older ideas of 'progress' and 'development' – for example, from the nineteenth-century writings of Auguste Comte – highlight cyclic patterns of growth and renewal and notions of trusteeship, each engaging with the uncertain conditions of the time, rather than a version of unilinear 'development' towards a singular, modernist goal realized through 'stages' (Cowen and Shenton 1996). Accepting uncertainty therefore means rejecting both the determinism of such simplistic evolutionist thinking, as well as narrow deterministic interpretations of Marxism. Instead, a view of a transformative politics of uncertainty means 'a plural vision of progress, defined according to different standpoints, with multiple modernities at play' (Scoones and Stirling 2020: 2). This is what Ashish Kothari and others (2019) call a 'pluriverse', where subaltern visions have a platform within a 'decolonized' vision of development and change (Sultana 2022). Such a stance therefore rejects a globalizing vision of modernity that colonizes the future, with technocratic managerialism and top-down control foreclosing alternatives.

However, a view centred on a progressive politics of uncertainty is not without dangers. Uncertain spaces can, for sure, act as prefigurative sites for experimentation and innovation, opening up to hope and opportunity and a new political 'common sense', as I argue in the closing chapter, but they can also be captured by regressive forces. Uncertainties can create fear and anxiety, and so authoritarian, populist narratives offering 'stability', 'security' and 'taking back control' may appeal to the vulnerable and marginalized. In the face of troubling uncertainties, offering apparent certainty through alternative 'truths' and misinformation is a tactic deployed by populist politicians and authoritarian regimes alike (Dotson 2021). The rise of authoritarian populism in many forms across the world is a stark warning of the dangers that lie ahead when uncertainties arising from the destabilizing of a set of norms, long-standing traditions and the undermining of a protective state are exploited for regressive ends (Scoones et al. 2022).

As the book's chapters explore in different ways, an alternative, transformative style of politics must emerge where responses to uncertainty are rooted in forms of solidarity, mutuality and care. This must be inclusive of those who are marginalized, offsetting the dangers of capture by regressive authoritarian populist forces. Such a perspective means seeing uncertainty not just as a feature of an individualist response to uncertain conditions but as part of a collective politics, reclaiming the idea of uncertainty as part of a progressive political project. Rejecting the fallacy of control means accepting that lack of knowledge, even ignorance, can be empowering, allowing for the imagining of multiple, open futures. As this book repeatedly discusses, it implies reinventing many accepted, mainstream ways of doing things, whether around approaching the economy and finance or confronting pandemics and other disasters or thinking about infrastructure and technology or the threats from climate change. As each of the chapters show, embracing uncertainty must result in radically rethinking approaches to science, bureaucracy, legal processes, policymaking and their intersections, as well as the ways we organize ourselves in society, raising big questions of governance and politics.

While being very aware of the dangers and limitations, in this book I want to offer a positive, hopeful liberatory position at the same time as pushing back against the techno-managerial tendencies of closing down to risk and control and standard ways of management and planning under a narrow modernist vision of progress and development, a theme that I return to in the final chapter. This means developing the capacities to navigate uncertainties – individually and collectively as part of society and through policy support – as an active response, not simply as passive, sometimes desperate, 'coping'. And it means, at the same time, responding to the deeply structured material conditions and relations that give rise to uncertainties differentially within and across societies.

Themes and questions

In order to do this, these rather abstract, perhaps excessively
idealistic, arguments for a new politics of uncertainty need to be
grounded. This is why this book is structured around concrete
themes, each full of real-world cases. The examples I draw on
are mostly ones that I have engaged with directly, and they come
from many different places – from Europe, Africa, Asia and the
Americas. The challenge of uncertainty is a universal one, so
this is not a book about risk and uncertainty in the technologically advanced global North or about so-called 'development',
frequently constructed as a challenge for places in the global
South. Uncertainty affects us all, and in surprisingly similar
ways, making it vital that we learn across contexts, encouraging
a conversation among diverse people.

What then are some of the core questions that are asked
across the chapters? Below I list four that are all central to the
diverse themes and contrasting cases that follow. In the final
chapter, I return to them and suggest an agenda for action that
we can all engage in. Together, they add up to a very different
way of doing things.

* How can we understand complex, non-linear systems and
  what sort of organizational responses make sense?
* What are the skills and capacities of both individuals and
  collectives that allow reliability to be generated in the face of
  uncertainty?
* How should policy processes be rethought for uncertain
  conditions, moving beyond assumptions of control to a more
  collaborative mode of co-production?
* What historical and political economy contexts give rise to
  what types of uncertainty, and who do they affect?

Through engaging with these questions across the chapters that
follow, I hope that you will be convinced of the arguments for
the centrality of uncertainty laid out above. Come back to this
chapter later and see if you are! The changes required will have
to happen in many spaces across multiple levels involving many
different players. As Mary Douglas and Aaron Wildavsky (1983:
1) commented over forty years ago: 'Can we know the risks we

face, now or in the future? No, we cannot; but we must act as if we do.' Responding to complex, uncertain systems subject to dynamic, turbulent change is not easy. But that is our task, as the intersecting environmental, economic, social and political challenges that affect us all are both very real and extremely pressing.

2

Finance: Real Markets as Complex Systems

It was the evening of Sunday, 14 September 2008, and employees of Lehman Brothers had heard about the imminent collapse of the investment bank. Over-exposed to sub-prime mortgage borrowing, its asset value had collapsed. Rumours spread that a Wall Street institution of over 150 years' standing would be declared bankrupt the following day. Employees, some accompanied by family members, were in the smart metal-and-glass building in Manhattan collecting their personal belongings. The now famous images of bankers leaving the building clutching boxes, picture frames and pot plants are etched on our memories.

At the same time, in the Horn of Africa, pastoralist livestock brokers and traders, such as Mohamed Hassan from Moyale in northern Kenya, had long been involved in what, at face value, seems like a very different type of market. However, there are some important parallels. Livestock markets are cross-border, high volume and are subject to many uncertainties. Just like global financial markets, they are complex systems par excellence. In contrast to the deregulated markets that collapsed during the global financial crash, they are, however, much more embedded in local societies, governed by cultural norms and subject to continuous real-time negotiations, rather than relying on high-speed transactions and fancy algorithms. As we will see, this makes a big difference.

Lessons from the financial crash in 2007–8 are many, but an important theme described in this chapter is the importance of embedding financial and market networks in ways that allow for human interaction and effective reliability management in the face of market volatility. In order to respond to inevitable uncertainties in complex financial systems, heroic assumptions about the efficacy of models and regulatory hubris should be avoided. Moving beyond a positivist 'economics of control' promoted by a neoclassical vision of economics, there is instead a need to understand 'real markets', which are social, cultural and political, and thus the adaptive, improvised and practical ways that inevitable uncertainties can be navigated (De Alcantara 1992). The real markets of the pastoral rangelands offer some important lessons for thinking about complex financial markets everywhere, the chapter suggests, as we all must learn how to navigate the uncertainties generated by market volatility.

A complex, opaque and poorly regulated financial system

Through 2007 and 2008, the contagion of the financial crisis spread across the banking sector in the West, fuelled in particular by the sub-prime mortgage lending arrangements in the United States, where in the preceding years the value of unconventional, securitized mortgages was around US$1 trillion (Tooze 2018: 63). Banks collapsed, massive bailouts were offered and the knock-on consequences across economies were huge. Was this the beginning of the end of financialized capitalism or just a bump in the road? Was there a possibility of a last-minute rescue as with Bear Stearns bank only a few months before? We were living in a time of unprecedented financial uncertainty. Interviews with bankers on the streets of Manhattan and London the following day suggested few knew what was going on, but rumours were swirling. Asked by a news reporter what was happening in the building, one quipped 'everyone's using up credit on their canteen cards . . . We don't know what's going on.'[1] The contagion that culminated in the crisis point was a long time in the making. It was the result of a long process of deregulation, from Margaret Thatcher's 'big bang' in 1986 onwards.

The consequence was a globalized financial system that was highly complex, opaque and poorly regulated (Tett 2009).

New financial instruments were devised to extract profit from the system from special purpose vehicles (SPVs) to credit default swaps (CDS), collateralized debt obligations (CDO), structural investment vehicles (SIVs), asset-backed commercial paper (ABCP), repo markets[2] and mortgage-backed securities (MBS). The bewildering array of acronyms and actors involved meant few understood the overall system and its dynamics. In individual banks and investment firms, people were trying to make money whichever way they could through a firm belief that they were able to manage risk and generate profit. The investment banks that later became household names – whether Goldman Sachs, Merrill Lynch or Morgan Stanley – perfected the art of managing the huge amounts of cash generated in the financial system through a range of derivative instruments, such as mortgage-backed securities. Here a bundle of mortgages or other debts is bought from banks and then traded, providing further funding for home buying as long as the underlying value of the asset is maintained.[3] They are, in other words, 'investments in investments, bets about bets',[4] which assume that the stock market behaves in predictable if random ways, without sudden, surprise 'black swan' events (Taleb 2007). This was a big error.

In the United States, the emergence of the sub-prime mortgage market fuelled a boom in home ownership and mortgage debt, backed by triple-A ratings as if these were assets literally as safe as houses. This in turn attracted more investors looking for safe assets in a volatile economy, trying to offset risks. Insurance companies entered the scene offering cover against highly risky assets, while some firms bought and sold financial products, such as mortgage-based securities, with no real assets behind them. Balance sheets were stacked with dodgy products, absorbing huge pools of cash on the money markets. The 'shadow banking' system was confusing and headed for disaster – a house of cards ready to collapse (Eggert 2008; Tooze 2018).

Yet few saw this coming. Confident statements were frequently offered by the leading lights of the global financial system. In May 2006, Ben Bernanke, recently appointed as chair of the Federal Reserve, highlighted the virtues of 'financial innovation and improved risk management', including 'securitization, improved hedging instruments and strategies, more liquid markets, greater risk-based pricing, and the data collection and management systems needed to implement such innovations'. He argued that 'these developments, on net, have provided significant benefits . . . Lenders and investors are better able to measure and manage risk; and, because of the dispersion of financial risks to those more willing and able to bear them, the economy and financial system are more resilient.'[5] Similarly, in 2002, Alan Greenspan, Bernanke's predecessor as Federal Reserve chair, commented approvingly of derivatives: 'These increasingly complex financial instruments have been especial contributors . . . to the development of a far more flexible, efficient and resilient financial system.'[6]

When Raghuram Rajan – then chief economist at the International Monetary Fund and later governor of the Reserve Bank of India – presented a paper with a more sceptical and cautious tone at the celebration of Greenspan's illustrious career at Jackson Hole in the summer of 2005, his comments were rejected out of hand (Tooze 2018: 67). His paper asked a simple question: 'Has financial development made the world riskier?' Exploring the growth of new financial instruments, he argued that the incentives for risk taking had increased within the financial system, potentially with dangerous consequences. It was a good question to pose, but the response was dismissed as backward looking and misguided. In retrospect the arrogant, hubristic complacency of the financial elite is extraordinary, but when you are overly confident that a risk-based regulatory system is firmly in place, uncertainties have the nasty habit of creeping up behind you and catching you by surprise, as they did only a few years later.

Models and mayhem

By the 2000s, financial systems were truly globalized. Everything and everyone was connected in a complex web. As the economic historian Adam Tooze explains in his celebrated book *Crashed*, understanding global finance was no longer a matter of looking simply at national accounts but the complex interconnection of large firms' balance sheets linked across the world. Trade in increasingly complex financial products was occurring continuously, with billions of dollars being exchanged and transferred globally. The arrival of high-speed internet had made such transactions almost instantaneous, and the old-fashioned style of traders and brokers exchanging across the floor, over the phone or in a bar after work had long gone. Rapid, impersonal trades were the standard, guided by complex algorithms and carried out on computers connected internationally. CEOs, central banks and governments had little clue how everything worked, yet mistakenly trusted the system and the light-touch regulation while enjoying the profits.

At the centre of this complex web were mathematical models generating operational algorithms that were used to manage such interactions. In the period leading up to the crash, the now notorious Black–Scholes–Merton equation dominated the way financial interactions were understood, and a massive derivatives market based on options trading was created (MacKenzie and Spears 2014).[7] As the mathematician Ian Stewart (2012) explains: 'The Black–Scholes equation changed the world by creating a booming quadrillion-dollar industry; its generalisations, used unintelligently by a small coterie of bankers, changed the world again by contributing to a multitrillion-dollar financial crash whose ever more malign effects, now extending to entire national economics, are still being felt worldwide.'

John Kay and Mervyn King (2020: 319) agree. They comment, 'models used by regulators and financial institutions, directly derived from academic research in finance, not only failed to prevent the 2007–8 crisis but actively contributed to it.' In particular, macro-economic forecasting models used by central banks tended to fail when major shocks occurred, precisely when they were needed the most. 'The search for a single comprehensive forecasting model of the economy is fruitless,' Kay and King conclude, because 'in a non-stationary world there is no underlying probability distribution or model to discover' (2020: 348, 350).

A particular challenge of financial models is the treatment of time. Many models assume that the future replicates the past, and so parameters are fixed, timeless and immutable, resulting in little or no forecasting errors (Davidson 1982). However, as economic historian Douglass North explains, 'For an enormous number of issues that are important to us, the world is one of novelty and change; it does not repeat itself' (1999: 3). Although assumptions are increasingly being challenged (Peters 2019), the convenient fiction of ignoring temporality creates a false sense of control, as the future is collapsed into the present through a set of potentially dangerous modelling assumptions (Walter and Wansleben 2020).

In the fevered world of globalized ultra-high frequency trading during the mid-2000s, in practice no one knew what was going on. Different narratives, associated with different levels of fear and confidence, competed with each other, with many forgetting that the past – where stability and growth reigned – did not predict the future. As Andy Haldane, then the chief economist at the Bank of England, comments:

> Securitisation increased the dimensionality, and thus complexity, of the financial network. Nodes grew in size and interconnections between them multiplied. The financial cat's-cradle became dense and opaque. As a result, the precise source and location of underlying claims became anyone's guess. Follow-the-leader became blind-man's buff. In short, diversification strategies by individual firms generated heightened uncertainty across the system as a whole. (Haldane 2009a)

The sophisticated market in complex financial derivatives was spread across a huge number of actors across the world. Beyond rapid electronic exchanges, there was limited interaction between them. The system was based on limited regulation, and banks and finance houses were offered what proved to be a dangerous amount of discretion.

As Haldane (2009b: 10) observes, 'network uncertainties make it tremendously difficult for risk managers to identify and price, and hence manage, balance-sheet risk.' The whole system was immensely unstable, and banks dramatically failed the stress test (Arinaminpathy, Kapadia and May 2012; Haldane 2012). As Stefano Battiston and colleagues (2016: 10031) show, 'small errors on the knowledge of the network of contracts can lead to large errors in the probability of systemic defaults.' This is the outcome of the dynamics of 'small world' networks (Watts and Strogatz 1998). Mathematical ecology showed us decades ago that complexity does not necessarily result in system stability (May 1973) – and this was certainly the case in banking systems (Gai, Haldane and Kapadia 2011).

In ecological systems – for example, forest fires, insect pest outbreaks and infectious diseases – there are a number of features that increase the robustness of networks (May, Levin and Sugihara 2008) and so help to avoid what are called 'systemic risks' (Beale et al. 2011), in fact uncertainties. These include, for example, redundancy in system design, as well as modularity (such as using firebreaks and movement restrictions), closing feedback loops through encouraging communication within networks and identifying super-spreaders, and so identifying the nodes that spread contagion.

In the pre-crash banking system, it was the very complexity of the algorithms and the associated models that caused some of the problems, even if practitioners were perfectly aware of the models' limitations (Millo and MacKenzie 2009; Wansleben 2012). Running on high-speed computers and servers, resulting in exchanges taking place globally in nanoseconds, meant that no one knew exactly what was happening in real time. Volatility in one part of the network could spread very fast to other parts, as 'evaluation cultures' were unable to cope (MacKenzie and Spears 2014).

In sum, the increased complexity and decreased diversity of the system meant that the financial network became more and more fragile. As we will see below, the resilience of pastoral-livestock market systems rests on the networks being diverse, yet stable, rooted in local social relationships. Points in a network can act as absorbers or amplifiers of shocks, depending on the configuration. In the case of the contagion that spread during the financial crisis, certain nodes became major amplifiers as uncertainty provided the basis for profit making and accumulation on the basis of 'escalating leverage, increased trading portfolios and the design of tail-heavy financial instruments' (Haldane 2010: 9). Haldane notes how 'Risks and counterparty relationships outstripped banks' ability to manage them. Servers outpaced synapses. Large banks grew to comprise several thousand distinct legal entities. When Lehman Brothers failed, it had almost one million open derivatives' (Haldane 2010: 12).

The result was the crash, which Haldane (2010: 12) argues emerged from 'an exaggerated sense of knowledge and control'. Assumptions of control and faith in the predictive power of models were so strong that the warning signs were missed by

nearly everyone, and unpredicted combinations of events desta
bilized the system. As Kay and King (2020: 7) suggest, 'The
inability of experts to anticipate the crisis was not simply the
result of incompetence, or wilful blindness, but reflected much
deeper problems in understanding risk and uncertainty.'

Regulatory manoeuvres

As the banking system globalized, the potential for instability
increased. The ratio of capital to loans issued became a key
concern, as the amount of capital could act as a buffer if the
loan portfolio became unstable. After much negotiation, the US
Federal Reserve and the Bank of England came to a deal known
as the Capital Accord, which set a minimum level of capital that
a bank should hold. However, what became called the Basel I
agreement was open to wide interpretation, and banks took full
advantage. Regulators applied risk weightings to different loans,
fatefully ranking mortgages and mortgage-backed securities as
low risk requiring less capital to be held against them. Flexible
interpretation of the rules resulted in a lax, ineffective system
that allowed banks to make profit from continued risk-taking
(Tooze 2018: 85).

Basel II followed in 2004. Although off-balance sheet risks
were brought into the accounts, banks were allowed to use their
own risk-weighting models to decide the extent of the capital
buffer required. Self-regulation was the watchword, but it was
basically a stitch-up by the industry as the global bankers' lobby
group, the Institute of International Finance, wrote the rules for
the Basel Committee (Tooze 2018: 87). Through a system of
risk-based regulation, based on their own proprietary models,
the big banks could expand their balance sheets, including
increasing the holdings of high-yielding mortgage-backed assets.
To reduce portfolio risk and reduce the requirements for capital
holdings against loans, default insurance products – 'regulatory
capital relief' – were bought in huge amounts, allowing banks
to reduce regulatory capital (the buffer), and so increase their
leverage in the markets, in turn generating ever greater profits
and generous bonuses for staff.[8]

The fallout of the 2007–8 crash was enormous. Economies
suffered, people lost their homes and electorates were furious.

The bailing out of the banks on a massive scale was regarded with deep scorn. The idea that supporting 'Wall Street to help out Main Street' was seen as absurd. The pressure for new regulatory systems was, as a result, intense. In the United States, the Dodd–Frank legislation became the cornerstone of a new, stricter regime to avoid a repeat. Passed in 2010, it offered a multitude of new rules for the financial sector and ushered in the Financial Stability Council to offer oversight, with the Fed undertaking 'stress tests' on the stability of the system. The international Basel III process that kicked off following the crash identified 29 finance firms, holding total assets of US$446 trillion that were especially important to global financial stability and so were required to meet tough capital standards, holding substantial liquid assets in order to stabilize the system (Tooze 2018: 312). Implemented from the beginning of 2023, the Basel IV framework has in turn constrained the use of banks' own risk models with the aim of restoring faith in the estimation of their risk-weighted assets.[9] While limiting the opportunities to cheat the system and encouraging a larger capital buffer, regulation through 'macroprudential supervision' of course remains premised on the basic but misplaced idea that such risks can actually be managed (Greenwood, Landier and Thesmar 2015; Aikman et al. 2018).

The assumptions of risk-based regulation, either through external state-imposed intervention insisting on capital buffers or on industry-led 'best practice', ignore uncertainty, where future likelihoods and consequences are unknown. Risk weightings, insurance, capital limits and so on are tools that assume that risk can be managed, yet the real challenge was 'systemic risk' (actually uncertainty), the product of system complexity. Being out of the scope of the ratings agencies and the oversight committees, uncertainty was therefore almost completely ignored in the confident proclamations of regulators and others. And, meanwhile, the banks continued to compete in largely unregulated markets to generate massive profits. As Tooze (2018: 88–9) comments, 'The complex financial instruments they produced exuded an energizing charisma. The clannish society of bankers created a social force field of common assumptions and an overweening superiority complex. They were masters of the universe. They could not fail.'

Political economies

The elaborate system of global finance that proved so vulnerable was centred on a narrow group of companies with connections globally, organized around a transatlantic axis. Huge profits were made, overshadowing many national economies. The leaders of such organizations had enormous lobbying power, framing regulatory provisions over decades. All this was premised on assumptions about the overall stability of the system: that it could never fail (Sorkin 2010). Even with oversight by central banks, instability was wired into the emerging model of financialized capitalism (Calhoun and Derluguian 2011; Wansleben 2023). Assumptions around 'risk management' – and the associated mechanisms of capital buffers, exposure weighting models and so on – gave a false sense of security. The power of the 'tight-knit corporate oligarchy' that made up global finance was immense (Tooze 2018: 13). Such power also breeds arrogance and in turn collective ignorance, and this inward-looking sense of invincibility all added to the factors that led to the 2007–8 crash.

Understanding the crash of course means looking at a much longer process that saw a fundamental shift in the relationship between the state and private finance, especially in the United States and parts of Europe, notably the United Kingdom. The so-called 'neoliberal' era allowed capital the space to accumulate in deregulated self-correcting financial markets. In the West, a disconnect was created between finance and the productive base of real economies. This enhanced the power of financiers and bankers within a new financialized political economy, reducing the influence of labour unions, consumers and others.

Private global finance was at the centre of the new economic architecture, but the state had a role too. Investors were allowed easy entry and exit from different asset classes that were 'de-risked' by the state. 'Development' became the process of 'de-risking' – for example, through public–private partnerships, subsidized insurance, micro-credit or direct cash transfers – to allow capital to find a foothold and generate profit and economic growth. As Daniela Gabor (2021) calls it, the 'Wall Street consensus' took hold. By making use of new financial instruments, which were backed by the agile financial sector, uncertainties could be suppressed, risks managed and economic development achieved. Or so went the argument.

The political economy of today's complex, global financial relations creates important power dynamics across diverse actors. Such actors are in turn supported by new technologies that apparently offer more opportunities for optimization and control. Supported by artificial intelligence and machine-learning neural network models, data are scoured for new insights and applied to the full range of human activity, including of course finance. As Louise Amoore (2019: 154) argues, even if there is uncertainty and so 'doubt' within the data, machine learning can generate 'a single value distilled from a teeming multiplicity of potential pathways, values, weightings and thresholds. It is this process of condensation and reduction to one from many that allows algorithmic decision systems to retain doubt within computation and yet to place the decision beyond doubt.' By eliminating uncertainties, machine-learning algorithms thus create new geopolitical orders, unsettling existing ways of responding to the world's uncertainties within the real economy (Amoore 2023). This, in the terms of Shoshana Zuboff (2019), creates a new form of 'surveillance capitalism', one that generates a controlling order through the extraction, collation and management of data on human populations, which can in turn act to undermine liberal democracies and the regulatory functioning of states.

Real markets in pastoral areas

Far from Wall Street and the 'square mile' of the City of London, others, such as Mohamed Hassan, must grapple with the uncertainties of complex markets beyond the reach of state regulation. How do they deal with crises? How do they manage risks and uncertainties? And what can we learn from such settings for rethinking financial systems more generally? The pastoral areas of the Horn of Africa – from Somalia to Ethiopia to Kenya and beyond – are the centre of a massive international market in livestock. Estimates vary, but each year around US$1 billion in trade in live animals passes through the ports along the Somali coast destined for the Gulf countries, notably Saudi Arabia (Catley, Lind and Scoones 2013). This is an internationalized, cross-border market affected by multiple uncertainties and so requires considerable financing, sophisticated coordination and complex governance arrangements. Markets operate almost completely informally, outside the grip of state regulation and taxation yet in a highly sensitive geopolitical arena (Hagmann and Stepputat 2023). In many respects, there are important commonalities with global finance, but there are also crucial differences.

Central to this complex international market is a network of traders and brokers who source animals from diverse locations across pastoral regions and organize their transport to and subsequent sale in terminal markets (Roba, Lelea and Kaufmann 2017). This requires a great deal of collective skill, as the uncertainties faced are huge. Rainfall variability – made worse by the effects of climate change – affects the production of animals across the rangelands, with frequent droughts reducing the possibilities of offtake or imposing significant mortalities, as during the last few years when rains have failed. Market uncertainties can upset plans as sale restrictions may be imposed due to disease outbreaks or new market regulations. Fearing the spread of Rift Valley Fever, Saudi Arabia suspended trade from the Horn of Africa for nine years following an outbreak in 2000, resulting in serious disruption to livestock markets across the region.[10] Political uncertainties impinge, too, as livestock movements across borders may be restricted by national governments, taxation by militias or by outbreaks of violence, such as that provoked by Al Shabaab across Somalia.[11]

Unlike with global finance, the web of interactions between actors in this market are based on close connections among kin and clan groups rooted in sustained social relations. Trade is dominated by particular actors, often those who are ethnically Somali, and mediated through social, cultural and religious connections stretching across borders (Little, Tiki and Debsu 2015). Facilitated by increasingly effective mobile-phone coverage, with finance moving by mobile money transfers, the system is remarkably effective, given the volume of exchanges in this 'informal', often 'illegal', cross-border trade. Those involved must negotiate with border police, customs officials and veterinary officers, so maintaining ambiguities around regulations helps ensure the flexibility of movement when the official rules would prevent it (Little, Tiki and Debsu 2015).

Those brokers who have more connections in their networks and come with more experience are relied on by traders for knowledge about conditions in production areas, prices in different places and connections to markets. Connected across far-flung networks, they make use of kinship and cultural connections to build trust between market players providing support for effective trade (Mahmoud 2008). By offering knowledge, credit and informal insurance, they help facilitate the operation of the market, reducing information asymmetries and other sources of uncertainty (Ng'asike, Hagmann and Wasonga 2021). Around 5,000 cattle per week pass through Garissa market in north-east Kenya. A broker based there explained, 'I have connections all over from Nairobi to southern Somalia. I have four customers at Kariobangi terminal market [Nairobi], five at Hulugho bush market, and almost ten at Garissa' (quoted by Ng'asike, Hagmann and Wasonga 2021: 180). As Hussein Mahmoud (2008) explains, *dilaals* or 'go-betweens' are essential in facilitating the market networks in the northern Kenyan borderlands. They can operate in multiple languages and can link producers and traders, measure livestock weights, recommend prices and prevent fraud. These market networks are based on trust, and this is fostered through close partnerships between producers and traders, as well as facilitation by intermediaries. Collective arrangements for trading animals also reduce risks and enhance capacities for financing and transportation. In sum, such real markets are always social – connected by trust-based relationships frequently over long distances, but with the end result being an efficient, effective market that can respond to multiple shocks, whether trade bans, price volatility, insecurity or drought (McPeak and Little 2006; Simula 2023).

Studies of such livestock markets in Marsabit county in northern Kenya show differences between 'long' and 'short' market chains, with the former being run mostly by men, while the latter are more local and more embedded in local social relations and involve women, particularly in the sheep and goat trade (Roba 2020). As uncertainties increase, it is the shorter, more locally managed chains that are increasingly important as they are the ones that can adjust rapidly and respond. A much more variegated pattern is emerging, now made possible through new forms of connectivity both for information and funds, which have replaced the 'big man'-dominated long chains of the past. With more players, connected in networks through more diverse social relations, the capacity to respond to uncertain events increases.

In contrast to the imaginary of the individualized, market-based risk management of conventional finance and regulatory practice, a more social basis for 'the economy' and 'the market', rooted in collective, networked responses, is key. This suggests wider lessons for how real economies and markets work in practice as part of complex, social systems (Gibson-Graham 2008). Such financial relationships may be supported by informal social interactions in a diversity of spaces: among extended families, in the mosque or in markets themselves, where diverse uncertainties are deliberated upon. In markets and informal gatherings, people exchange stories about what is happening in different parts of the market network. Gossip and rumour add to the narrative, while people will cross-check with others through a quick call or WhatsApp exchange.

All this may seem far from the challenges of global finance, but there are important lessons to be learned. Such real markets are also highly non-linear and complex, operate internationally and have limited formal regulatory control but, in contrast, remain firmly embedded in social settings. Rather than dismissing them as 'informal' and in need of 'modernization' through new infrastructure, 'better governance' and stricter regulatory control, we must recognize that pastoral livestock markets can and do deliver effectively in the face of often extreme and intersecting uncertainties. Incomes generated are significant to national economies across the region and generate huge numbers of livelihoods along the chain, from producers to transporters to processors to retailers, with brokers and traders at the centre of the story. Such markets must respond in real time to changing contexts and unexpected contingent events. Importantly, these markets are facilitated by the personal interactions and crucially culturally imbued social relations, while they also make use of technologies that support the efficient and rapid flows of money and information. A range of networked social practices are central as traders interact with brokers, transporters, financiers and others to grapple continuously with uncertainty and ignorance.

The human touch

What can be learned from the real markets of pastoral areas and the likes of Mohamed Hassan who must continuously negotiate uncertainty? There are some important parallels, centred on the significance of social relations and what might be called the 'human touch'. Despite the failure of the financial models, the lax regulatory system and the political economy of finance that saw a small elite control the system with extraordinary hubristic arrogance, things didn't completely fall apart during and following the crash (Grabel 2017). Within the banks, on the trading floors and across financial institutions, people were able to navigate uncertainties during the financial crisis, generating a variety of pragmatic innovations responding to what Ilene Grabel (2017) calls 'productive incoherence' in the system. The skill to differentiate, to find local solutions, to communicate and share these and learn from experience then becomes absolutely essential, features we see again and again in pastoral markets. While not succeeding everywhere, in both pastoral settings and global financial markets such routes to generating reliability in the face of extreme uncertainty are rooted in people with particular skills: the ability to scan the horizon, see the dangers and translate this into ameliorative action within a complex system and through professional and personal networks (Roe 2013, 2016; see chapter 4).

Just as in the real markets of pastoral areas, ethnographic accounts of the financial crash show how, despite the infrastructure of failed control and inadequate regulation, there were mechanisms, rooted in social behaviours and collective practices, which allowed for survival and sometimes remarkably effective responses (Leins 2018). A fairly basic lesson emerges: economic activity everywhere is social, rooted in practices and behaviours and forms of professionalism that go beyond the understandings of markets simply as abstract mechanisms of exchange. Even modern, technologically driven, financialized markets are therefore more like the old-fashioned bazaar and the livestock markets of the Horn of Africa than many think (McMillan 2003).

Cultures, rituals, emotions, performativity, 'tribal' affiliations and beliefs all play an important role in understanding financial systems (e.g., Zaloom 2006; Holmes 2013; Christophers, Leyshon and Mann 2017). There is an 'emotional logic' of capitalism, as morals, ethics and feelings are central to the functioning of the economy. Following Karl Polanyi (1944), far from being disembedded, capitalism is always social and relational (Könings 2015). The everyday practice of finance and banking involves, for example, rules of thumb, practical heuristics and experimentation (Akerlof and Shiller 2010; Tuckett and Nikolic 2017), while the adaptive responses of financial regulators, supervisors and traders are seen in hindsight to have been essential in offsetting the worst effects of the crisis (Grabel 2017). Given the complexity of the market, financiers can never understand the range of implications of the new products they are trading in (Lépinay 2015) and so make sense of their world by constructing narratives, always telling stories about complex dynamics (Beckert and Bronk 2018). Despite these coping strategies, firmly held beliefs based on experiences from the past – for example in the 'liquidity' of markets and their ability to self-correct – were central to the knowledge cultures of bankers and financiers, and generated blinkers to wider realities (Ho 2009; Tett 2021), generating a 'cult' of risk (Tett 2019), a sense of 'disaster myopia' (Haldane 2009c) and so dangerous self-confidence.

How do the experiences of grappling with uncertainty and ignorance during the crash suggest ways forward for global finance and its regulation? Clearly, the original Basel framework, based on a complex, layered web of risk-based measures, was found seriously wanting, but what are the alternatives to standard risk-based regulation? Haldane observes, 'because complexity generates uncertainty, not risk, it requires a regulatory response grounded in simplicity, not complexity' (Haldane 2012: 19). This, he argues, means rethinking network configurations and facilitating new practices and behaviours among those involved, in turn requiring new skills to enhance reliability. This suggests a shift from reliance on opaque and highly complex risk-based models to allowing supervisors more discretion and judgement and so be accepting of uncertainty, even ignorance. This in turn requires deliberation on appropriate responses in the face of inevitably incomplete information, encouraging a wider view rather than a narrow focus on tick-box rule compliance and restrictive regulatory protocols. By breaking up the network into more modular units, he argues, human relationships and interactions can be encouraged and sustained, and wider crises spotted, just as happens daily in pastoral market settings.

Once the hard-earned experience of confronting the uncertainties of the financialized market head-on is absorbed, a very different relationship between bankers, financial institutions and the state is suggested. The hubristic overconfidence of the liberalized laissez-faire ideal of neoliberalism is fundamentally challenged. By breaking up the financial network, the power of large institutions must be confronted while bringing the human touch back into the management of complex financial systems. A voluntary, industry-led system of regulation is clearly inadequate as speculative gambling and significant accumulation results in extreme system fragility. Against the grain of much neoliberal thinking, the role of the state in facilitating responses to uncertainty is once again regarded as essential. In other words, the experience of the crash has challenged some of the shibboleths of economic policy – risk-based management and regulation of complex financial systems using models, algorithms and technologies were not the solution. Alternatives have to be found. Just, maybe, some of these can be discovered in workings of the real markets of pastoral areas. While clearly very different, there are more commonalities between the trading floors of global financial networks and the remote markets of the Horn of Africa than you might think (Scoones 2021b).

Conclusion

The lessons from the 2007–8 financial crash are many, but central among them is the importance of recognizing how uncertainties are generated through non-linear interactions in complex systems and that social, networked responses are key to navigating uncertainties and confronting ignorance. The radical forms of financial deregulation seen during the neoliberal era also made market interactions extremely opaque, adding to the number and speed of interactions, and therefore the uncertainties generated. Reforms that assumed the management of risk (not uncertainty) and so control – whether through external regulation or clever algorithms – were quickly undermined as diverse uncertainties and forms of ignorance were ignored.

Assuming that temporalities were irrelevant was also deeply flawed, and this only added to the challenge of responding to extreme volatility.

The disembedding of financial systems from the real economy of production and consumption allowed for accumulation among a rich, powerful, networked global elite, operating outside and across states. This meant that, in contrast to pastoral settings, complex financial systems became detached from local political-economic contexts, generating a new financialized geopolitical order centred on 'Wall Street' (and its equivalents), not 'Main Street'. Unlike in pastoral areas, where market traders, such as Mohamed Hassan, are rooted in local societies, the new financial elite escaped any form of social or political accountability. A focus in the West on finance, not production and manufacturing rooted in the real economy, meant that productive sectors were ignored, and the political influence of labour and consumers alike decreased, adding to the disconnection of finance from society.

As economic relations reconfigure due to financialization, new uncertainties emerge. A focus on finance as a core sector in the West has meant that production capacities have shifted elsewhere, notably to Asia. The result is a new, more multipolar geopolitical and economic order, with different axes of power and influence. This raises questions, for example, around the hegemonic power of the US dollar in the global financial system, the role of the expanded BRICS grouping in addressing financial crises and of course the role of China as an economic power (Woods 2023). This means that future global economic crises will look very different, but some basic lessons from thinking about the 2007–8 crash, together with pastoral markets, remain, with some profound implications for how we think about economics, finance and development.

Central among these is the importance of taking uncertainties and the embedded social responses to them seriously. However, uncertainties are largely ignored in conventional approaches to economic analysis and development practice. As discussed in chapter 1, the neat assumptions of 'rational expectations' of neoclassical economic theory eliminate uncertainty, rejecting the distinction made by Frank Knight between calculable risk and uncertainty, where futures are not known. The assumptions of predictable dynamics and timeless patterns where the future is folded into the present, making it calculable, have proven deeply problematic.

The assumptions of risk management and control, backed by calculable models that fail to take account of system and network complexity and uncertain events, proved disastrous, with the financial crash reverberating across the whole world economy. But such perspectives have not always been central to economic thinking as I discussed in chapter 1. John Maynard Keynes (1937: 152) in his *General Theory*, for example, argued that specifying value in a market 'cannot be uniquely correct, since our existing knowledge does not provide a sufficient basis for a calculated mathematical expectation.' Yet Keynes's insights on uncertainty are only now being recognized. As Robert Skidelsky (2011: 3) reflects, 'Keynes' view that uncertainty about the future is the root cause of financial crisis may be contrasted with today's conventional view that the recent banking collapse was caused by the "mispricing of risk".'

As was discussed in chapter 1, other economists from very different traditions appreciate the importance of uncertainty as distinct from risk in macroeconomic thinking. It was probably George Shackle who articulated thinking about uncertainty for economics most effectively, arguing that any person confronting the future confronts 'the void of unknowledge' (1992 [1972]: xi), highlighting that economic questions are largely ones about contested ideas rather than settled facts. Unfortunately, such cautions and qualifications were largely lost in the pursuit of a narrow version of mathematically oriented neoclassical economics (DeMartino, Grabel and Scoones et al. 2024), which fed through into thinking about finance, resulting in the elaboration of models to manage risk through an ever more complex set of financial instruments.

Away from the frenzied setting of the investment banks, in the rangelands of the Horn of Africa, livestock markets continue to respond to diverse uncertainties in ways that do not reduce the challenge to calculable risk through obscure models and complex algorithms. Here social relationships between multiple players such as Mohamed Hassan mediate market interactions for livestock sales, with credit and insurance often being offered as well as secondary markets for a range of livestock products. Prices are negotiated on the spot, facilitated by good connections by mobile phones, but crucially through relationships of trust that are reinforced by ethnic, clan and kin networks. Connecting short and long market chains, and managing transactions across multiple countries, in important ways, the form and functioning of such markets is not in practice hugely different to those seen in the global finance system.

Of course, global finance trades in far larger amounts and much faster, but the important lesson from Africa's rangelands is that social relations are always the basis for transactions and the ways uncertainties must be navigated. In global finance, as we have seen, uncertainties are too often wished away and managed as calculable risk. The bigger system and its uncertainties are not understood and, because so much of the activity is managed through computers and via models and algorithms, the human, face-to-face interactions so essential in the complex livestock market and trade networks of the Horn of Africa are not central. This is a crucial gap, as the development economist Albert Hirschman recognized long ago. Hirschman's vital insight was around the importance of adaptation, flexibility and learning-by-doing as responses to uncertainty in development policy and practice (Hirschman 2013 [1970]). Whether during the financial crisis or within pastoral markets, all actors have to navigate uncertainty. They must experiment, innovate, improvise and adapt to generate reliability in the face of high levels of market volatility. This requires diverse practices, involving human inter-action and drawing on social relations.

The problem with the finance and banking sector is that such capacities go unrecognized, are often hidden from view and are not part of the core approach to managing financial networks. Regulatory reforms focus on attempts at control through risk management, not facilitating the practices central to responding to uncertainty. By contrast, in livestock market networks in the Horn of Africa, such reliability practices are crucial to the success of a massive livestock trade where, in the context of a complex market network, uncertainty has to be taken seriously (Catley, Lind and Scoones 2013).[12] In other words, despite the apparent sophistication of global financial markets, they have proven less effective at responding to market complexity and the arising uncertainties than pastoral market settings because of the ignoring or suppression of the very practices that enhance reliability in complex, real markets. That said, the success of pastoral markets in responding to uncertainties can easily be disrupted by misplaced 'development' interventions that attempt to formalize, manage and control, in much the same way that regulatory approaches in banking and finance have done.

Building on such experiences, new (although still marginal) perspectives in economics are challenging mainstream neoclassical approaches and the associated 'analytical monocultures' that have ignored uncertainty for too long (Bronk and Jacoby 2016), as discussed in chapter 1. New lines of work are exploring, for example, network dynamics (Anand, Gai and Marsili 2012), the role of emotion and imagination (Bronk 2009; Tuckett 2011; Beckert 2016), the importance of narratives and storytelling (Beckert and Bronk 2018), new approaches to forecasting (O'Mahony et al. 2023) and patterns of co-evolution, adaptive management and innovation (Rammel, Stagl and Wilfing 2007) – in other words, seeing markets and finance as complex systems, with a social dimension, just as livestock traders and brokers in the Horn of Africa always do.

All such new approaches necessarily make perspectives on uncertainty central, and so suggest a more grounded, interdisciplinary approach to economics and finance, rejecting the reliance on simplified models of risk and control. Unfortunately, standard economic texts and much training in economics, finance and banking cling to outdated perspectives and the ideal of an 'economics of control' (Lerner 1944; Colander and Freedman 2018). While overarching regulatory and governance systems are of course needed as a guiding framework, the search for a fail-safe system of management and control is foolhardy. Instead, a more decentralized approach is required where social interactions, human judgement and deliberation about future uncertainties are needed. As thinking in economics and finance returns to some their older traditions and so reclaims the importance of taking uncertainty seriously, conversations between bankers, financiers, economists and livestock traders in Africa – all of whom must be experts at managing uncertainty – might, this chapter suggests, offer some interesting insights for the future.

3

Technology: What Is Safe and for Whom?

Introduction

How to regulate new technologies in the context of uncertainty, even ignorance, is a central challenge for governments across the world. Advances in science and technology hold out much promise, but how to regulate their use so that benefits outweigh potential risks is immensely challenging. Risk-assessment, management and communication approaches have been honed into elaborate procedures for risk governance, but too often they assume that we can predict or at least anticipate future risks. What happens when we don't know what the likelihoods of such risks are, and we are dealing with uncertainty or ignorance? How do we assess what is safe, and for whom? How should inevitable risks and harms be distributed through society, or indeed across the world? What roles should accredited experts, lawyers and lay publics play in assessing what technological futures are desirable? How do political cultures, institutional histories and contextual political economies play into regulatory design and decision making?

None of these are easy questions to answer, but reflections on past experiences of scientific and technological change can be helpful in identifying where the problems lie and what opportunities exist for new approaches that truly embrace uncertainty. This chapter explores the politics of risk and uncertainty around a number of technologies, focusing in particular on genetically modified (GM) transgenic crops. In addition, mobile-phone wireless technologies and, just briefly, deep learning artificial intelligence (AI) are touched upon. But the debates that emerge could equally be applied to 'gene-edited' crops using CRISPR technologies (Ely et al. 2022; Rock et al. 2023), 'geoengineering' and other technological solutions to the climate crisis (Sovacool 2021; see chapter 7 below), driverless cars (Stilgoe 2021) or modular nuclear reactors (Steigerwald et al. 2023), among many, many others.

Grappling with how to navigate uncertainty is therefore central to thinking about how to regulate technologies for societal benefit and, in the process, balance safety with usefulness and the demands for technological development.

Risk assessment and management: attempts at control

There are a number of standard approaches to addressing risk and uncertainty in decision making (Jasanoff and Wynne 1998; Millstone 2007). Most attempt to control the future by assuming that risks can be controlled and managed, with publics being passive recipients of science-led decision making.

The first, and still surprisingly common vision, is a science-led, technocratic model, whereby a neutral science is assumed to feed directly into policymaking and in turn into risk communication to a public assumed to be suffering a 'deficit' in knowledge and understanding (Wynne 2016). This approach was implicitly assumed by some in the GM crops debate discussed below. This included frustrated biotechnology scientists convinced of the efficacy and safety of their products and politicians and others who wished to see the technologies accepted and were exasperated by what they saw as an ignorant, irrational public.

A second approach is labelled the 'decisionist model' and corresponds to the US National Research Council's 'Red Book' approach (NRC 1983). Here science is important but is not everything. Risk assessment, evaluation and management are all central and, while informed by science, the process is also influenced by socio-economic considerations too. Importantly, though, there is a separation of scientific risk assessment and more social risk evaluation and management. The assumption is that risk can be appraised objectively through technical, scientific processes, and that uncertainties and contrasting perspectives are not a concern.

Finally, there is a more transparent, collaborative model, where the wider risk-assessment policy – including its framing – is defined by socio-economic and political considerations. Risk assessments and their evaluation are in turn an interactive process, where science and broader socio-economic aspects are thought about together. Risk management and policy and regulatory outcomes then follow from this process. This was influential, for example, in revisions of the global Codex Alimentarius regulatory framework for food safety (Millstone 2009), where specific questions are asked about what counts as a risk, what is regarded as relevant evidence and how interpretations of evidence should be carried out. Going beyond a technocratic, risk-based decision framework towards one that required wider participation and deliberation was an important move, although still not one that has been widely adopted.

For many commentators on risk governance (e.g., Renn 2008; Burgess, Alemanno and Zinn 2016; Zinn 2016), it is this latter, more transparent and collaborative model that provides the most appropriate approach for contemporary regulatory challenges. Elaborations of such risk governance approaches, both for technology-specific risks and more systemic, combined and cascading risks in wider, complex systems, acknowledge the importance of 'stakeholder participation' along with 'risk communication', even if these are often envisaged in a quite instrumental way (van Asselt and Renn 2011). Most risk governance models, however, still assume that risks can be defined and assessed using standard approaches, with prediction central to a managed, controlled and ordered process, even if involving 'stakeholders' in the process. Uncertainty can, it is argued, be managed or reduced to make risk governance feasible.

In sum, attempts to govern and control nearly always resort to assumptions about risk, even when collaboration and partici-pation are notionally included. Such technocratic approaches rarely countenance, let alone accommodate, uncertainty, where futures remain unknown. Uncertainty therefore presents a special challenge for the regulation of technology, as we just don't know what the risks will be.

What about uncertainty?

Of course, when considering especially new technologies being deployed in diverse contexts, many uncertainties exist. A compilation of 63 studies looking at health and environmental risks across different energy technologies showed how individual studies had a relatively narrow 'uncertainty range'. However, taken together, there was massive variation, offering no clear view for any decision maker (Stirling 2010). Making a simple choice based on such uncertain scientific evidence is clearly impossible. For this reason, a different approach for navigating uncertainty in technology assessment is required.

Fortunately, a number of methodologies acknowledge divergent views and multiple uncertainties. Inclusive scenario approaches, for example, allow different people, drawing on different forms of expertise and sources of knowledge – statistical, experimental, experiential, tacit, indigenous and so on – to debate future options. Citizen juries or panels – along with deliberative mapping, polling and inclusive focus groups – can help with deliberation on available knowledge and claims and come up with views on what courses of action can be followed, with appropriate caveats and cautions applied (Chilvers and Kearnes 2016). These need not be consensual – as in consensus conferences or some types of jury process – and indeed the divergent views may be useful in constructing ways forward that accommodate diversity, thus opening up debate (Stirling et al. 2007; Stirling 2008). Qualitative social science methods, such as Q method, multi-criteria mapping or narrative analysis, allow for the elaboration of different positions and views, linked to different groups of people. Highlighting how and why they exist can help others coming from different places to appreciate how uncertainties are defined, identified and approached by different people from different standpoints (Stirling and Mayer 2001). Focusing on diverse users, 'constructive' or 'real-time' approaches to technology assessment allow for engagement with stakeholders across innovation processes (Rip, Schot and Misa 1995; Guston and Sarewitz 2002). Meanwhile, 'post-normal' technology assessment is geared to crises, where decisions are urgent but uncertainties dominate (Sinozic-Martinez, Weinberger and Hahn 2023). All such approaches facilitate

wider debate about regulatory options for technologies (or
indeed other choices) under conditions of uncertainty. In the
end, choices are made, but these are informed, qualified and
incorporate diverse – perhaps conflicting – understandings of
uncertainty.

Arguments follow that not only is public debate necessary at
the sharp end of regulatory decision making but also upstream
around the framing of science and the choice of investments
in technology (Wilsdon and Willis 2004), allowing for wider
participation in technology development more generally (Irwin
2001). Rather than a rush to modernization based on rapid
technological development at all costs, a more inclusive notion
of progress is better served by a 'slow race' (Leach and Scoones
2006), involving diverse actors and substantive deliberation
around the directions of technological change, the diversity of
technologies and the distribution of costs and benefits (Stirling
2009).

As discussed in more detail in chapter 7 in relation to climate
change challenges, Sheila Jasanoff (2004) argues that a more
serious approach to 'co-production' is required where different
knowledges are treated equally, and these combine to construct
new approaches to technology regulation, rooted in diverse
cultures and understandings. In so doing, the sites for regulatory
action are dispersed, involving more participants and diverse
knowledges. This goes way beyond the instrumental deployment
of 'participation' and 'deliberation' within risk governance and
moves towards an engagement with how science (and technological innovation) links with democracy (Smith and Stirling
2006). 'Citizen science' is as a result much more than an add-on
but rather a fundamental recasting of the relationships between
science and citizens (Leach, Scoones and Wynne 2005). This in
turn raises important questions of 'cognitive justice' (Visvanathan
2005) in the context of democratic struggles around the directions of innovation, the sources of technology and the role of
science in societal transformation.

It was exactly these themes that became central to the
biotechnology battles fought in the late 1990s and early 2000s
as a new generation of GM transgenic crops became available,
associated with much hype about how they were going to
transform agriculture and feed the world (Scoones and Glover
2009).

Biotechnology battles

Across Europe in the late 1990s, a huge debate about GM crops raged. In the United Kingdom, it was especially tense. The new Labour government seemed divided on which way to go: follow the Americans and encourage the commercialization of the new crops or take the more precautionary stance of the rest of the European Union. Prime Minister Tony Blair and his science minister Lord Sainsbury were gung-ho. Science showed that these new technologies were the way forward, they argued. Others were more sceptical, reflecting a wider public disquiet about the potential risks of such crops. There was a big divide, reflecting deep uncertainties around how such technologies would affect people's health, the environment, trade relations and wider food security. Many arguments were deployed both for and against, with some, such as the vocal advocacy group 'Sense about Science' and its head, the British peer Dick Taverne, arguing that restricting GM crops would be tantamount to being against scientific progress. Those opposing GM crops shared stories about the disastrous effects of 'Frankenfoods', with pictures of weird tomatoes and other vegetables printed in the tabloid press. Others took a more measured line, emphasizing the uncertainties and the need for more deliberation before leaping into the unknown.

In October 1999, the Global Environmental Change programme of the United Kingdom's Economic and Social Research Council, of which at the time I was co-director, released a report, *The Politics of GM Food: Risk, Science and Public Trust*,[1] which was based on extensive research. Among others, the then environment minister, Michael Meacher, was dragged into the media studios to debate the findings on the BBC *Today* programme. Unlike some of his colleagues in government, he was remarkably balanced. Along with the minister in the Cabinet Office, Mo Mowlam, he understood the importance of thinking about the uncertain consequences of a new technology and bringing the public along with any government decision. Aligning with a Europe-wide commitment to the 'precautionary principle' and, unlike the Americans, accepting that there was no 'substantial equivalence' between GM crops and others produced by different breeding processes, the UK government eventually upheld a moratorium, pending further field trials. Aiming to gain a wider buy-in to any new policy, in 2000 it established the Agriculture and Environment Biotechnology Commission (AEBC), in parallel with the Advisory Committee on Releases into the Environment (ACRE) that was tasked with approving releases.

In addition to studies on the science and economics of GM crops, a process of wider public discussion about GM crop policy – GM Nation? – was initiated in 2002.[2] This was an important innovation. Rather than assuming that science could resolve all uncertainties, there was a need to deliberate on them in a more rounded fashion, with new uncertainties inevitably emerging in the process. Robin Grove-White (2006: 174), one of the commissioners, observed that public concerns 'reflected unease about likely contingencies outside the purview, or even the imagination, of *present* scientific understanding. This extended not only to potential environmental or epidemiological issues as yet unidentified by science, but also to potential ripple effects, whether political, social, economic or ethical in character.' As Grove-White pointed out, there were no provisions within the existing regulatory framework for addressing such uncertainties, meaning that they were effectively evaded by government and industry until later when the public became involved in the debate.

The GM crop controversies at the turn of the millennium were a prime example of how debates about new technologies throw up numerous uncertainties, which are seen by different actors in highly divergent ways. Expecting these to be resolved by some process of 'sound science' led by elite experts away from public scrutiny and sanctioned by politicians as 'evidence-based' policy-making was and remains naive in the extreme. There are multiple uncertainties, different views and inevitably an intense politics around the 'evidence'. This is why open public deliberation is essential, and standard, technocratic models of risk governance, even with performative concessions to consultation and participation, are inadequate. The standard approach to science–policy interactions, where scientists offer closed-down 'results' without any expressions of doubt, will not do. Indeed, as any scientist will confirm, such an approach runs counter to the scientific method, where doubt and 'organised scepticism' (Merton 1973) are central features.

How does this play out in policymaking? My colleague from
the Science Policy Research Unit at the University of Sussex,
Andy Stirling, described a meeting in the UK Cabinet Office
before which he was told by civil servants in harsh terms that he
should not share his results with the minister on diverse views on
agricultural biotechnology emerging from multi-criteria mapping
in ways that suggested there was uncertainty. Instead, he should
offer a clear, definitive direction.[3] There was no need to confuse
or cause alarm. Luckily, the minister was Mo Mowlam, whose
recent experience as the UK minister for Northern Ireland meant
that she knew a lot about divergent viewpoints and was highly
receptive, dismissing the concerns of the civil servants. What
followed was an open discussion about alternatives that allowed
scientific evidence to speak to diverse uncertainties, allowing
more humble, informed and effective decision making to follow;
something that may have been prevented by over-eager civil
servants trying to protect their minister from what they saw as
the confusions generated by uncertainties.

The GM debate, even if exceptionally heated and highly
divisive, is not unusual. As new technologies throw up divergent
views, rather than closing down around a narrow assessment
of 'risk' led by elite science as the basis for a controlled, instrumental form of 'risk governance', a wider debate is needed
(Stirling 2008). This requires a different approach to policymaking, embracing the sensibilities of Meacher and Mowlam
rather than Blair and Sainsbury, and offering publics a chance to
deliberate on how the future should look. This is not a rejection
of science and evidence, far from it; instead, such a stance offers
a more effective approach, allowing uncertainties to be aired
and diverse forms of knowledge making to engage with them.
Such knowledge may emerge from established, accredited science
but also from other forms of insight, which may be incredibly
valuable when dealing with uncertain settings.

Regulatory contexts

What unfolded in the United Kingdom and more widely in
Europe for a period reflected in turn a located political economy,
one where precaution and public debate were central in deciding
on future directions. In the United Kingdom, the GM crops

debate was played out in the shadow of the disastrous failure around BSE (bovine spongiform encephalopathy) a few years before (van Zwanenberg and Millstone 2005). Confident proclamations about the safety of beef being produced on UK farms were offered, based on a closed expert committee without the requisite expertise. Following this, the agriculture minister, John Gummer, famously offered his four-year-old daughter Cordelia a beefburger on television in 1990, just to show how sure he was of the product's safety.[4] When the government acknowledged in 1996 that people had become seriously ill as a result of vCJD (variant Creutzfeldt–Jakob disease), this all looked rather rash and stupid.

The Phillips inquiry on BSE that followed showed how a narrow form of scientific advice had been blind to the uncertainties, resulting in the government regulators failing to act when warning signs were increasingly evident.[5] Across a voluminous report in multiple volumes, the inquiry recommended that in future more openness in advisory committees and expert reviews was needed; that trust is generated through such openness and that the public can be expected to respond rationally (Stilgoe, Irwin and Jones 2006). This echoed the 2000 House of Lords Select Committee Report on Science and Technology, which observed that 'policymakers will find it hard to win public support on any issue with a science component, unless the public's attitudes and values are recognised, respected and weighed along with the scientific and other factors.'[6]

By the time the GM crop discussion emerged in full force, the disaster of BSE thus made many in the United Kingdom (although by no means all) increasingly cautious and more open to debates about uncertainty, while the public expressed a lack of faith in the regulatory institutions and associated expertise that were notionally tasked with ensuring their safety (Ballo et al. 2022). This provided the context for a much more open, vigorous debate about GM crops in the United Kingdom than had happened around other technological risks in the past and, indeed, since.

In other settings, there were different perspectives reflecting contrasting political and public cultures around science, technology, risk and uncertainty, each based on different historical experiences. The United States was the most obvious contrast to Europe, with its commitment to science-driven, industry-led development of biotechnology. Regulation was framed not by a commitment to precaution but a focus on the 'equivalence' of different products, despite their emergence from different processes with different risks and, somewhat in contradiction, their recognition as 'novel' and so presumably not 'equivalent', through patent protection (Millstone, Brunner and Mayer 1999). This US perspective on GM crops was pushed across the world through 'development' and 'capacity building' programmes, such as the Agricultural Biotechnology Support Projects hosted by Cornell University and supported by the US aid agency, USAID.[7] Some saw this as an attempt to shift regulatory systems globally towards what was proclaimed to be a 'science-based' model as promulgated in the United States. It was no coincidence, of course, that such programmes also had the effect of opening up opportunities in the developing world for US corporations, such as the notorious push by Monsanto of its insect-resistant *Bt* (*Bacillus thuringiensis*) technologies, as well as herbicide-tolerant crops such as 'RoundUp Ready' soya (Glover 2010; Stone 2022; Dowd-Uribe 2023).

Not everyone played ball, however, and different regulatory responses emerged across the world, reflecting both different national contexts and influences of processes of globalization. In the early 2000s, I explored how the regulation of GM crops was negotiated in Brazil, India (mostly Karnataka state) and South Africa/Zimbabwe (Scoones 2002, 2006, 2008). This was the time when the first GM products were being commercialized, with herbicide-resistant soya released in Brazil in 2002, insect-resistant *Bt* cotton released in India also in 2002 and *Bt* yellow and white maize released in South Africa in 1998 and 2000. All were Monsanto's much-hailed transgenic products. Regulatory systems had been established through the 1990s as GM crop trials were undertaken in all countries, but the contests over commercial release were hard fought, even if, as in India and probably Brazil, there were GM crops already in circulation.

Overall, government regulators were largely cautious, resisting the pressure from Monsanto (and the US government) to commit to GM agriculture. Large-scale agricultural producers in Brazil and South Africa were strong advocates for GM crop approval, while it was medium-scale, relatively richer cotton producers in India who were the first adopters of GM crops. In all countries, a growing urban middle class, conscious

of health and environmental issues, was also important in
mobilizing against GM crops, along with farmers' movements,
labour unions and others. Protests included crop burning, port
blockades and consumer boycotts, as well as intensive media
engagement and endless civil litigation, as multiple uncertainties
about the new technologies were highlighted (Scoones 2008).
Networking among anti-GM activists internationally provided
the basis for sharing perspectives on these different uncertainties.
Particular controversies around health and biodiversity impacts
were widely shared across networks, for example.[8] A major fear
was the consequences of a takeover of the seed industry through
the patenting of proprietary transgenic products by US multina-
tionals and so a feared marginalization of local seed systems and
small-scale agriculture. Regulatory decisions about GM crops,
many argued, had national consequences, not only for the local
development of appropriate capacity in crop breeding and seed
supply, but more broadly for food security and agricultural
incomes. Debates about risks and uncertainties were therefore
framed more widely than the immediate health or environmental
impact of the technology.

Rather than adopt a generic approach to regulation, policies
that were appropriate to country contexts emerged through
complex front- and backstage political negotiations and evolving
practice, always reflecting different uncertainties and public
concerns. In Brazil, the election of the Workers' Party (PT)
government with Luiz Inácio Lula da Silva (better known just
as Lula) as president in 2002 was expected by many – most
notably the MST, the Landless Workers' Movement – to result
in radical commitments to agrarian reform and the banning of
GM crops in favour of local production systems, rejecting the
Argentinian model next door. However, the incoming minister
of agriculture proved to be a fervent GM advocate, backing
large-scale commercial farming, and so prioritized promoting
Brazilian agriculture in a globalized world. In India, economic
liberalization from the early 1990s had resulted in a declining
agricultural sector, with GM advocates arguing that improved
productivity, farm consolidation and the adoption of new
technologies would result in a revival of fortunes. Nevertheless,
nationalist sensibilities in India raised concerns about the foreign
capture of a key sector, while other NGOs (non-governmental
organizations) and campaign groups highlighted environmental

and health questions around GM crops. In South Africa, largely white, large-scale commercial farmers made the case for GM maize, both for feed and food, while the ANC (African National Congress) government remained wary about land reform, fearing the collapse of agricultural production, and implicitly backed larger commercial producers. Although middle-class environmental activists campaigned effectively against GM crops, policymakers aimed for careful compromises, balancing different uncertainties and outcomes. By contrast, further north in Zimbabwe, a moratorium on GM crops persisted, although crop trials continued. This reflected a wider commitment across much of the continent to the hard-fought agreements by African negotiators under the 2003 Cartagena Protocol on Biosafety, which established a precautionary stance for regulation.[9] Underlying much of this caution was a real antagonism to the perceived 'colonization' of African agriculture by external powers and the need to protect local food systems, including following the radical land reform in Zimbabwe after 2000 (Scoones et al. 2010). Even by 2023, despite much wider acceptance of GM and 'gene-edited' crops globally, Kenya's Court of Appeal upheld the long-term GM crop ban, rejecting the government's plans to extend GM crops in the country with US support on the basis that the public had not been involved in the discussions.[10]

In all these cases, regulatory decisions around a contested technology represented different contextual responses to uncertainties, refracted through public debates, government policy priorities, class and commercial interests and wider political cultures of regulation, as well as histories of colonization and past experiences of exploitation and external domination. As discussed in chapter 1, uncertainties are therefore not neutral, somehow 'out there' in the world. They are always conditioned by context and circumstance and require an engaged, open political debate about impacts and consequences, galvanizing diverse knowledges and views. A standardized, instrumental form of risk assessment and governance is always insufficient.

As Jasanoff shows in her 2005 book, *Designs on Nature* (Jasanoff 2005a), which contrasted the policies around GM crops in the United States, Germany and the United Kingdom, regulatory responses to risk are co-constructed with wider public debate and politics, the law and tendencies to litigate and the embedded institutional, bureaucratic procedures that generate regulation. As with Brazil, India and South Africa, different bodies of knowledge were deployed in each country, with the United States dominated by a rhetoric of 'sound science', while the United Kingdom relied much more on 'common knowledge' and Germany on 'public knowledge'. This reflected contrasts in styles of expertise and regulatory institutions across countries, as well as the lobbying power of commercial interests and their influence on public policy. In the United States, the system was dominated by a group of highly accredited scientific experts linked to formal institutions, with a constant concern about potential litigation. In the United Kingdom, the 'safe hands' of the professional civil service was more relied upon to deliver on a wider 'public good'. By contrast, in Germany an emphasis on the 'public sphere' and wider representation within institutional settings was evident. Although highly stylized, such contrasts reflect embedded public cultures of policy and what Jasanoff calls 'civic epistemologies', or the way that citizens engage with policy knowledge and decision making. Wherever in the world, risks and uncertainties around technologies, and thus regulatory cultures and practices, are therefore never independent of long histories of institutions, politics and society, meaning that a one-size-fits-all regulatory response to technological uncertainties will never work.

Science and the law

In the end, many questions about how societies address uncertainty – and with this the role of science in assessing risk and safety – are addressed in the courts. Legal frameworks provide the basis for confirming regulatory approaches and opportunities for their challenge by citizens.

In March 2023, Mrs Justice Stacey of the King's Bench of the High Court of Justice of England and Wales handed down a judgement on a case raising questions about the safety of 5G wireless technologies as part of a judicial review.[11] The case revealed the many limitations faced by the courts in opening up debates about uncertainties around potential harms. Within a judicial review, only administrative questions of illegality of the proposal, procedural unfairness and irrationality of the arguments are admissible. There is therefore no scope for debating what are deemed to be settled scientific findings on the risks of 5G technologies as presented by government science. While acknowledging the real concerns that the claimants had, the judge was unable to open up debate about the science as the ruling had to follow the position of government science – and the international organizations that government scientists relied upon – even if these findings were vigorously contested. The government view was basically that the 5G technology was safe, and uncertainties, as expressed by the claimants and the evidence that they had accumulated as part of their campaign including their own lived experience, were not germane to the judgement, even if the judge acknowledged that scientific advice included voluntary precautions that could be followed. In most cases, whether in Europe or the United States, uncertainties are excluded from such judicial review considerations, as the courts rely on what is deemed to be authoritative science.

A decade earlier, a very similar debate emerged around the earlier 3G mobile-phone technology, and once again this was deemed to be safe. The National Radiological Protection Board, the scientific body in the United Kingdom charged with reviewing safety and providing guidance for regulation, ensured that uncertainties were addressed within the scientific domain, far from public scrutiny. According to Jack Stilgoe (2007: 56), at that stage, 'The public were viewed as homogeneous, cognitively deficient and passive, demanding reassurance rather than engagement.' The Board lost credibility as concerns increased, resulting in the establishment of an Independent Expert Group on Mobile Phones, which explicitly addressed wider uncertainties and public views. What ensued was a process of co-construction between public concerns, scientific risk assessments and legal cases. This confirmed the regulatory position, now with considerably more credibility and without an unhelpful separation of scientific risk assessments and social and political debate (Stilgoe 2007).

As sites for knowledge making, both science and the law offer important spaces for deliberation about risk, uncertainty and technology (Jasanoff 1997). Neither should be captured by political or commercial interests; both are independent and disinterested and based on the adjudication of 'truths' found in multiple sources of information; and both are governed by ethical conventions of openness, transparency and fairness. In these ways, science and the law have many similarities, yet they remain separated, with the legal process often seen as subservient to accredited formal science, being required to follow established scientific expert consensus. This was seen in the judicial review of the 5G case but is also evident in the United States where, for example, the 'Daubert' case of 1990 ruled that only accepted science was admissible in court (Jasanoff 2005b).

However, given how science works and how uncertainties increasingly impinge on daily life – and so court decisions – there is evolving acceptance that uncertainties should be considered. For example, in a judgement on badger culling in 2019, the Court of Appeal for England and Wales noted, 'By its very nature, scientific knowledge is a developing concept. Contrary to popular thinking, scientific knowledge cannot always deliver certainty', arguing that 'The dichotomy . . . between scientific certain[t]y and scientific opinion is a false one.'[12] This hints at an important move, opening up the opportunity for the courts to engage more concretely in questions of scientific uncertainty, even under judicial review processes, exploring how values and science combine – in this case around culling – across different options (Lees 2020).

As Jasanoff (1997) argues, there are many opportunities for confronting uncertainties, addressing public disquiet and co-constructing regulatory decisions through deliberation within a court setting, without decisions reverting to problematic science-led, technocratic regulatory decision making. In rethinking the role of the law, Jasanoff (1997: 214) suggests that 'The law can render transparent domains of contingency and constructedness in science that science's culturally bounded querying procedures could not have brought to light. Through repeated and incremental, if conflictual, interactions with science and technology, the legal system plays a vital part in exposing the presumptions of experts and holding them accountable to changing public values and expectations.' As she argues, 'the legal process should develop a more searching, self-critical awareness of its own pivotal role in producing new knowledge (and potentially hindering its production). Only by admitting its agency, and its limitations, in this regard will the legal system position itself to use science as it should be used in legal environments: for doing justice' (2005b: S51).

In stark contrast to much current practice, she thus sees the potential for opening up the courts as spaces for free deliberation about uncertainty in science, mutually reinforcing the scientific process and systems of accountability around the regulation of science and technology, with the key challenge being 'how courts can better render justice under conditions of uncertainty and ignorance' (Jasanoff 2005b: S49).

Regulation, precaution and ethics

As we saw in the European debate about GM crops, the precautionary principle has become a core approach for addressing uncertainty and even ignorance when surprises come from nowhere. This is not an excuse for inaction, as some critics argue, but for a more deliberate approach to regulation. Instead, a major study of lessons from 'early warnings' from a huge array of fields showed how 'misplaced "certainty" about the absence of harm played a key role in delaying preventive actions' (Harremoës et al. 2001: 4). This was the lesson from BSE but also from many other cases.

The precautionary principle was central to the 1992 United Nations Rio Declaration on environment and development, stating that 'where there are threats of serious or irreversible damage, lack of full scientific certainty shall not be used as a reason for postponing cost-effective measures to prevent environmental degradation.'[13] The principle also became a defining feature of European environmental policy, setting Europe apart from the United States on GM crops, as we have seen. Key lessons from past experiences – laid out in the important report *Late Lessons from Early Warnings* (Harremoës et al. 2001) – include the need to acknowledge and respond to risk, uncertainty and ignorance in the appraisal of technologies and in policy. This has to be supported by long-term monitoring to identify early warnings in any area, linked to a process of learning and the identification of knowledge gaps and blind spots across different types of expertise. By looking at diverse options to meet needs, robust and adaptable alternatives can be identified that do not result in single-track technological trajectories. While assuring accountability and independence in the regulatory system, there is also a need to avoid 'paralysis by analysis', acting to reduce potential harms when concerns arise.

In recent years, the massive growth of artificial intelligence (AI) has given rise to concerns that the negative consequences could outweigh the many positive benefits that might be realized. In 2023, hundreds of scientists and entrepreneurs, from Elon Musk onwards, argued for a 'pause' – a temporary moratorium – so that regulatory policy could catch up with the technology. Another colourful statement suggested that AI could lead to human extinction, that it was an 'existential risk' requiring urgent regulatory action.[14] The arguments for greater regulation, including from some of the biggest proponents of the technologies, should, however, not be a brake on innovation but a moment for wider discussion about pros and cons, and the systems of precautionary regulation and democratic accountability that might work for such a revolutionary technology that affects us all. And such deliberation must, above all, confront uncertainty and not expect technocratic regulation to save the day.

How we collectively act in the face of uncertainty (and ignorance) raises questions of ethics and justice. Whose knowledge counts? What use is the technology, for whom? Whose needs and concerns matter? What are the consequences of alternative solutions? What are the potential costs of action and inaction? None of these questions can be answered purely by scientific appraisal and elite expert deliberation as they all rest on ethical and political choices. This becomes especially the case when the potential harms are huge, amounting to 'existential risks' for society and indeed the planet (Rees 2021). For example, are large-scale geoengineering solutions to the climate crisis justifiable, whether solar panels in space or iron filings in the sea, when we really don't know the consequences of such massive interventions at the same time as other solutions to climate change are possible (Biermann and Möller 2019)? What are the political implications of such interventions for particular places where the impacts may be felt especially acutely? Under such conditions, ethical deliberations must combine with an open, inclusive debate among scientists and wider publics, with the precautionary principle firmly in play (Maynard and Stilgoe 2020).

Science, technology and society

Questions of uncertainty therefore raise old debates about the appropriate relationships between science, technology and society. As Winston Churchill was reputed to have commented, 'science should be on tap, not on top', with political account-ability in a democratic system offsetting the dangers and assuring safety for populations. Others disagree, arguing that science and technology offer a vision of progress and modernity that we should never eschew. Accepting some risk is inevitable and, given the challenges of climate change, food insecurity and poverty, we should not hold back, they argue. The 'ecomodernist' visions of the Breakthrough Institute and similar organizations suggest that GM or gene-edited crops, climate geoengineering, nuclear energy, lab-grown foods, artificial intelligence and more can combine into a positive, modern future that rids the world of last-century challenges (Asafu-Adjaye et al. 2015). Such a view emerges from a context of science, technology and innovation that is increasingly privatized, globalized and centred on extraction for profit. This neoliberal perspective on technology sees science as expanding the frontiers of accumu-lation, with questions of safety, ethics and justice relegated to secondary considerations.

Such a brave new world of techno-modernist, neoliberal futures, however, rarely engages with the multiple uncertainties it generates. Even if uncertainties are acknowledged, they are either dismissed or relegated to a challenge for science rather than a wider political debate for society. Instead, as discussed in chapter 1, a different type of science is required under these contested conditions of uncertainty, one that Silvio Funtowicz and Jerry Ravetz (1990, 1993) many years ago termed 'post-normal science'. This does not reject science and technology as a source of solutions but takes a more humble attitude. Thirty years on, such an approach, I would argue, is even more necessary, as the conditions they describe are extremely relevant to many different contemporary challenges.

A post-normal science proceeds through embracing complexity and uncertainty, and this requires new forms of evidence and a different style of review of diverse forms of evidence. What are called 'extended peer communities' – lay and other experts working together – become essential in evaluating knowledge claims and suggesting policies. As Funtowicz and Ravetz argue:

> This plurality of perspectives and commitments does not deny the special competence of people with special expertise; nor does it mean anything like the importation of some token laypersons onto a review committee. However, it does mean that there is a mixing and blending of skills, partly technical and partly personal, so that all those engaged on an issue can enrich the comprehension of the whole. There is no sharp line dividing the 'expert' constituency from the 'lay', particularly since each expert will be 'lay' with respect to at least some of the others. (Funtowicz and Ravetz 1994: 204)

What does all this imply for the style and organization of scientific advice in ongoing debates about technology regulation under conditions of uncertainty and ignorance? First, there is a need to accept different types of expertise, ones that are plural and conditional, open and transparent and subject to wide deliberation. Second, advisory processes must allow diverse memberships, not just with nominal 'lay' contributions but also ones where discussions between different groups, maybe with highly conflicting positions based on different experiences and different sources of evidence, are encouraged. Third, such advisory processes need to operate both 'upstream' – framing the focus and direction of science – and 'downstream', addressing questions of application and regulation (Stilgoe, Irwin and Jones 2006). By acknowledging uncertainty, a commitment to co-production where knowledge and social/political orders are mutually constituted is required (Jasanoff 2004), allowing for diverse public imaginaries and a commitment to cognitive justice (Leach, Scoones and Wynne 2005). This is as essential for the challenges of regulating new technologies as it is for the response to pandemics, disasters or climate change, as subsequent chapters confirm.

Many have therefore called for 'responsible innovation' (Macnaghten 2020), which allows for public deliberation on the future of technology. This requires anticipation, reflexivity, inclusion and responsiveness in the process of innovation and technology regulation. In the process, as Michel Callon and colleagues argue (2009: 9), 'hybrid' institutions have to be invented that allow for democracies to be 'enriched, expanded,

extended and . . . more able to absorb the debates and controversies surrounding science and technology'.

Conclusion

Given the ways that science and technology are debated
currently, dominated by heroic visions of modernist technical
solutions and singular pathways to science-led innovation and
progress governed by controlling forms of 'risk management',
all this may seem too idealistic and pie in the sky. Yet many
important lessons have emerged from our collective engagements
with GM crops, mobile-phone technologies, artificial intelligence and many more examples where new forms of science
and technology expose uncertainties and so genuine and valid
areas of public concern. As this chapter highlights, opening up
spaces for wider democratic deliberation is vitally important –
as part of technology assessment processes, within regulatory
decision making, in the courts and as part of broader public
debate. This must go beyond performative consultation or the
nominal addition of a 'lay' person onto a committee. Equally,
such spaces must always be geared to particular social, political
and cultural contexts, steering away from one-size-fits-all
governance arrangements, respecting local political economies.
More open processes, in a variety of forms, will help us navigate
uncertainties thrown up by new developments in science and
technology, meaning that many potential benefits are assured
while errors are avoided.

Not closing down to risk but rather opening up to uncertainty and being ready for surprise in the face of ignorance is
therefore central to effective regulation of new technologies. Just
assuming that risks can be assessed, managed and communicated
through a top-down, expert-led, instrumental approach to risk
governance is misplaced and sometimes dangerous. There are no
simple, standard solutions, but lessons from past experiences,
some of which have been discussed in this chapter, show how it
is important to draw on plural but conditional knowledges and
diverse sources of expertise; to deliberate on contested issues and
bring normative questions of values and ethics centrally into the
debate about science, technology and progress. Limiting debate,
whether in policymaking spaces or in the courts, constrains the

possibilities of more robust decisions, and in the case of the law may also undermine justice.

Navigating uncertainty is challenging and uncomfortable, but would not a government minister or a High Court judge be in a better position to come to effective policy decisions or deliver justice if uncertainty is embraced, not shied away from, with deferral to inevitably limited and narrow scientific expertise? I think so. To do this will require a shift in the cultures of science, policy and the law, with new roles for particular actors – whether ministers, judges, civil servants, scientists or the public – and new institutions where open deliberations around uncertainty become central. This represents a huge challenge, but one that will be taken up if we genuinely embrace uncertainty in the crucial arena of regulating science and technology where uncertainties are of course inevitable.

4

Critical Infrastructures: How to Keep the Lights On and the Animals Alive

Introduction

What is the difference between Jerry Marshall, a control-room operator in an electricity supply system in California, and Rahma Mahmoud, a livestock herder in northern Kenya? Less than you would think. Both manage complex systems together with others in order to achieve a reliable supply of goods and services – in one case, electricity for homes and industries and in the other case, milk, meat and other livestock products for local use and the market.

Both are part of what is called a 'critical infrastructure', large-scale systems that are so essential for day-to-day life and wider society that they must not fail. Whether it is variations in electricity supply or demand or variations in available fodder due to changes in rainfall patterns or patterns of insecurity, both systems must continuously respond to high levels of variability in the environment in order to deliver relatively stable outputs. In order to do this, both Jerry and Rahma, and their families, friends and colleagues, have to scan the horizon for unexpected challenges, garnering multiple knowledges across networks, at the same time as being responsive to rapidly changing situations in real time.

This chapter will delve into the practices of both Jerry and Rahma and of the many other 'reliability professionals' working tirelessly in diverse critical infrastructures across the world, acting continuously to avert the next potential disaster. They are what Jens Zinn (2016) calls 'in-between' practices, which are central to risk management, focusing neither on rationalist perspectives on science, evidence or utility nor on non-rational faith or ideology. Such practices are centred on intuition, trust and emotional intelligence, supported by long experience and continuous learning and deliberation around options. As we will see, reliability professionals are central to the management of uncertainty and the avoidance of danger, yet their skills, aptitudes, knowledges and practices are rarely recognized in the standard designs of infrastructural systems and development projects. This chapter draws in particular on work by Emery Roe, Paul Schulman and colleagues and emerges as a result of many years of productive conversations about critical infrastructures, reliability and the similarities and differences between electricity supply systems (and other high tech, 'modern' critical infrastructures) and pastoralism in dryland areas of Africa (see Roe, Huntsinger and Labnow 1998; Roe 2020).

Normal accidents

Critical infrastructures include electricity and water supply systems, but also nuclear power stations, air traffic control and other infrastructures where the consequences of failure are large. They are usually complex, technologically sophisticated systems managed by many people. Reliability emerges when there is the safe and continuous provision of services such as electricity, water, natural gas, industrial chemicals or telecommunications (Schulman et al. 2004; Roe and Schulman 2008; Roe 2013, 2016; Schulman and Roe 2016). The supply of each is subject to uncertainties, including those generated by volatile demand, sudden system failures or natural hazards affecting the system.

The design-centred, risk management and engineering response to critical infrastructures is to develop a series of optimal protocols that assure services with no disruption, based on the modelling of event scenarios, predicted as regular or, say, once-in-a-decade occurrences. Highly trained engineers will be on call to fix problems when shocks and emergencies occur. The risk analysis and management approach is the standard response but, beyond the protocols, procedures and regulations, there are other things going on, as managers operating within such systems must deal with risk and uncertainty continuously.

Regulatory protocols are aimed to ensure that accidents do not happen, but of course, inevitably sometimes they do. The cases of the nuclear meltdown at Three Mile Island in 1979, the chemical release at Bhopal in 1984, the *Challenger* space shuttle explosion in 1986 and the *Exxon Valdez* disaster in Alaska in 1989 have all been well studied. Despite the lessons learned, since then there have been many more, whether the *Deepwater Horizon* disaster in the Gulf of Mexico in 2010 or the Fukushima explosion in 2011. Charles Perrow calls these 'normal accidents', in the sense that they are somehow inevitable in tightly coupled, complex systems. The argument runs that, in order to reduce the likelihood of such accidents happening in the future, systems need to be re-engineered in order to increase redundancy, spatial extent and reduce complexity and coupling. Standard safety procedures are often inappropriate, as they often add to system complexity, making matters worse.

Another strand of literature focuses on wider organizational arrangements and makes the case for 'high reliability organisations' (La Porte 1996), where systems are designed to avoid particular, catastrophic failures, whether a nuclear leak or failure of a water or electricity system. In contrast to the more fatalistic analysis of Perrow (1999), such analysts argue that, with the more effective organizational redesign and appropriate skills and training, catastrophic, systemic failures can be avoided (Pidgeon 2011). Such organizations attempt to instil cultures of trust, coordination and reliability, with design-based redundancy allowing flexibility under conditions of emergency. Collective approaches are essential, joining together experiences, knowledges and practices (Weick and Roberts 1993). A drive to improve performance continuously is also important in such organizations, with lessons learned from past experiences or 'near misses'. These are in turn articulated as 'best practices', which are 'fail-safe' and 'foolproof', contrasting with the 'optimized' designs imagined by engineers and economists. Close supervision is linked to well-designed protocols, procedures and standards in carefully run organizations that avoid error so that the system doesn't fail (Rochlin 1993; Schulman 1996). The aim is to create, in today's terms, more resilient organizations and systems that can weather any storm. These literatures offer important reflections on the design of critical infrastructures and the organizations that support them, but they sometimes fail to engage with the agency and practice of reliability and the people involved, such as Jerry and Rahma and their colleagues. A focus on 'high-reliability *management*', not just design or organization, suggests a complementary focus.

Roe and Schulman (2008) argue that a focus on the professionals (and their networks) at the centre of critical infrastructures is crucial. They must move between different 'performance modes' – or ways of responding to uncertainty – and shift between different cognitive frames and practices in so doing. This all must happen in real time, continuously. In conditions when the input variability is high – which is most of the time – and when there are options available to respond, then a 'just-in-time' performance mode is the most common. When options decline, just-for-now will do, but the challenge is always to create new options, so that responses to uncertain conditions can be both rapid and effective. In order to be responsive in real time, reliability professionals must switch between scanning the horizon for unforeseen dangers, looking for emerging patterns and testing options against potential scenarios and reactive, case-by-case response at the micro-level. In all instances, reliability professionals connect people, mobilizing expertise and support. Learning, communication, networking and being aware of the situation as it unfolds are all essential skills.

The next two sections look at what this all looks like in practice in an electricity system in California and a pastoral system in Kenya.

Electricity systems: keeping the lights on in California

Based on a fascinating longitudinal study of the California Independent System Operator (CAISO) (Roe and Schulman 2008), we can ask the simple question: how are the lights kept on?[1] The context for the study was the deregulation of the state's electricity supply system from 1998. This involved breaking up integrated public utilities and creating a market for all aspects of electricity generation, transmission and distribution. Following deregulation, private electricity generators sell electricity to distributors on a wholesale market who in turn sell it to retail customers. Within the new complex network are engineers, software suppliers, transmission managers, line maintenance experts and multiple traders and brokers. CAISO became central to the overall system, being responsible for managing a high-voltage grid across the state.

CAISO employs about 600 people and at its centre is the 'control room' where in the early 2000s about thirteen people sat around different computer consoles. The wider network linked to the control operations included engineers, software experts, purchasers and schedulers, transmission dispatchers, input suppliers, safety consultants, repair teams and others. The job of those in the control room, linking to this wider network, was at heart to balance load and generation across a complex techno-logical network to ensure reliable electricity supply. As a CAISO control-room official observed, comparing the system before deregulation, 'To operate the system now, it's so dynamic. It's a full-time challenge. It's very volatile . . . The biggest challenges are all the unknowns in all your decision factors and forecasts. A lot of decisions have to be made fast, in a short time. . . .There is a lot of intuition involved, and a lot of experience coming in.'[2]

However, the policy design for the deregulation did not account for the uncertainties it created but was driven on the basis of simplistic economic assumptions about the benefits of privatization and deregulation. The danger posed by deregu-lation was mass blackouts causing economic havoc, dangers to public health and even deaths. Yet, despite the dire predictions, this did not happen to the extent feared. Why was this?

The short answer is reliability professionals and their networks. How did they generate reliability given such volatility and within a complex, technologically sophisticated infrastructure with many moving parts? In other words, what do control-room operators do all day (and night) to avert disasters and ensure reliable supplies of electricity most of the time? The answers are fascinating. In sum, these systems aren't reliable unless they are managed in ways that go beyond design and technologies.

Transforming high input variability to low output variability requires a range of options to be available to controllers and operators. Even in a highly complex, tightly coupled system like deregulated electricity supply, the many reliability professionals such as Jerry Marshall can navigate their way, substituting, improvising and experimenting with different options, often at the last minute. So, for instance, changes in the weather, failures in one part of the generation system, the breaking of a line or load fluctuations due to changing demand result in a highly unpredictable and uncontrollable situation.

In an electricity supply system, many challenges are faced. Load and generation capacity is balanced across the grid to avoid insufficient generation resulting in power outages or too much generation burning out key facilities. All this needs transmission pathways through the grid to be assured. Overheating of lines that could cause fires and accidents should be avoided so loads must be managed carefully. Voltage levels across the grid must be regulated so that they are neither too high (and so potentially destroy equipment of electricity users) nor too low (resulting in transmission failures). In the same way, frequencies must be modulated so as to ensure that electrical equipment functions effectively. All these challenges and more are managed in the CAISO control room, where operators monitor information on everything from voltage and frequency readings across the system, to load and generation balance across the grid, to the status of path transmission across each of the regional networks (Roe and Schulman 2008: 27–8).

CAISO employees explain how the challenges increased after deregulation as, for example, electricity was being sold by private traders but was not necessarily available to meet demand at a particular time due to delays in trading bids. CAISO operators had to experiment, creating proxy bids to fill the gap temporarily (Roe and Schulman 2008: 62). It meant that responding to uncertainty and managing reliability had become intense and stressful, requiring new skills and personal and social resources, along with much experimentation and improvisation along the way.

A gen dispatcher observed, 'As long as you keep the big picture, things are good . . . Stability of attention is important – you can't lose focus.'[3] Another commented, 'It's a massive amount of multitasking, you've got to be analysing what's moving, how fast can it move, you've got to have a good overall picture of what's going on, all this simultaneously.'[4] There are no 'normal' patterns, as everything changes fast, and this has accelerated since deregulation. This means operating in 'peak' mode more often, which requires a lot of time spent on coordination, ringing people up and ensuring that information is shared, what operators call 'firefighting' (Roe and Schulman 2008: 37). As the gen dispatcher noted, having an eye on the 'big picture' is essential, but it means switching between interpreting emerging patterns, testing out scenarios under a whole range of potential future contingencies and facing real-time challenges around particular cases in the here and now. As another gen dispatcher commented, 'I have two or three decisions ahead (three on a bad day). I have to be aware: what are my options.' Their colleague summed it up: 'I have to worry about the future at the same time I am doing the present.'[5] It is in this 'middle ground' where reliability professionals operate, both looking ahead and anticipating the future while responding in the now to uncertain events as they arise. As Roe and Schulman put it (2008: 67), they are 'neither system designers nor narrowly focused reactive operators', but they operate in between these classic and recognized roles in a space that receives very little formal acknowledgement.

Shifting between performance modes is essential, and this requires rapid learning and quick responses. As one interviewee, a control-room manager in a transmission operations centre, explained, 'You don't learn as fast as you can until you have to respond to something that requires fast responses.'[6] For most of the time, operators were operating in 'just-in-time' performance mode. This meant rapidly adjusting. But occasionally, when options were not available, temporary options were applied, and occasionally resort to old-style command and control became necessary. But for nearly all occasions a flexible, rapid, continuous style of response was seen, and this was essential for keeping the lights on, even in the face of extreme uncertainty.

Reliability professionals must guard against complacency and must always be aware of the judgements that they are making. They must always have alternatives at hand and must ensure that all staff members in the network are engaged in a focused mission of ensuring the safe, continuous provision of electricity to the grid. Roe and Schulman (2008) point out that staying out of unstudied conditions is essential. As a control-room supervisor observed, 'I'm always uncomfortable.' This is a good thing and helps to increase safety and reliability in the system.

As Roe and Schulman observe, traditional approaches tend to rely on elaborate investment in the design of anticipatory

systems in order to generate system resilience, supported by
various models, standards and protocols. However, in the
context in which Jerry Marshall and colleagues work, this is
not appropriate and would slow things down and undermine
effective responses to immediate, rapidly unfolding situations.
Responding to the blackouts that occurred during California's
electricity crisis, a shift supervisor commented, 'We're trying
to write the rules for something that's just happened, but each
rolling blackout is new. It was a nightmare.'[7] Under conditions of
uncertainty, predictions are impossible, and generalized anticipatory approaches fall down when it is the specific, real-time
contexts that are important. Rules have to be continuously
reinvented. Widespread experimentation and adaptive improvisation are therefore vitally important to just-in-time working
practices when navigating uncertainty.

Pastoral systems: responding to drought and disease

Despite the obvious differences, a pastoral production system in
northern Kenya is in many ways quite similar to an electricity
supply system. The reliable provision of goods and services
under conditions of deep uncertainty is the same mission.
Pastoralists are confronted by many challenges – droughts,
floods, conflict, disease, market volatility and so on – none of
which are predictable. This means they must continuously avert
disasters and so generate reliability in the system.
    Rahma Mahmoud, introduced earlier, is a female herder from
Kinna in Isiolo County in northern Kenya who manages about
fifty cattle.[8] In February 2023, she was planning how to keep them
alive, given the terrible drought that was enveloping the region.
She had assessed the risks and developed scenarios about how to
respond. She had listened to those who were predicting drought
but was hedging her bets. She had invested in relationships that
would allow her animals to survive if things got worse, making
deals with farmers in Meru and prospecting near the national
park where she had relationships with guards and rangers to
access grazing (illegally). She lives in Kinna town but regularly
travels to see her animals (at least every two days) to monitor
the herding labour. The motorbike drivers whom she employs

to transport her are also involved in scouting further afield to see if there are better opportunities for water and grazing. She has a reliable M-Pesa (mobile money) dealer in Kinna who can advance her cash if there is an immediate problem (say, a fine from the national park, a sudden payment required at a farm, the need for emergency feed), and she has sustained this relationship over years. She knows the agrovet and the *Chilres* (traditional animal healer) and will consult them if the animals are feeling sick, responding rapidly if there is need. As she explains, 'It's a difficult time now. The herd has been split, between the weaker and stronger animals. Some are grazing about halfway to Meru. We fear the rains will fail, so we have to be ready to move to the farms or the national park.'

Just like the real-time operators and dispatchers in the California electricity system, she was developing scenarios about the future, responding to diverse contingencies. She was expanding her options – through making contacts with farmers in Meru and keeping in touch with national park guards and others. She had funds available and the ability to transfer them when needed. All this meant that she could respond rapidly if things got really tough and rains did not come in March or April. Given that the network is dispersed – just like the deregulated California electricity supply system – good communication is vital, and mobile phones as well as motorbikes mean that everyone can be contacted quickly, as soon as the need arises. Monitoring the situation carefully is essential so she always keeps an eye on the condition of her animals.

As it turned out, heavy rains came in late March and this caused new, unexpected problems. With fresh grass suddenly available, the animals became ill as they were not in good condition, and some were lost. Disease also spread, and Rahma had to make connections with the agrovet and local healer to ensure that animals were saved. Rains came more steadily in April and, although the animals had been split into two groups with some moved further south, there was no immediate necessity to hire grazing on the farms, although she had earlier bought in hay for calves and pregnant females.

Rahma's experience is typical. At the centre of the reliability network is the herder, with others enlisted to help out, be they those who can offer advice and technical knowledge, supply finance or ease access to key resources. The tracking between wider horizon scanning and immediate response requires skill, combined with good social relations and, in Rahma's case, some funds generated from the sale of animals. The challenge for a reliability professional in a pastoral area is to balance animal condition with fodder and water supply in a highly variable system. The objective is to ensure animals survive a drought (or heavy rainfall, disease outbreak or any other source of uncertainty) so as to generate a reliable flow of livestock products (mostly milk and meat, but also manure that can be exchanged for access to fodder with farmers) and income from sales. Rather than electricity load and generation supply, other variables have to be balanced in a complex system (a critical infrastructure), but the principles are the same.

Mobile herding combines skilled labour, flexible fodder provision from different sources and disease control in pastoral strategies to confront the highly variable, non-equilibrium environments that characterize pastoral areas. The result is – hopefully – a stable flow of livestock services and products that continues to support livelihoods. Uncertainties dominate pastoralists' lives and are seen by these communities not as hazards to be avoided, adapted to or coped with but to be embraced and even lived off (Scoones 1994; Krätli and Schareika 2010; Scoones 2023a,b).

Central to the generation of reliability in pastoral settings – as in electricity supply – are networks. These are built through social relationships and can be drawn on when challenges are faced. Five hundred kilometres to the north, in North Horr in Marsabit district, herders who keep camels, goats and sheep must work together to tackle livestock diseases. There are many diseases that can undermine production or even kill animals; some are seasonal, some episodic, some continuous. For example, *peste des petits ruminants* and contagious caprine pleuropneumonia strike small stock, while brucellosis and tuberculosis, along with diarrhoea and worm infestations, are significant in camel populations.

Looking at knowledge interactions around managing uncertain livestock diseases, research led by Alex Tasker identified three interlocking networks through a detailed mapping of knowledge exchanges analysed by 'social network analysis' (Tasker and Scoones 2022). The form and functioning of such networks tell us a lot about how reliability is constructed. First, there is what we called the 'locally embedded' network. This involves largely informal knowledge exchanges between pastoralists and service providers, including some key brokers who act as 'high-reliability professionals'. Next, there is the 'development project' network, where exchanges occur around an NGO-led partici-patory disease surveillance programme. And, third, there is a smaller but still significant 'political' network, which is used to engage with political actors outside the local area.

Across these three networks, knowledge flows in different ways. The actors in each network differ, but the overlaps and connections between the networks are crucial. Within the locally embedded network, flows of knowledge are based on two-way exchanges. Issues are deliberated upon collectively, and infor-mation from other areas is brought in by key players who have wider links and cross-ethnic and language connections. Crucial in such exchanges is the *Chilres*, who is a traditional livestock healer but importantly also a knowledge broker who helps to address livestock disease challenges. His connections with Boran, Turkana and Samburu herders allow knowledge and experiences to be shared across wide areas. As a high-reliability professional, he is able to scan the horizon for future challenges and better practices while also garnering information for immediate cases. The knowledge exchanges recorded with the *Chilres* were broad and discursive, often involving the telling of stories, exchanging poems and relaying anecdotes. Reliability emerged through a collective process of sharing, rooted in a vernacular style, where uncertainties were deliberated upon from different perspectives and were not assumed to be definitive risks emerging from expert assessment.

This contrasted starkly with the development project network, where the state veterinary department or the NGO delivered singular, technical recommendations in a one-way, top-down exchange, rather than having responses emerge through a more open discussion. The community disease-reporting approach involves the channelling of information from the community upwards for experts to interpret and provide recommenda-tions about disease risks. This is a classic, technical form of risk assessment and management, rather than one rooted in real-time responses of reliability management. A young herder contrasted the advice from the *Chilres* with that from NGO employees:

I know him [the *Chilres*] well, he is a good man, a clever man. He and I talk about many things, he knows about animals very much ... You may ask him many things that he can tell you ... When you go to [the NGO] ... you can ask them for their knowledge, but they follow the programme that they have. If they are digging wells, then you have water. If they are vaccinating, then that is what you will have.[9]

The *Chilres*, however, did not operate alone. His reliability network relied on key relationships with the local Animal Health Assistant (AHA) and the Community Animal Health Worker (CAHW) – themselves both herders from the Gabra ethnic group. Their employment allowed access to veterinary care from state services. Both the AHA and CAHW therefore have multiple identities, allowing them to become important knowledge brokers. As a local pastoralist explained when discussing the AHA:

You cannot sit with [the NGO] people, you cannot talk with them as we [the Gabra] talk. He [the AHA] sits every night, he herds his animals, he is at weddings and he will be with us when it rains and when it does not. But he is clever and he has a good job, a job that means he can talk to the NGO, to government. He can make them hear us and can tell us what they say and what they do not say. What is good for him is good for us.[10]

In the same vein, when describing the CAHW's role, another herder noted, 'The CAHW knows the animals and the government well, he has many friends and people who he knows and works with. He is a good man for North Horr as they [the government] will know us and our problems.'[11]

In North Horr, the capacity to respond to uncertain livestock disease events therefore is assured by a locally embedded network, which is linked to two other overlapping networks through local brokers, in turn facilitated by technologies, notably mobile phones and WhatsApp groups. The locally embedded network has all the characteristics of high-reliability management, including the scanning across knowledge domains (tacit, experiential, vernacular, scientific), active learning and collective deliberation, local experimentation and innovation and flexibility in responses. Due to connections across networks, including to the state, to NGO projects, to other ethnic groups and even to diaspora connections of Gabra who can offer support, the overall system becomes more reliable. Facilitation of cross-network interactions by reliability professionals is essential, not only for galvanizing knowledge and support but for responding in real time to challenges when they arise. While the state and the NGO contribute through their projects, these efforts would not be effective without the locally embedded network and the associated brokers.

However, this process of reliability generation reliant on local actors is not acknowledged or recognized by the NGO and the state. It is an important lesson for how to understand external interventions in context: without local action and support, such interventions would go nowhere. Here, too, livestock disease responses would not be reliable if they were not managed beyond official designs and technologies. A critical infrastructure has many parts, and focusing just on the formal ones, symbolized by project signs, shiny cars and fancy offices, misses perhaps the most important elements needed for ensuring reliability in the face of intersecting uncertainties.

The knowledge of locally based, networked reliability professionals for ensuring reliability under difficult conditions therefore requires skills, expertise and situational, contextual awareness rooted in social relationships. To label this knowledge as 'indigenous' or 'traditional' is missing the point, as it is always hybrid and deployed as part of a networked professionalism geared to addressing uncertainties. In this sense, reliability can be seen as the networked capacity to mobilize knowledge to confront uncertainty and avoid ignorance, where conditions have not been studied or experienced before (Tasker and Scoones 2022).

In this case, the study focused on responding to livestock disease uncertainties, but there are many different and overlapping reliability networks addressing livestock water provision, livestock and product marketing, fodder management, herding labour organization, responding to insecurity and conflict, off-farm income earning or indeed any other aspect of pastoral development.[12] Such networks require different reliability professionals – some involving mostly older men, some largely women or younger people – working in different ways with different sources of knowledge, but the principles are the same. There are of course no guarantees, but 'development' projects, with their focus on formal design, hierarchical knowledge flows and risk management and control, rarely match the capacities of local reliability networks, and they ignore them at their peril.

Beyond the politics of design and control

Rather than seeking to enhance locally embedded networks, centred on reliability professionals – whether in control rooms of electricity supply systems in California or the rangelands of northern Kenya – most efforts to 'improve' such systems do the opposite. By pushing an illusion of control, such interventions try to restructure and streamline in order to increase efficiency and provide improved technocratic oversight, focusing on risk, not uncertainty. This usually acts to undermine existing practices of reliability, requiring new experiments and innovations by reliability professionals and their networks to avoid disasters ironically often made worse by 'development'.

In the California electricity system, the deregulation designed by economists, engineers and policymakers committed to a 'free market' solution caused a whole array of problems as market transactions took over. This required the reliability professionals at CAISO to improvise and innovate fast. The reduction of the bandwidth for operation by efficiency 'improvements' and technological 'upgrading' acted to reduce options for reliability professionals to work with, as they continued to manage uncertainty and avoid ignorance. Real-time monitoring, artificial intelligence-generated data and elaborate risk-assessment protocols may be useful, but only if embedded in existing and emerging reliability practices, rather than being seen as a design response to generate greater control over the system (Roe and Schulman 2008).

In the same way, in pastoral systems, investments in expensive and elaborate 'early warning' systems may give the impression of greater knowledge and therefore control, but actually the link between satellite-derived information on drought impacts, for example, and local action is often broken. The information may not 'downscale' effectively to local situations; recommendations fail and the system is therefore not trusted (Buchanan-Smith and Davies 1995; see also chapter 6 below). By assuming that risk can be managed through technological developments, reliability is undermined by the complexities and uncertainties of the real world. Ignoring the reliability of professionals on the ground creates a disconnect between development efforts and actual practice, galvanized by a hubristic illusion of control.

This is of course not to say that reliability professionals reject innovations and improvements; they are constantly striving to improve but in a prospective, challenge-oriented way responsive to uncertainties as they unfold, rather than premised on attempting to control the uncontrollable. When new technologies emerge – such as mobile phones and WhatsApp capacities for group-based conversations in the pastoral rangelands – they are grasped with great enthusiasm as they provide the basis for doing what reliability professionals require: sharing, learning, experimenting, improvising and adapting.

High-reliability management is intensely political. The knowledge relationships and socio-technologies at the core of reliability networks are shaped by power and politics. The systems within which reliability professionals must operate, and the array of options they have to play with, are structured by wider processes of political economy. These may be ideological proclivities of policymakers and politicians who commit to ideals of 'efficiency' and 'optimization' through 'deregulation' or the patterns of globalization that refashion knowledge networks and technological possibilities in new ways. While the focus of this chapter has been on the agency of particular professionals and their networks, these wider structural relationships are always important.

The point is that reliability professionals are not just passive recipients; they must respond, reshape, recast and reinvent continuously within wider political economic contexts. CAISO control-room professionals and pastoralists in northern Kenya therefore do not sit by and passively 'cope'; they must always reimagine 'the system' within which they operate. For electricity control-room staff, the move to deregulate has reshaped operational requirements entirely, requiring new ways of balancing load and generation. For pastoralists in northern Kenya, the increasing intensity and frequency of droughts due to the combined effects of climate change and land encroachment does not mean that they just give up, but pastoral livelihoods must be reconfigured, with migration to other areas and the adoption of new livelihood strategies generating a diversified response to expanding uncertainty with new standards of reliability (Scoones and Nori 2023). For both, the response is not to imagine a new 'optimal' control solution that can be designed by outsiders and imposed as part of a 'will to improve' (Li 2007), but instead new options have to be continuously created, not as fixed design and standardized development but as flexible management and practice.

Emery Roe summarizes how pastoralists, like control-room operators, are reliability seeking, not risk averting:

> Reliability professionals manage their operations *because* they do not have entire control of the system at any one time, where however any coping passively to system-wide shocks outside of direct control is not an option either. Instead, they must actively manage risks they cannot control as well as actively manage key uncertainties so as to stay out of unstudied conditions. More, if and when they find themselves in unstudied conditions, they cope by planning the next step ahead. (Roe 2020: 18)

Conclusion

As reliability professionals in very different systems, Jerry and Rahma share some common skills. Within the system that they are operating – an electricity supply system and a pastoral system supplying livestock products – working together with many others, they seek to reduce variability and so uncertainty, and to encourage stability and so reliability in flows of goods and services, just as we saw in the 'real markets' discussed in chapter 2 when financial and market volatility was being tackled. There are many others like Jerry and Rahma in many other 'critical infrastructures' around the world. Think of any that you are familiar with – supplying water, food, energy, transport, financial services, liveable buildings, clean air, biodiversity conservation or whatever – and you will find similar people, with similar capacities, linked in complex ways to different networks. In subsequent chapters of this book, we meet reliability professionals confronting pandemics, disasters and climate change, for example.

In whichever case, you need to ask what system is it that is being managed and to what standards – is it only certain events that need to be precluded, is some disruption acceptable and what forms of catastrophic collapse need to be avoided at all costs? What forms of variability are important, so what uncertainties must be managed and what areas of ignorance need to be avoided? And what networks need to be built and what practices must be deployed in order to keep goods and services supplied continuously and reliably? Navigating uncertainty and generating reliability requires different skills – knowledge of what is possible, based on the building of scenarios and the scanning of horizons, as well as real-time responses in the moment to unfolding situations. It's always a messy, complex situation with no clear rules, and most responses are informal, unrecognized, below-the-radar practices, yet are crucial to generating reliability (Roe 2013). Tacit, experiential knowledge, case studies, scenario analysis and pattern-recognition skills combine with astute vigilance and accumulated experience, held both by individuals and in common within networks (Roe and Schulman 2008).

As already emphasized, the practices of the reliability professional therefore go beyond the macro-design of the policymaker or planner but also differ from the micro-operations of the 'street-level bureaucrat' on his or her own. Reliability professionals, therefore, must neither get lost in the micro-management of immediate operations, nor focus only on the wider policy context and future scenarios; instead, they must tack between these frames, learning continuously and spotting problems and responding in real time. All this requires flexibility, adaptation and customization, as well as being able to recognize what works from past experience (Roe 2016).

No single individual can undertake all these tasks so, as we have seen, reliability emerges from lateral networks, ones that are linked by personal contact, trust and collegial or familial relationships. In an electricity system, this will be among control-room operators, engineers, data analysts, suppliers, regulators and others, while in a pastoral system, networks are formed between pastoralists, local government officials, veterinarians, hired labourers, mobile money operators, agro-dealers, traditional healers and weather forecasters, among others. Collective recognition of the mission – the 'performance regime' – helps avoid complacency and catastrophic failure.

The continuous averting of disasters in critical infrastructures is a vital task in an uncertain world. Yet high-reliability professionals, whether in California or northern Kenya, are – to repeat – often not recognized. Standard responses to risks and uncertainty rely on risk assessments, safety regulations and operational protocols or are imposed as externally designed 'development' projects that can actually undermine the resilience of pastoral systems in the face of shocks and stresses. Formalizing the informal out of existence, when critical service reliability is at stake, is always a big error. In sum, a better recognition of high-reliability professionals, their knowledge, skills and aptitudes along with the networks that they are embedded in, is a far better route to responding to diverse uncertainties faced by any critical infrastructure and requires a very different approach to staffing, training, reward systems, organizational design and external support.

5

Pandemics: Building Responses from Below

By March 2020, COVID-19 had already reached Europe and was causing devastation across northern Italy. The terrible scenes from China were already on everyone's television screens and newsfeeds. In London, a number of specialist scientific committees had been formed to review the evidence and inform politicians about a plan of action. No one knew what might happen or whether in the United Kingdom it would be different to elsewhere. As a UK parliamentary inquiry from September 2021 put it, decision makers were operating in a 'fog of uncertainty'.[1]

Central among the UK committees was SAGE – the Scientific Advisory Group for Emergencies – which was convened in January 2020 and was linked to other committees, including the Scientific Pandemic Influenza Group on Modelling.[2] SAGE was co-chaired by the Government Chief Scientific Advisor, then Patrick Vallance, and the Chief Medical Officer, Chris Whitty. The core members of SAGE were scientists, and particularly epidemiologists with knowledge about how diseases spread and how they affect human populations. Meetings were also attended by a number of civil servants and advisers, including Dominic Cummings, a notorious fan of 'super-forecasting'.[3] In the early months of the pandemic, the star among the SAGE scientists was Neil Ferguson of Imperial College in London, whose group had developed a model for COVID-19 in the United Kingdom, drawing on their long experience with influenza, foot-and-mouth disease and other outbreaks. This of course was not the only model, as others contributed from the London School of Hygiene and Tropical Medicine, Warwick, Oxford and Edinburgh. SAGE, as Patrick Vallance explained, was a setting of intense debate across many uncertainties.[4]

On 16 March, Ferguson presented a new paper.[5] It had a rather boring title – *Impact of Non-Pharmaceutical Interventions (NPIs) to Reduce COVID-19 Mortality and Healthcare Demand* – but it was a bombshell. The model had been adapted to incorporate data from Italy on hospitalizations from COVID-19, rather than using the earlier data from influenza outbreaks. This changed the results dramatically. If the disease spread as they expected, with an R_0 of 2.6, it would overwhelm the National Health Service and, without any mitigating measures, up to 510,000 people could die in Great Britain. Some mitigation would result in 250,000 deaths and total suppression could reduce mortality to 20,000. Rather than managing the disease with the aim of achieving some level of 'herd immunity', the results suggested much more dramatic action and an immediate lockdown.[6] On 23 March, in a sombre televised address, the Prime Minister Boris Johnson finally announced the first full lockdown.[7]

Meanwhile, over 8,000 kilometres away in Harare, Joseph Mlambo was in Parirenyatwa hospital as part of his student training for becoming a nurse. The first cases in Zimbabwe were all imports, including from the United Kingdom. But everyone had seen the news from China and Europe and heard what was happening from relatives in the diaspora from the United Kingdom and elsewhere. No one knew what was going to happen, and there certainly were no COVID-19 models for Zimbabwe to offer any type of prediction.[8] As Mlambo explained, 'We were scared, but as students we had no choice; we had to attend to the sick. We had no PPE [personal protective equipment], no experience, no knowledge.'[9] Over the coming weeks, together with his fellow students, other nurses and doctors, he had to deal with a rise in COVID-19 cases. Very aware of the consequences of previous epidemics, they followed international World Health Organization guidelines, and soon the government responded with its own lockdown measures. Everyone seemed to expect the worst, even though at that time there were only a handful of reported cases in the country and very limited local transmission.

Here we have two very different settings, each confronting profound uncertainties where the future was unknown. In the United Kingdom, a highly qualified cadre of scientists was on hand, linked to a well-established system of 'science-based' emergency response. A populist government with a strong libertarian streak under then Prime Minister Boris Johnson was ill-prepared for dealing with the pandemic, as the subsequent public inquiry has starkly shown.[10] Ministers resisted state impositions, and obfuscation and delay characterized the response. A big fear was that the National Health Service would be overwhelmed, a consequence of decades of policy neglect and underfunding. In Zimbabwe, by contrast, the public health system barely existed, due to the ongoing economic and political crisis that had persisted since the late 1990s, exacerbated by economic mismanagement, corruption and international sanctions imposed after Zimbabwe's land reform. The president, Emerson Mnangagwa, and his vice-president and health minister, Constantino Chiwenga, were from state security and military backgrounds, and an authoritarian, top-down response came easily. At least early on, this was supported by public health professionals who were deeply concerned that if the virus spread, the consequences could be devastating. They had lived through the worst of the HIV/AIDS pandemic and knew a lot about how to handle epidemics.

So, in one case, epidemiological modelling offered one way of thinking about the future; in the other, people had to find their way without concrete predictions while drawing on past experiences. While the UK scientists couched their predictions with all sorts of qualifications, inevitably it was the numbers of potential deaths that hit the headlines. In Zimbabwe, there were no models, but the international guidelines were what the government fell back on, following a standardized, prescribed approach to responding to a pandemic. Yet in practice in both cases people on the ground had to get on and deal with what was an uncertain, threatening and incredibly scary future.

Epidemiological certainties?

The revised Imperial College model became the central basis for the UK response, prompting the sudden switch from a laissez-faire approach to one of strict, state-led intervention. While ultimately it was elected politicians who decided on what to do, the scientific-bureaucratic elite was highly influential. As we saw in the case of the financial and banking crisis in chapter 2, models can take on a life of their own.[11] They of course are only as good as the assumptions that structure them and the data that they make use of. In the case of Imperial College, it was a fairly standard SIR compartment model, where susceptible, infected and recovered/removed populations were looked at. Such models are widely used to investigate disease dynamics, extended sometimes by agent-based modelling that looks at the interactions between people and disease agents over time.

However, the standard compartment models have limitations. They are mostly deterministic, providing a singular output from known starting conditions. They therefore often do not account for dynamic, stochastic properties, including sudden changes and random events. They assume aggregate patterns across varied geographies, including of movement and mixing. And they often fail to account for non-normal patterns, including super-spreader events (Hinchliffe 2020; Shen, Taleb and Bar-Yam 2020). At the beginning of the pandemic, all modellers were dealing with multiple uncertainties – about incubation periods, asymptomatic transmission, viral evolutionary dynamics and more – so much had to be assumed. If those making use of models are not careful, they may give a false sense of precision when in fact things are uncertain. This in turn can give the mistaken impression to politicians that a disease can be controlled when in fact ambiguity and complexity reign (Heffernan 2021). This was a big problem in the early stages of the pandemic in the United Kingdom.

Another problem with the initial modelling work was the lack of data. The first versions of nearly all models used experience and data from influenza outbreaks as a benchmark, assuming no asymptomatic infection and easy control. In retrospect, this was a mistake. As Sally Davies, former UK Chief Medical Officer observed, 'we underestimated the impact of novel and particularly zoonotic diseases.'[12] Assumptions based on influenza led to delays in response, with some arguing that letting the virus selectively run through the population would ultimately offer a level of herd immunity.[13] However, with high hospitalization and mortality rates from the SARS-CoV2 virus in the first wave, especially among old people and ethnic minority groups living

in multi-generational housing, this would have been a disastrous option. Using data from Italy shifted the models' outputs
dramatically, and different decisions followed. As others pointed
out, you had only to look at the television to see that this was
nothing like flu. Richard Horton, a medical doctor and long-time
editor of the journal *The Lancet*, angrily argued that scientists
in the United Kingdom knew what was going on as early as
December when Chinese colleagues were discussing the Wuhan
outbreak. Why did they wait until nearly the end of March to
lock down?[14]

It was not as if these discussions were not part of the debates
within SAGE – and by then also its counterpart, the Independent
SAGE, which was set up in May 2020 by the former UK Chief
Scientist David King to offer complementary scientific views
and a more open debate. As Jeremy Farrar, himself a member
of SAGE, then director of the Wellcome Trust and a very well-
respected medical scientist, shows in his book *Spike*, there was
intense debate, with the rather anodyne SAGE minutes not
reflecting the profound nature of deliberations (Farrar and Ahuja
2021). However, as the inquiries into the pandemic response
have clearly found, the dangers around disciplinary expertise,
over-reliance on models and lack of structured challenge undermined the capacity of the UK science advice system to address
uncertainty.[15]

Complexity, uncertainty and grounded experiences

The problem was that the epidemiological models (and there
were by then quite a number) dominated the discussions,
leading to what statistician David Spiegelhalter called 'number
theatre',[16] performed in the regular televised briefings by officials.
Meanwhile, those who were dealing with the uncertainties
on the ground across the United Kingdom were largely not
being listened to. The composition of the SAGE committee
has been much criticized because in the crucial initial stages of
the pandemic, before the first lockdown, it was almost wholly
dominated by epidemiologists and medical scientists from the
United Kingdom, with a scattering of behavioural scientists on
the sidelines. There were no social or political scientists at all

at that stage and, more importantly, seemingly no mechanisms for listening to those on the front line, whether in Birmingham, Bergamo or Beijing, and learning from their experiences.

Underpinning the dominance of a technocratic decision-making structure was the rather arrogant assumptions of 'British exceptionalism': we have top scientists, we know best and therefore we are prepared. That there was considerable experience emerging from East Asia in early 2020 was, it seems, simply ignored or deemed irrelevant. The United Kingdom had prepared extensively for a future pandemic, but this (again) was modelled on influenza. In 2016, a major civil emergencies simulation, Exercise Cygnus, was undertaken, involving more than a thousand civil servants and others. This built on a previous exercise in 2007, Winter Willow, involving some five thousand participants. Such simulation exercises may have helped in some ways, but they may also have been a distraction and generated a smug complacency and a false sense of confidence. As the then Secretary of State for Health, Matt Hancock, explained to the UK COVID-19 public inquiry on 27 June 2023, it turned out that the reassurance that the United Kingdom was the 'best prepared in the world' was simply 'wrong'. There was a 'flawed doctrine' at play, influenced by the flu modelling and emergency simulations, he explained, with it being assumed that a full pandemic could not be contained and suppressed. When probed, whether the models and risk assessments 'simply failed to identify a sufficiently broad range of scenarios', his answer was, simply, 'Yes'.[17]

Models, of course, have social and political lives; they are not just neutral collections of mathematical equations, but once they gain traction in policy they get intertwined with social and political processes (Leach and Scoones 2013). This happened to the Imperial model big time. Over several crucial months, the model became central to UK political decision making, provoking tussles between those who preferred the libertarian approach and no state intervention and those who urged caution and early action by the state, even in the face of opposition. By finally recommending a major lockdown in mid-March 2020, it set the tone for the rest of the pandemic and many of the challenges that ensued.

Although there is a pretence that models are simply techno-cratic 'evidence-based' tools that are offered to policy for decision making as in the tired adage 'science advises, politics decides', the relationship is of course much more complex. The neat separation of science and policy, especially when things are urgent, complex and contested and the stakes are high, has been much disputed (Funtowicz and Ravetz 1993; Sarewitz 2004), as discussed in earlier chapters. Scientists are rarely the neutral arbiters of undisputed knowledge, as sometimes imagined; they can be advisers, advocates, brokers and more, often shifting between roles as part of the science advice process (Pielke 2007). Operating across the boundaries of science and policy, many researchers have contrasting perspectives on uncertainties, based on experience in different domains. In the realm of science and modelling, a high acceptance of uncertainty is standard, and the important skill is to know when predictions make sense and, importantly, when they don't (Yates 2023). By contrast, when scientists are advisers on committees, the incentive to move into the 'certainty trough' (MacKenzie 1998) is high, where advice is frequently narrowed and uncertainties ignored (Pearce 2020).

The famous slogan, repeated endlessly in the United Kingdom at the beginning of the pandemic, 'Follow the science' begs many questions, as I reflected in an opinion piece in mid-March 2020: which (singular) science, who leads, who follows?[18] As Helen MacNamara, the United Kingdom's deputy cabinet secretary at the time, commented at the public inquiry in November 2023, the slogan was used to put pressure on scientists and shift blame and responsibility in a context when key figures making the ultimate decisions seemed not to have a clue what the science was.[19] Inevitably, models have embedded within them assumptions about how society functions and how individuals behave. Simplifications are necessary, and so assumptions about homogenous mixing, standard travel patterns and so on are common. Models, therefore, are intimately entwined with social and political assumptions – for example, about age, gender, racial or occupational dimensions – ones that are not necessarily questioned by the epidemiological modellers whose expertise lies elsewhere. This must be the job of others, but in the United Kingdom at that time they were not at the table or, if they were, they were clearly not competent.[20]

Especially in emergency situations, where modelling efforts frequently happen at night under great pressure in advance of meetings the following day, the way science and policymaking become entwined is important to understand. Models are in this sense 'performative'; they offer another element of the drama, and the actors involved become centrally involved in the play. Models therefore act as 'boundary objects' (Star 2010) and are situated relationally between the intersecting practices of science and policymaking (Rhodes and Lancaster 2020; Cairney 2021). Through offering the prospect of 'taming' chance and uncertainty (Hacking 1990), models can also close down debate, narrowing the framing and limiting the sources of data (Christley et al. 2013; Saltelli et al. 2020; Stirling and Scoones 2020). In the construction of models, publics are imagined often as passive and ignorant, in need of reassurance and direction and, in the UK case, as unwilling or unable to follow collective rules, preferring instead independent, individualized liberties (Ballo et al. 2022). By providing prediction and direction, epidemiological models offer security and certainty in the face of uncertainty, creating subjects disciplined by scientifically prescribed interventions. In this way, they act as a disciplining tool of anticipatory governance, especially in emergency settings (Guston 2014; Lakoff 2017).

The predictions that emerge, no matter what the qualifications and nuances, can gain extraordinary purchase in public and media debate – as with the models around possible mortalities in the United Kingdom from COVID-19. They thereby escape the confines of qualified scientific calculus to become 'real' in policy debates through their performative effects as they travel in society (Latour 1987; Callon and Law 2005). Models therefore are co-constituted with politics, acting to define citizens and wider society. As models travel, it is their 'situational fit' rather than their precise empirical validity that becomes important, as they gain 'agency' in the wider debate (Rhodes and Lancaster 2022a). In this sense, the science is 'emergent', the product of the process of knowledge making by multiple actors through time, creating in its wake an affective sense of urgency, scale and impact among wider publics.

Zimbabwe: where there are no models

Beyond the somewhat rarefied debates about model predictions among expert committees, people were confronting the virus across the world. By early 2021, when the 'Beta' variant wave hit Zimbabwe, Joseph Mlambo was stationed in Chikombedzi in the far south-east of the country. Based in the township, the government hospital, which has two doctors and a dozen nurses, serves a huge area. With his experience of the first wave in Harare during his training, Mlambo became the point person for COVID-19 in the hospital. He recalled, 'Even the doctors were scared, they did not know what was coming. We set up a separate ward for COVID patients, required everyone to be masked and allowed only a limited number of people into the hospital compound.' He continued, 'At the beginning we had no protective clothing ourselves, and we had no ability to test.' Vaccines became available from February 2021, thanks to Chinese support, but coverage was limited as availability – certainly in places like Chikombedzi – was constrained, at least initially. Many local people were sceptical about the Chinese vaccines. One villager from nearby commented, 'China has economic and political interests in our country. They can now expand and exploit our resources.' Another observed that China 'is known for sub-standard goods. This makes us worried . . . We definitely don't rule out fake vaccines from China' (Bwerinofa et al. 2022a: 80–1).

In other words, uncertainties were everywhere. In fact, basic forms of ignorance (where neither outcomes nor likelihoods are known) and ambiguities (where contestations about possible outcomes are played out) were also central, making the whole setting highly challenging for anyone, be they a health professional, local government official or local villager. As one villager observed in relation to the vaccines, 'COVID-19 is man-made; the vaccines alter our DNA and can kill us.' Others commented on the financial gains to be made: 'This is about money. There are trillions to be made. How can we trust those companies?' (Bwerinofa et al. 2022a: 81).

Far from the Ministry of Health headquarters and with limited support, Mlambo – and many others like him across Zimbabwe and indeed the world – had to improvise, innovate, learn and adapt to the unfolding pandemic. As he explained, 'We had to start from scratch. I linked with the local community through local authorities, religious leaders and others. This helped gain the trust of people. We all had to learn together.' Important in this process was the use of different forms of local knowledge and remedies, not just the accredited medical knowledge that he had been trained in. As he put it, 'When I come home, I leave my uniform in the bathroom, and of course the whole family takes local remedies' (Bwerinofa 2022b: 8). After all, his nurse's training curriculum did not cover COVID-19 or anything like it. Unlike in East Asia, where experience of an earlier coronavirus, SARS (Severe acute respiratory syndrome), had primed people to some degree, this disease was new. That said, the long experience of the HIV/AIDS pandemic in Zimbabwe had provided many important lessons about building trust with affected communities, avoiding stigma, coordinating responses and building on local innovations for improving care, themes that were widely acknowledged in our discussions across Zimbabwe (Bwerinofa et al. 2022a: 16).[21]

With COVID-19, there were no treatments available, vaccines were scarce or not trusted so people had to innovate. In response to these uncertainties in Zimbabwe, there was an explosion of innovation focused on COVID-19 treatments, making use of traditional herbs, tree bark and concoctions involving mixes of everything from Coca-Cola to chilli. Of course, the efficacy of many of these could be questioned, but people swore by them. In particular, the *Zumbani* (*Lippia javanica*) plant was much in demand. Used for steaming and in teas, it improved breathing and alleviated symptoms. Markets sprung up selling the plant, people packaged it in different forms and it even began to be sold in shops and exported to Zimbabweans in the diaspora (Bwerinofa et al. 2022a).

As the pandemic evolved over a number of 'waves' of different variants, responses changed. Innovations had to be rapid, adaptive and quickly shared. For example, when the Omicron variant emerged in South Africa at the end of 2021, those living near the borders, such as in Chikombedzi, had to respond first. They then shared their experiences with others, including friends and relatives, through WhatsApp or Facebook groups. Within days, the information spread across the country and to the diaspora through complex networks. While social media was full of rumour and much false information, trust in particular forms of knowledge from local experience shared by those who people knew was important. As a result, a broad understanding of the implications of the Omicron wave were known by Zimbabweans across the world long before official scientific reports emerged (Bwerinofa et al. 2022a: 130).

As a newly qualified nurse, Joseph Mlambo did not have the authority and experience of others, but he had other qualities important to responding to the pandemic in a place like Chikombedzi. Central among these was his ability to use experience, including from observing what was happening locally, triangulating it with his recent exposure in Harare a year earlier, and to learn from this. He had important qualities of what others have called 'adaptive leadership', the ability to network, galvanize others, use diverse forms of information and facilitate decisions (Ramalingam, Wild and Ferrari 2020). During the pandemic, he was what others would call a 'high-reliability professional', able to scan the horizon for future dangers, manage uncertainties and respond in real time, together with others, just like similar professionals dealing with 'critical infrastructures' described in the last chapter. He would never describe himself in these terms; he was just a nurse doing his best in difficult circumstances. But very often the real heroes of the pandemic were people just like Joseph Mlambo.

Unsung heroes

Similarly, in the United Kingdom, the unsung heroes of the pandemic were the front-line health professionals, social workers, care providers and local government officials in places like Leicester in the East Midlands where the pandemic had a devastating impact on local populations. Yet, as the mayor of Leicester, Peter Soulsby, complained in mid-2020, the data that would help in a targeted response were not being shared by central government authorities.[22] A combination of working and living conditions made British-Asian communities especially vulnerable to the rapid spread of the virus, and a series of extended lockdowns was imposed on the city of Leicester in particular.

At that stage, no one knew how the virus affected people differently, whether in relation to pre-existing health conditions or genetic predispositions, and most reports excluded assessments in relation to ethnicity (Pareek et al. 2020; Pan et al. 2021). Ethnic minority populations in Leicester and similar cities are frequently employed in essential worker and health-care roles, as well as in service roles such as in shops and in other precarious and low-paid work where exposure was high. Many more recent migrants worked in informal garment factories in the city, which continued to operate through the lockdowns.[23] Cultural-religious events, such as Eid al-Fitr in late May 2020 at the end of Ramadan, brought people together, and many lived in multi-generational households, again enhancing transmission risks, especially to older, more vulnerable people. Media stigmatization of such communities at the height of the pandemic made many distrust public health messages, encouraging people to confront COVID-19 uncertainties within communities. This made the work of front-line professionals trying to navigate uncertainties in a complex social and political context that much harder.

The simple models that were being used to define policy had no way of encompassing such complex settings; they didn't even try. Models assumed a population-level biopolitics that defined a particular strategy for confronting the disease, while taking some account of different sub-populations (Hinchliffe 2020). Sensitivity to particular conditions and individual experiences was not part of the epidemiological whole-population frame. By contrast, this more disaggregated view was very central to the perspectives of clinicians, front-line health professionals, care home workers, commuters and patients living with the disease in diverse environments. They knew about how particular settings generated significant vulnerabilities resulting in illness and death among often already marginalized populations. The models, however, did not even consider such information. And why? Because the sort of expertise that would offer such insights was not at the table in the expert committees like SAGE. And because the type of models being used to define policy didn't engage with such disaggregated dynamics, commonly assuming instead homogenous populations with even mixing among individuals.[24]

Luckily, there were many equivalents of Joseph Mlambo in the UK Midlands and elsewhere, and it was they who were able to reduce the impact of the virus through their networks and combined efforts, often without much support from the central state. One critique of the UK response was the failure to decentralize and encourage localized responses, adapted to local social, political circumstances. A centralized track-and-trace system failed catastrophically at huge expense, while the central procurement of PPE and other equipment lined the pockets of some with the right connections. Meanwhile, care homes were seemingly ignored, with terrible consequences. Empowering local authorities, decentralizing roles and allowing real-time tracking, tracing and flexible responses might have worked much better, as occurred so effectively in parts of East Asia. Global experience has shown a highly variegated picture, ranging from the laissez-faire stance of Sweden to full surveillance and rigid lockdowns in China to the elaborate test-and-trace systems of Singapore, Taiwan and South Korea; all with varied, context-specific outcomes (Sridhar 2022).

Certainly, the United Kingdom suffered badly. Despite being one of the most 'prepared' nations on the planet,[25] the United Kingdom still experienced huge numbers of deaths from COVID-19 (estimated at over 230,000 by late 2023)[26] and many other negative effects on schooling, mental health and the economy. Many continue to suffer the condition of 'long COVID', and the impacts of the pandemic were felt very unevenly across class, race, gender, age and disability, with long-term consequences. By contrast, in Zimbabwe as elsewhere in Africa, the feared spread and levels of mortality were not experienced. While there was of course massive under-reporting, the total reported cases and mortalities in Zimbabwe were about 260,000 and 5,725 respectively.[27]

The contrast is nothing to do with the type of response as both countries followed (more or less) the standard approach, combining lockdowns with other non-pharmaceutical interventions and, later, mass vaccination (respectively, 80 per cent and 39.5 per cent of the population receiving at least one dose in the United Kingdom and Zimbabwe).[28] Many hypotheses exist to explain the 'African paradox', whereby outside South Africa many fewer mortalities occurred than most expected. Explanations suggested in discussions in Zimbabwe included demography (a young population), prior exposure to different viruses, limited mobility, living outdoors, along with good, local food and indigenous treatments. In comparing the rural experience where we worked with the situation in town, people argued that this was a 'rich people's disease' and that 'poverty protected us' (Bwerinofa et al. 2022a, 2022b).

The politics of pandemics

During the AIDS pandemic, public health activists urged people to 'Know your epidemic, know your response and act on its politics' (De Waal 2021). This is useful advice for any disease, and during the COVID-19 pandemic it was crucial. Whether in the United Kingdom or Zimbabwe, politics impinged from all sides. Politics influenced the state of the health services and the level of care that could be offered. Politics impinged on the science, and vice versa. And politics framed the style of interventions that ensued.

Lockdowns, movement restrictions and vaccination programmes were all intensely political. In the arguments for intervention in the name of public health, uncertainties in the science were deployed to implement restrictions on people's normal freedoms. The argument was we must act with precaution, now. In this process, the authoritarian streak of governments came to the fore. Freedom of speech and of association, along with the space openly to critique public health measures, became constrained, including in the United Kingdom (Price and Harbisher 2021). As the human rights lawyer Adam Wagner put it, by using emergency procedures without widespread scrutiny, 'the lockdown law restricted our rights more than any other in history' (2022: 3). In Zimbabwe, many thought that the endless lockdowns were increasingly less to do with public health protection but more to do with constraining opposition politics and generating a politics of control (Bwerinofa et al. 2022c). When the Zimbabwe government insisted on vaccines for certain government officials, many rejected this again as an attempt to discipline and control rather than protect public health.

When things are so uncertain, authorities wishing to impose public health measures must be trusted. In Zimbabwe, this increasingly became less the case. The state was seen as distant, corrupt, uncaring, and the authoritarian responses as part of a pattern of suppression of dissent, just as had been the case during the 2008 cholera outbreak (Chigudu 2020). While the initial lockdown in March 2020 was accepted by most as the images from China and Italy had created a sense of panic and foreboding, later, as the disease failed to spread and already highly constrained livelihoods became more and more difficult, trust in the state declined. Uncertainties generate a variety of cultural and political responses. Resistance to lockdowns increased as people ignored or evaded the rules and comic sketches ridiculed the police trying to implement them.[29] Tensions spilled over into daily life: among families, across generations, between rural and urban residents, across religious dominations. People complained bitterly about the lockdowns, especially into 2021: 'It's government, the WHO, corporations who are in control. The powerful. The messages come one-way from them to the masses. We are bombarded with messages and instructions, which require adherence without question.' Another person commented, 'It's just don't, don't, don't; it's terrible for us, we are trying to live. How can we live a life of lockdowns?' (Bwerinofa et al. 2022a: 135). In rejecting the authoritarian lockdowns imposed in the name of public health 'science', recourse to 'tradition' and the 'spirit world' and other forms of knowledge were sought through local leaders, religious prophets, traditional healers and spirit mediums, as uncertainties were negotiated through daily social life (Bwerinofa et al. 2022a: 105; see also Parker, MacGregor and Akello 2020).

In other parts of the world, lockdowns were largely avoided. What has been termed 'civil libertarian' science dominated (Fuller 2020). Here the uncertainties over potential impacts were downplayed, and a more relaxed approach to intervention was followed. This was the tendency within the United Kingdom before the switch in policy, but was most evident in Sweden, where epidemiologists argued openly for a 'herd immunity' strategy, allowing the virus to spread through the population. Uneasy about imposing restrictions following what some saw as uncertain science, this perhaps reflected the liberal politics of the country and commitments to individual freedoms.

In this way, the diverse and changing responses to uncertainties in the science internalized relationships between the state and society, mirroring underlying cultures, patterns of inequality and politics across nations (Zinn and Brown 2022). Pandemics are always important windows on society. The models and the associated scientific debates therefore take on a politics reflective of the context, emphasizing certain elements while downplaying others. As Alex de Waal (2021: 45) explains, 'Pandemics are the occasion for political contests, and history suggests that facts and logic are tools for combat, not arbiters of the outcome.'

The links between poverty, inequality and disease are well established (Farmer 2001) and were highly evident during COVID-19. Exposure to the virus was highly differentiated. Across the world, older people, those with disabilities, people of colour and those with few resources suffered the most (Sutoris et al. 2022). Uncertainties and their effects are not evenly distributed; they are experienced quite differently, depending on who you are, as the evidence on COVID-19 from both the United Kingdom and Zimbabwe clearly shows. It is no surprise then that epidemics can also be a site of struggle between classes, as shown by the 'cholera revolts' starting in the 1830s when the urban poor rose up, challenging the elite (Cohn 2017).

By focusing narrowly only on how diseases spread and infect human populations, the wider structural political-economic relations that create disease uncertainties in the first place are usually left outside of the discussion. For example, most debates about COVID-19 excluded any discussion about how, for instance, market forces accelerate deforestation, drive the expansion of agribusiness and large-scale commercial agriculture and displace and impoverish people, thus generating the conditions for the emergence of zoonoses and their subsequent spread, probably including SARS-CoV2 (Wallace 2020). In focusing on the epidemiological specifics of R_0, doubling times and patterns of infection and so on, the way disease models are framed inevitably distracts attention from the wider political economy of disease dynamics and the uncertainties that arise from highly politicized human–nature entanglements (Rhodes and Lancaster 2022b).

A colonial-style, medical-military approach to tackling epidemics has long dominated public health responses (Tilley 2016). The language of 'war', 'combat', 'suppression' and so on is not inadvertent. With strong historical precedents, the COVID-19 period in most countries – including, but in different ways, the United Kingdom and Zimbabwe – saw the emergence of a particular type of science of pandemic control. In this, risks could be assessed and managed through control-oriented interventions, such as lockdowns, border controls and movement restrictions. Yet, as we have seen, with all the will in the world, the ability to predict, manage and control the virus was fanciful: there were just too many uncertainties. As discussed many times in this book, recognizing uncertainty is not an excuse for inaction, but a recognition of the limits and perhaps the futility of control is an important lesson (Stirling and Scoones 2020).

Other approaches, with a different politics, are, however, possible. As Paul Richards (2016: 145) argues in relation to the experience of Ebola in West Africa, 'It is striking how rapidly communities learnt to think like epidemiologists, and epidemiologists to think like communities.' In Zimbabwe's rural areas, people's understanding of the disease evolved through the different phases, with new responses and treatments emerging over time through a combination of local innovation, sharing across networks and inputs from the formal health systems. Responses included suggestions around eating habits, focusing in particular on 'strong', local foods such as small grains rather than processed maize meal; the taking of local medicines to boost immunity and strength; and a huge array of treatments, from breathing and steaming regimes to a variety of concoctions that helped with disease symptoms, adapted as they changed between the variants (Bwerinofa et al. 2022a,b).

This was a plural health system par excellence, with preachers, prophets, spirit mediums, herbal healers and others combining with hospital and clinic-based support from nurses and doctors. This was not at all a rejection of formal science and public health and a retreat to the local and 'indigenous', but an acceptance that uncertainties – combined with genuine apprehensions and anxieties – required a more diverse, collective response. Instead of 'following the science' (singular), it meant negotiating between multiple sciences (plural) and the associated uncertainties. Over time, people rejected the control-oriented politics of lockdowns, casting them as authoritarian and unnecessary, and instead adopted a more caring, inclusive approach, which drew on local forms of 'moral economy' and collective solidarity, reinforced through social networks (Bwerinofa et al. 2022b). In this way, the politics of uncertainty was redefined in the process, suggesting possibilities of new forms of mutual aid and solidarity in the absence of state protections long removed through neoliberalism and state collapse (Leach et al. 2021). This is a dynamic we see in many 'disasters', as explored in the next chapter.

Rethinking pandemic preparedness

In both the United Kingdom and Zimbabwe, despite the disparities in science advice, qualified personnel and health infrastructure, and the hugely different political-economic contexts, in the end responses to the pandemic ultimately relied on people on the ground working together, making use of social relationships and practices, developing trust, responding in real time and adapting flexibility to fast-changing circumstances. While epidemiological models can provide the basis for thinking generally about the future, offering different scenarios, they are poor at providing prescriptive directions for action under conditions of deep uncertainty, even ignorance. As we saw in the United Kingdom, a hubristic over-reliance on models and limited sources of technocratic expertise can instead be dangerous, diverting attention from real-world contexts, diverse knowledges and practical experience.

What then should an approach to pandemic preparedness and response look like if uncertainty (and ignorance and ambiguity) were taken seriously? As Sheila Jasanoff (2005c, 2021) argues, rejecting 'technologies of hubris' in favour of 'technologies of humility' is essential. This requires a different type of professional expertise and new forms of network at the centre of pandemic response. The narrow version of the SAGE-style expert advice system as used in the United Kingdom is inadequate and, as experienced through the COVID-19 pandemic, may actually have undermined the capacity to respond effectively. In Zimbabwe, a plural response evolved, with people relying on diverse sources of knowledge and innovation in response to uncertainties. This was partly through force of circumstance as the state health system was unable to deliver, but the types of treatments and forms of support that people made use of helped everyone navigate uncertainties across the phases of the pandemic and so created forms of local resilience (Bwerinofa et al. 2022b). In this sense, people continuously performed and practised preparedness and generated resilience, even if this was very localized.

The argument, though, is not to abandon modelling efforts and just rely on local initiatives, nor to formalize all the impromptu, creative practices of informal responses, but instead to recognize the important limits of science-based prediction in the face of deep uncertainties. Instead of searching in vain for the perfect 'evidence' to feed into 'policy' in a linear way, a different approach would be to accept, as scientists of course do, that epidemiological modelling is always messy, contested and uncertain, and so requires opening up the debate to greater scrutiny and wider engagement. This would mean not only using the modelling efforts to encourage a plurality of models – embracing a 'critical promiscuity' (Anderson 2021) – but to encourage the challenge of all model framings from different angles. What assumptions are being used? What data are relevant? Is this appropriate to my setting? Rather than seeking 'evidence-based consensus' and then 'communicating' the results to 'the public' with an assumed 'deficit' of knowledge (Wynne 1993), seeing modelling as a space for deliberation (and disagreement and contest) allows for a more robust and inclusive debate about how to respond.

Further, all diseases must be understood in context. In the United Kingdom, it was in care homes, in crowded factories, in multi-generational homes and at large sporting events where COVID-19 spread the fastest. In rural Zimbabwe, it was at markets, at tobacco selling points, at beer parties, in crowded buses, during funerals and at church services where transmission especially occurred. Local people and front-line professionals were able to identify these sites, along with the ways that the disease spread. In Zimbabwe, for example, it was the informal transporters (*malaicha*) who moved people and goods, including across the border to South Africa, who were recognized as important conduits of disease. In all settings, those living with the disease have a good sense of its epidemiology and can identify ways of controlling it if empowered to do so (Bwerinofa et al. 2022c).

Recent experiments in 'participatory modelling' show how a triangulation between different types of models, with different assumptions and data inputs, can help open up debates around public health responses (Scoones et al. 2017; Lancaster, Rhodes and Rosengarten 2020; Adams, Rhodes and Lancaster 2022; see also chapter 6 for other examples). Through engaging with 'contingency' and 'mess' (Law 2004), this allows models to work 'not simply as epistemic boundary "crossings" – moving across different versions of expertise – but as modes of enactment

– by altering and making new versions of expertise' (Rhodes and Lancaster 2020: 187). Through co-producing not only knowledge but also the institutions, interventions and forms of action required, a different approach to modelling for public health has radical potentials for shifting the way uncertainties are encountered and responded to.

This requires much deeper contextual knowledge of diseases than usually possible in generic models, asking, for example, how infection occurs in private spaces through ceremonial and informal practices at funerals, as was highlighted by Paul Richards (2016) for Ebola in West Africa.

As the world contemplates future pandemics, have these lessons about understanding and confronting uncertainties from COVID-19 been taken on board? The short answer is no. Many initiatives have sprung up, ranging from global 'pandemic treaties' to the development of 'vaccine banks', but these tend to emphasize control and management, not the embracing of inevitable uncertainty. In a similar vein, a focus on tackling misinformation – what has been termed the 'infodemic'[30] – emphasizes the elimination of doubt and the transmission of 'correct' scientific information, forgetting that negotiating pandemics always involves confronting multiple uncertainties in specific social and cultural contexts.

In sum, the many lessons from the COVID-19 pandemic – and Ebola, avian and swine influenza, SARS, MERS and other outbreaks before – have not been learned, and a technocratic and centralized system is being reinforced, where too often uncertainties are ignored. We must always remember that pandemics are as much social and political phenomena as they are biological and medical, and so require open, inclusive reflexive spaces for debates about knowledge and action before, during and after a pandemic. Technical solutions are important but are just not enough when thinking about pandemic preparedness (MacGregor, Ripoll and Leach 2020; Leach et al. 2022). While epidemiological models can certainly offer useful insights, they blind and obscure if too much faith is put in them; models are after all just models. As this book argues across very diverse cases, where uncertainty, ignorance and ambiguity dominate, technocratic risk-based decision making is inadequate, and a major rethink is required. As the UK COVID-19 Select Committee Inquiry argued, 'it is the nature of preparing to face future risks that there will be much that must be unknown about them. Perfect foresight, and therefore a perfect response, is not available.'[31]

More effective preparedness for future pandemics – which will surely arise, but not necessarily in the form of a rerun of COVID-19 – must instead rely on a number of core principles. These must be central to new approaches to public health policy and development practice. Principles include the use of and respect for multiple knowledges, including those outside accredited science; the recognition and support of professionals and their networks – often informal and community based – who can generate reliability in the face of uncertainty and a decentralized, flexible approach responsive to local contexts and changing circumstances that facilitates responsive, collective action within plural health systems (Michie et al. 2022; de Graaff et al. 2023; IDS 2023). Building resilience for future pandemics requires all these elements now, long in advance of the identification of an 'event of concern' by the WHO. Such capacities, as discussed throughout this book, are relevant too for navigating other uncertainties, and must be central to any investment in 'pandemic preparedness'.

6

Disasters: Why Prediction and Planning Are Not Enough

Introduction

The news is full of disasters: droughts, floods, earthquakes, volcanoes, tsunamis, chemical spills and more. They are more frequent and their scale of impact is growing, according to UN reports (UNDRR 2022). A whole industry has grown up around disaster risk and its management, aimed at reducing the risks and offsetting the worst. But can such disasters be predicted and therefore managed? Can the suite of new tools for early warning, disaster risk reduction, risk management, insurance and antici-patory early action work when we don't know what is around the corner?

In March 2015, in Sendai, South Korea, the world agreed a new framework that shifted the emphasis from managing disasters to managing risk.[1] Building on the Hyogo framework for action and other predecessors, the Sendai framework has been the basis for global policy since, overseen by the UNDRR (United Nations Office for Disaster Risk Reduction), which reports on progress annually. The framework makes many useful recommendations on monitoring, response and governance, but it's all centred on risk, not uncertainty. Within the main framework document, 'risk' is mentioned 434 times, but tellingly 'uncertain(ty)' does not appear at all, even if many references to risk actually mean uncertainty in the terms of this book. Too often, the assumption is that, with better information, improved predictive tools and effective anticipatory management, disasters can be averted.

The risk framing suggests a technical, managerial solution, focused usually on a single hazard and event. However, since the original 'environment as hazard' approach (Burton, Kates and White 1978), increasingly sophisticated approaches to 'Disaster Risk Reduction' (DRR) have been developed, such as various adaptations of the pressure and release 'crunch' model, which highlights how risks are generated when hazards collide with underlying vulnerabilities, generated by root causes, dynamic pressures and unsafe conditions (Pelling 2003; Blaikie et al. 2004). Within this framework, others highlight the importance of behavioural and cultural aspects of risk perception (Krüger et al. 2015), as well as the political economy of root causes (O'Keefe, Westgate and Wisner 1976; Cannon 2015).

Despite such developments, the focus remains on predicted risks – seen as the product of hazard and vulnerability. The argument goes, if we only knew more about the risks and their causal effects through patterns of vulnerability, then we would have a better response system. But what if uncertainties were more centre stage, what would a different approach look like? What do disasters look like in places where they are experienced? What are the everyday practices that help avert them? How do external interventions, including those emerging from the disaster and development industry, support or hinder people's own responses?

From Sendai to southern Ethiopia

To answer some of these questions, we will move from the conference halls of Sendai and the UN offices of Geneva to Yabelo in Borana, southern Ethiopia. This is an area inhabited by pastoralists, some relying only on animals but many with diversified livelihoods and farming and trading too. Boru Galgalo and his family own a few cattle and a number of goats and have a small farm plot of a few hectares. In the past few years, they have suffered many 'disasters' – in 2020, there was a major locust plague that eliminated crops and grazing; from 2020, COVID-19 stopped movement and closed markets, seriously affecting their livelihoods, even if they didn't get sick themselves; between 2020 and 2022, they suffered drought, when grazing was short and agricultural production was poor, yet in 2023, after multiple seasons of drought resulting in the loss of about twenty of Boru's cattle, there were heavy rains, causing flooding, with a rise in animal diseases. Talking about this experience, Qaballe Malich, a 38-year-old woman from the same village, commented, 'I worry about risk. These problems and challenges hinder my family and me from leading a decent life. God will deal with uncertain events. My daily routines are dealing with problems, and I live in poverty.' She continued, 'Uncertainty is your limited knowledge (*jilbii hinbanne*) of when and how vital resources for your livelihood will diminish . . . in most cases, the availability of those resources is meaningless unless you have command over them' (Taye 2022: 162, 164). Uncertainties are therefore part of everyday experiences; they interact and combine, and their impacts are deeply influenced by social and economic circumstances.

This is very different to the hierarchical, administrative linear framing of disaster and emergency management coming from Sendai-inspired plans. Pastoralists such as Boru and Qaballe must manage highly variable environments over huge distances with mobile herds and flocks. They must always respond to the more complex, contingent, fluid flows of everyday life in such settings. Their experience of time – whether through a day or across the seasons and between years – can be quite different to the focus on specific events or hazards of disaster management experts and planners (Maru 2020); for pastoralists, unfolding time is a flow not an event (Adam 2013). Local, everyday experiences of course intersect with fast-paced 'modern' life, endlessly projected through the ubiquitous smartphone. Responding to uncertainties therefore means negotiating multiple temporalities. Memories of past droughts, floods or disease outbreaks loom large, while expectations of the future are shaped by cultural beliefs and cosmologies.

In navigating uncertainties, pastoralists must combine deep knowledge of the social, technological and ecological system, drawing on experiential and more formal knowledges, while responding in real time to challenges as they unfold. To avert disasters, pastoralists such as Boru and Qaballe must scan the horizon for danger – whether an impending conflict, a waterhole drying up or a key grazing area diminishing – recalling at the same time past experiences and remembered histories, while always being attuned to the immediate, practical challenge of keeping animals alive and healthy right now, just as the high-reliability professionals dealing with critical infrastructures we encountered in chapter 4.

Within the Yabelo area, there are many development projects focused on reducing the risk of 'disasters', usually arriving after a major drought. Big investments have been made in early warning systems that use climate models and meteorological predictions to assess the likelihood of drought in the hope that droughts can be anticipated and early actions follow. Humanitarian relief and cash transfers are frequently used by the state and NGOs to help the needy, while a plethora of so-called 'resilience-building' projects try and encourage pastoralists to shift out of 'risky' livestock production towards 'diversified' livelihood opportunities. In the last decade, livestock insurance has also been offered as part of the suite of external interventions, aimed at offsetting the risks of drought for those still keeping livestock. Boru, Qaballe and their families are involved in some of these projects, as we will see, but the big question is: do the external constructions of risk and disaster match those living with and indeed from uncertainty in the Borana rangelands?

Techno-managerial solutions

The disaster risk reduction industry that takes the Sendai framework as its starting point has introduced many terms, methodologies and institutions. It's frankly all a bit bewildering. In one UN progress report, there were five pages of acronyms in small type at the beginning![2] But the standard framing can be boiled down to a few key points.

'Hazards', according to this framework, are what need to be measured and understood. They may be 'natural' (such as droughts, floods and so on) or 'human induced' (such as nuclear accidents, chemical spills or biohazards). They may combine as 'multi-hazards', but the big challenge is to predict the frequency of their occurrence and their impact (in other words, their risk). Their impact in turn relates to people's 'vulnerability'. This will of course vary between different places, but a big focus must be on making people more 'resilient' to the impact of disasters, whether through improving housing or farming practices or livelihoods in general. Thus, interventions may focus on reducing the hazards, for example through engineering efforts that reduce flooding or reduce the likelihoods of chemical spills. However, many hazards will continue, and with climate change it is recognized that they will only increase. Another strategy is to develop the capacity to predict disasters so that people can respond early before major losses occur. Here early warning systems become important so that anticipatory early action is possible. Contingency plans based on models, scenarios and role-played exercises are central, allowing authorities to be prepared in advance of an inevitable disaster. Ways of mitigating the impact may in turn include insurance, which shares the risks across a group, or vulnerability-reduction and resilience-building measures with affected communities.

In sum, the assumption is that, with better knowledge and improved early warning, preparedness and response systems, then disasters can be managed and risks reduced. A whole panoply of technical interventions is in turn proposed, with the big tech and insurance companies offering their skills in data management and prediction. For example, the major reinsurer, SwissRe, offers CatNet®, a proprietary software for location-based identification of hazards and as a tool 'for efficient, accurate underwriting and risk management'. In the same vein, Google FloodHub – a free-to-use interface – forecasts riverine floods based on artificial intelligence models of river flow and flooding to allow for early anticipatory action, offering flood maps for early warning efforts globally.[3]

In this standard disaster risk-reduction framing, disasters are usually seen as singular, catastrophic events – a drought, an earthquake and so on – although what are termed 'slow onset' disasters are also increasingly recognized. Emergencies that arise are the focus of mobilization of resources, deployment of equipment and people, and the provision of humanitarian relief for those in need. The military-style response, involving complex logistics and rapid response, allows external actors, including states and humanitarian agencies, to respond quickly, or so the argument goes.

Of course, there are many variations to this brief, necessarily simplified, version of the standard disaster risk-reduction and management approach, but the basic elements are well entrenched and are associated with substantial investments across the world. However, as with other cases discussed so far in this book, there are many questions raised as to whether this risk-focused, techno-managerial approach is appropriate for addressing uncertain conditions, where we don't know what will happen when, and probably can't. An acknowledgement of uncertainty – rather than accepting everything can be managed as risk – raises some difficult questions for the type of interventions usually proposed.

Can we ever have an early warning system that can offer accurate predictions that are appropriate for defining local-level responses? Can we calculate risks so that insurance products can be designed and sold? Can we have effectively targeted humanitarian and social assistance approaches that reduce vulnerabilities to risks? The science of seismology is, in the words of earthquake scientist Susan Hough (2002), often fruitlessly engaged in 'predicting the unpredictable'. This makes negotiating uncertainties in the context of early warning volcano alerts incredibly challenging (Fearnley 2013). The same applies even when prediction capacities are improving, whether for droughts in East Africa and modelled links to Indian and Pacific sea-surface temperature changes (Funk et al. 2023) or as a result of training historical data through artificial intelligence learning models (Lam et al. 2023).

The same challenges of uncertainty for prediction, early warning and action apply to nearly every hazard. Even with improved data and modelling, uncertainties will always exist. Interestingly, during the mid-term review of the Sendai framework, some of these questions emerged, and a greater focus on systemic risk and uncertainty in complex, multi-hazard settings where risks combine, compound and cascade was emphasized (UNDRR 2022). The report comments:

> The planning systems and institutional culture of the twentieth century worked towards fixed time frames, for known outcomes in contexts that were largely stable and linear or were assumed to be. The complexity of today's world and the destabilization of global ecosystems through climate change and other direct human impacts

require that twenty-first-century institutional cultures must become more comfortable with uncertainty. (UNDRR 2022: 202)

Compared to the original Sendai framework document, the mid-term review text has 98 mentions of 'uncertain(ty)', although still 1,968 mentions of 'risk', but this is surely progress!

As this book has argued across the chapters, taking uncertainty seriously signals a very different approach. This in turn raises wider questions about the politics of risk management and disaster risk reduction. How is a risk framing in disasters and emergencies used as an excuse for control and management by external actors? How do resulting processes of securitization and militarization affect the style of response and the construction of disaster 'victims'? And what does the reliance on externally defined systems of risk management and control mean for local agency and vernacular, everyday responses centred on uncertainty by the likes of Boru and Qaballe?

Before returning to these themes, the following sections will look in a bit more detail at two areas central to disaster management and response – disaster preparedness and insurance. Critical reflections on each offer insights into what a reframing around uncertainty might look like.

Preparing for the worst

Disasters may be inevitable and cannot be prevented, let alone fully controlled, so the most important thing to do is be prepared. Preparedness planning is central to disaster management systems globally but emerged as a core state practice during the Cold War, when the United States became convinced that a nuclear attack by a hostile Soviet Union would happen. Preparedness involved the elaborate playing of war games by military and civil officials, the development of scenarios for what might happen, the carrying out of exercises to simulate responses and prepare the key agencies and the elaboration of civil contingency responses in case of attack (Collier and Lakoff 2021). A whole set of techniques, practices and rationalities with particular historical roots therefore define 'anticipatory action' and 'preparedness' as part of emergency and disaster planning today. It was these that were played out during the COVID-19 pandemic, as we saw in the previous chapter.

Since its Cold War origins, preparedness planning has become standard in a whole array of fields. A central argument is that advanced planning, including the allocation of finance, the training of response teams and the easing of bureaucratic constraints in times of emergency, will allow more effective responses to what Dan Clarke and Stefan Dercon (2016) call 'dull disasters'. With most disaster and emergency responses coming too little, too late to be effective, the argument is that preparedness can lead to early action and more effective, rapid response, even when events are uncertain. This argument has much merit, given the dismal record of emergency humanitarian responses to too many disasters, but it also has its limits. It again relies on an interventionist response by the state or other agencies to stabilize and control an imagined and planned-for future that may not arise. Such imaginaries of the future do not necessarily articulate well with how local understandings of uncertainties are understood, felt and experienced and so responded to in places like Yabelo.

In southern Ethiopia, there has been much investment in preparedness planning. Elaborate early warning systems for drought have been developed through large investments in such facilities as FEWS NET (the Famine Early Warning System Network) and the IGAD Climate Prediction and Application Centre (ICPAC).[4] These provide important sources of information, but how are they used? In nearby northern Kenya, one of those involved in drought early warning and management commented, 'With early warnings, you are telling them what they already see. We are ambassadors for what they already know!' As we found when discussing with officials in Isiolo and Marsabit counties in early 2023, those working on the ground know when there is a drought (livestock are dying in numbers, and there's no grass and water), so they don't need information that the situation is dire.[5] The problem is that there is often a big gap between early warning information and action on the ground, what Margie Buchanan-Smith and Susanna Davies (1995) term 'the missing link'.[6] The information is not trusted, or experience suggests that, for particular conditions in particular places, it may not be accurate and therefore not useful.

Boru, Qaballe and other pastoralists, however, often have
no idea that such information exists at all. The early warning
bulletins used by the aid agencies and NGOs to develop their
plans and raise funds exist in very separate spaces. Instead, they
use local signs – of clouds, stars, plants, birds and animals – to
get a sense of what the weather might bring. Religious leaders,
elders and traditional forecasters and healers are those who
are central to the local early warning and response system,
but recommendations always emerge from a collective, deliberative discussion. For again, it is uncertainty – where the
future is not known, at least for mere mortals – not risk that
is being addressed. Of course, just like the predictions coming
from the official meteorological models, local predictions may
not always be accurate, but by contrast they are usually more
trusted. Emerging from discussion and debate within the local
community, building on much historical experience, such advice
becomes part of an ongoing response to a drought as it unfolds
over time, rather than something that is associated with a time-
delimited 'warning' and 'response'.

Other investments in 'preparedness' in Borana, as well as
northern Kenya to the south, focus on building 'resilience'
among pastoral communities. There are huge numbers of
projects, usually initiated in the aftermath of an earlier disaster.
They focus on creating groups, ideally of women and youth,
and very often emphasize generating 'alternative livelihoods'
on the assumption that pastoralism is no longer viable. In
our discussions with some of those involved in such projects
in northern Kenya, we found that many are disillusioned and
frustrated. One project officer noted, 'It's resilience, resilience,
resilience in proposals. The word "resilience" just attracts the
donors.' Another observed, 'We have spent billions and billions,
but we have nothing to show, even if we try our best. There's
something we are not getting right.' Reflecting on the projects
themselves, another argued, 'You go to a village and there are
so many groups – water, rangeland and so on. It's confusing the
community. The roles and people are almost the same. They are
just funded by different projects.' An NGO project lead summed
it up: 'This word resilience is so ambiguous. We must understand
it better. There is a gap – the projects don't work.'[7]

'Resilience' has many definitions, ranging from the classic
version of the system 'bouncing back' following a disaster to

a former assumed stable state to ones that focus more on the relational properties of resilience and the importance of transformation through the process of responding to shocks and stresses (e.g. Walker and Salt 2012; Brown 2015; West et al. 2020; Reyers et al. 2022). What ends up in the preparedness plan very much depends on how resilience is defined. In some cases, 'resilience' projects may reinforce existing patterns of poverty and marginalization, aiming for people to cope and survive, while in others, systems are transformed and underlying vulnerabilities are addressed. Local, vernacular understandings of resilience point to the capacities to respond to diverse challenges through the use of local knowledge and forms of collective, social responses (Wandji, Allouche and Marchais 2021). This is very different to the externally defined 'project' response of the NGOs and aid agencies frequently centred on an imaginary of a stabilized and controlled future around 'resilient', alternative livelihoods, where existing practices of pastoralism, for example, are replaced, refashioned and modernized through 'development' interventions (Scoones 2021a).

In this way, preparedness planning frequently imposes a particular solution around an imagined future, where the techniques and practices of early warning, scenario planning and contingency arrangements define how things could be. This then generates a politics of expectation and anticipation in disaster and emergency settings that sees the emergency as a moment separated from the everyday. Exceptional interventions around disasters are in turn designed to return things to 'normality', when the hopes of a progressive, modern future can be realized (Adey, Anderson and Graham 2015). In the terms of Michel Foucault, such practices of 'governmentality' – 'the conduct of conduct' – frame how disasters are responded to, disciplining subjects in the process (Lawrence and Wiebe 2017; Joseph 2018).

All this is very far removed from the local, vernacular understandings and practices of disaster preparedness and resilience of Boru, Qaballe and their colleagues across the pastoral areas of southern Ethiopia, where futures are much more constrained and disasters are experienced as 'slow' (Nixon 2011; Anderson et al. 2020), 'quotidian' (Sharpe 2016) and processes of continuous or anticipatory 'ruination' (Stoler 2013; Paprocki 2022). This therefore once again creates an uncomfortable and unavoidable disconnect between local experiences and external policies and programmes, very often undermining trust in and so effectiveness of disaster and emergency responses.

Insuring against disaster

Insurance has long been a route to offsetting the impacts of disasters. You take out insurance to protect your property from flood, fire or theft; to protect yourself or your car against accidents; to insure your family against ill health, early death and so on. This is classic indemnity insurance that is paid out once the insured event has occurred, with the payouts based on a loss assessment. Premiums in turn are calculated according to actuarial analyses of the likelihoods of such events happening, based on past occurrences.

Other types of insurance pool risks in different ways, but the principles are the same. For example, sovereign insurance allows for insuring against risks at a country level, with states taking out premiums (Christophers, Bigger and Johnson 2020; Johnson 2021). Catastrophe insurance is focused on particular events, such as cyclones or hurricanes, allowing states or other parties to insure against damage (Grove 2012). These may be linked to parametric or index-linked insurance where payouts occur once a certain trigger point is reached, rather than after the loss occurs. In the case of drought, this may be when satellites monitor vegetation cover and a drought is predicted once a threshold is reached. Such index-based insurance can be sold to individuals and linked to losses of a particular asset (Carter et al. 2017).

Index-based livestock insurance has been touted as a great solution to reducing the impacts of drought disasters that affect pastoral populations and has been heavily promoted in southern Ethiopia and northern Kenya (Jensen, Barrett and Mude 2015). In Ethiopia, it is offered as a commercial product, supported by the Oromia Insurance Company and backed by an international research and development institute, the International Livestock Research Institute (Taye 2022). Index insurance relies on an assessment of the risk of a poor season based on satellite-image assessments of vegetation through the year. In Ethiopia, the correlation with patterns of livestock mortality has been established through past data and a trigger level is set for payouts. Insurance areas are established where such measurements take place, and those who buy insurance get payouts according to what happens there. Payouts in turn are intended to be used to keep animals alive through buying fodder, for example, but may be used for a number of things.

Boru bought the product soon after it was introduced, but no longer buys it as he felt the premiums were too high and he had other priorities. Given the drought last year and the loss of many animals, he now has some regrets, but says it was too expensive and didn't always pay out when expected. Similarly, Jilo Wako, an elderly man from the same area, explained:

> During my second-year investment in livestock insurance, there was a payout [2019] and I received some cash for the ten cattle I insured. It was very small. The drought was so severe that we were forced to migrate to an area where there was better pasture. I was surprised and disappointed due to the fact that policyholders in the area I migrated to were paid higher than us. I lost the trust I had in the system. (Scoones, Mohamed and Taye forthcoming: 5)

As with any insurance product, index-based livestock insurance makes a number of assumptions. First, it assumes that the estimates of vegetation cover are accurate and reflect fodder availability. This may be a problem if the assessments pick up green vegetation that is not palatable or underestimate the importance of particular grazing patches, for example. Second, it assumes that a singular 'peril' – a seasonal deficit of vegetation – is the major problem for livestock keepers and that drought affects the whole insurance area and all people uniformly. Other risks are deemed to be 'idiosyncratic' rather than 'covariate' and are expected to be addressed by individualized coping strategies (Chantarat et al. 2013). Third, it assumes that livestock remain within the insurance area and do not move. This may mean that animals registered for insurance in a particular area do not experience the vegetation patterns assessed, as they move to other areas. And, finally, it assumes that the insured asset is privately held by an individual, rather than part of a more collective form of ownership and management (Johnson et al. 2023b; Taye 2023).

In other words, by developing a calculative model for a singular risk and then financializing it in an insurance product, a set of assumptions are imposed on pastoral ecologies, societies and politics. Commercial insurance is par excellence a reflection of an individualized society governed by the market, which is arguably why it has become so popular today as a solution to humanitarian and development challenges. As François Ewald (1991) describes, insurance has always been a reflection of existing dominant social and political relations.

However, this private, financialized model of commercial insurance has not always been central. Today's individualized commercial insurance – including that offered to Boru and others in southern Ethiopia – evolved from other forms. To trace the origins, we have to go back to the eighteenth century in Europe. At this point, the emergence of life insurance was seen as 'gambling', betting on life (Clark 2002), and widely frowned upon, with the Life Insurance Act of 1744 in England proscribing such practices. While Calvinist Protestants rejected insurance as a challenge to providence, others argued that insurance offered a positive route to enrichment and expanding entrepreneurial capitalism (Baker 2002). Collective mutual and friendly societies established a more social version of insurance from the late eighteenth century, centred on the ideals of 'friendship, brotherly love and charity', as Nob Doran (1994) describes for the Manchester Oddfellows Society. Focusing on life, burial and sickness insurance, thrift, saving, family security and good conduct were the moral values promoted for the artisans and working classes. In the nineteenth century, actuarial visions and a more commercial basis were established. Risk calculations, insurance premiums, agents, collectors and advertising had become central features of insurance practice by this time (Alborn 2009). Only in the early twentieth century were such practices socialized again, this time by the state. In Britain, Prime Minister David Lloyd George introduced a national insurance scheme, and later William Beveridge advocated for a state-supported welfare system for universal needs (O'Malley 2002).

Insurance is therefore not just about protecting yourself from individualized risk, open to the temptations of selfish, careless behaviour and moral hazard, but insurance can be seen in a more positive, hopeful frame. Jointly working through a collective sharing towards a common goal of protecting others, the values of mutual aid and cooperation are highlighted. This in turn can provide a focus for mobilization and collective action, emphasizing moral hope, not hazard, as well as opportunity and not just negative risk (Stone 2002). Certainly, this was the vision of early pioneers of insurance in the friendly societies, one taken on by the solidarity politics of the welfare state, where preventing harm and supporting the whole population, no matter what their means, was the aim (Ewald 2020).

However, when disaster risk management experts talk of insurance today, it is individualized, commercial insurance that is most commonly referred to. In this, what can be termed a risk assemblage is constructed through a network of insurance companies, reinsurers, risk management consultants and state or aid agencies providing support. They are connected through risk models and actuarial logics that define both the subjects (the insured) and the objects (hazards) (O'Malley 1996), generating a form of what Foucault (2008) called a biopolitics around insurance (Collier 2008; Grove 2017). The practices and techniques of today's commercial insurance operate at a distance and through the market, offering therefore a neoliberal, individualized solution to risk (Isakson 2015; Christophers, Bigger and Johnson 2020; Collier, Elliott and Lehtonen 2021).

So how does this play out in Borana, Ethiopia, and how does this interact with other forms of 'insurance', more linked to collective support and mutual aid? When Boru and others were buying livestock insurance, it was not the only thing that they were doing to protect themselves from the impacts of drought and other disasters. Indeed, Boru took out premiums only for a small number of animals. The insurance only offers payouts under certain conditions and, as Boru complains, many droughts that they experience are simply not covered. The problem is what is called 'basis risk' – the difference between what the insurance covers through its calculative models and what is actually experienced. In Kenya, this turned out to be much larger than expected in the initial design, with only about 30 per cent of high-loss drought risk covered by the product on average (Jensen, Barrett and Mude 2016). For most of the time, even for insured assets, you are on your own.

This is why alternative local responses to drought and other disasters are essential. As Boru explains, the worst problems are faced when droughts occur season after season and are combined with other challenges, notably conflict with neighbouring groups. As is increasingly recognized in the disaster risk and reduction community, hazards always intersect, accumulate, cascade and compound, making insurance a blunt and partial instrument for addressing such complex challenges. In southern Ethiopia, responses to drought and other intersecting disasters include moving animals to other grazing areas; redistributing and restructuring flocks and herds through loaning systems to relatives and others; shifting herd composition to more drought-hardy livestock; selling animals in local markets and investing the proceeds in other activities; and diversifying livelihoods, whether locally through farming, trading or charcoal making or elsewhere through migration to urban areas (Taye 2022). For pastoralists in Borana, these are the elements of risk and uncertainty management that go way beyond purchasing insurance, although they may be combined with it.

Collective forms of mutual support among families, extended kin networks and within wider clan groupings are especially important. This may involve raising funds for those who have lost animals or loaning animals to allow for herd and flock recovery. These are strongly embedded cultural practices, and there is an expectation that everyone will contribute, with those who isolate themselves from collective forms of solidarity being frequently rejected by the community (Mohamed 2023). For most, the best way to navigate uncertainty is together, not alone.

Complex herd-management practices, livelihood diversification and culturally rooted forms of moral economy are what allow pastoralists to respond to uncertainties, adaptively and flexibly averting disasters on a continuous basis in order to navigate uncertainties in Borana (Taye 2022). As Golicha Galgalo, a wealthy male pastoralist from Gomole in Borana, explains:

I sniff out opportunities and grab them. I am not afraid. . . . I received livestock insurance payouts . . . but despite the fact that it helps during stress periods, it has been three years since I dropped out . . . I now have other opportunities that I am almost sure I will make a profit from. I have feed reserves for my animals that can last . . . I have never seen a drought for the past three years. (Taye 2022: 175)

Commercial livestock insurance may be part of the response for some – as it turns out mostly richer, male herd owners – but because it focuses on calculable risks around a singular peril it cannot address the unfolding uncertainties of complex disasters as experienced on the ground. Other complementary options, embedded in social relations and a local 'moral economy', must be found (Johnson et al. 2023b).

The politics of disasters

Both commercial insurance and standard approaches to early warning and disaster preparedness therefore sit uneasily with the local practices that pastoralists in places like Borana use to avert and manage uncertain disasters. This creates tensions and contradictions, and with this a politics of disasters.

A new politics of risk and uncertainty generated by interventions such as preparedness planning and insurance is of course not exclusive to pastoral settings. Take flood protection through insurance in poor neighbourhoods in New York City in the United States, where flood-risk maps act to exclude and marginalize through the pricing of insurance. This in turn raises many questions about how 'loss', and so 'risk', are understood, and who is responsible (Elliott 2021). In the same way as poor residents of New York City draw on powerful forms of 'moral economy' alongside increasingly expensive insurance options, in urban South Africa individualized insurance intersects with collective forms of belonging and identity, creating a politics of both inclusion and exclusion. Those with insurance identify as 'modern' and 'independent' and may reject what they see as burdensome collective forms of solidarity, while those without insurance, relying on local forms of support, regard those who reject the community with scorn (Bähre 2020). Meanwhile, in France in 2003, there were around 15,000 excess deaths due to a major heatwave, many of whom were elderly residents of the suburbs of Paris. This was an 'unnatural' disaster as these victims were already vulnerable, and their ability to cope with extreme heat was undermined by the social architecture of the city. The health and social care metrics that were supposed to protect the elderly were totally inadequate, as were the formal city preparedness plans. This was therefore a social and political heatwave with devastating consequences, a stark reminder of the likely future under climate change (Keller 2019). Reflecting on the 2010 *Deepwater Horizon* oil disaster in the Gulf of Mexico, Michael Watts (2016) again highlights the politics of disasters, arguing that a corporate focus on containing risk by technical means undermined a culture of safety, as practices of secrecy and rule breaking took hold, exposing the oil extraction operation to almost inevitable disaster. Watts argues that, in the context of expansion into a resource frontier and an aggressive pursuit of profits, multiple uncertainties and insecurities inevitably arose.

In all these cases – and there are many, many more – the vision of disaster risk reduction and management, with its models, risk management plans and insurance protocols, creates a moral and political order – often driven by profit seeking and cost cutting – and a set of expectations often at odds with those facing disasters themselves or with a wider culture of safety. As we have seen, disaster management acts to control the future in the present through a range of techniques and practices aimed at offsetting the impacts of disasters when they strike (Grove et al. 2022). Through this process of 'governing through emergencies' (Adey, Anderson and Graham 2015), disasters are separated from the everyday and ordinary through technical and political interventions, at least for the privileged. An open-ended, liberal view of the future underlies this, where offsetting 'exceptional' disaster events can offer progressive opportunities both for business and for living a 'modern life' (Dillon 2007). The 'emergency' or 'crisis' thus becomes the modus operandi of the liberal state, protecting citizens through humanitarian efforts while imposing regulations, plans and limits (Calhoun 2010). 'De-risking' society through the financialization of disasters – involving the public funding of private investment – in turn provides opportunities for some to exploit disasters for profit, sometimes creating predatory forms of 'disaster capitalism' in the wake of disasters (Klein 2007; Le Billon et al. 2020; Gabor 2021).

All disasters are of course political in that their impacts are unevenly distributed. As widely discussed, Hurricane Katrina, which hit New Orleans and surrounding areas in August 2005, mostly affected poor, black neighbourhoods (Braun and McCarthy 2005). In the same way, during the floods that covered Pakistan in 2022, it was a failure of governance rather than the floods themselves that was the real cause of injury, death and loss of livelihoods (Mohmand, Loureiro and Sida 2023). Similarly, while the earthquake that struck

Turkey and Syria in 2023 affected everyone, it was those living in housing constructed with poor building materials and to inadequate standards that were worst affected.[8] In all these settings, long-term neglect by state authorities, corruption and ineffective and unevenly implemented regulations mean that disasters are experienced differently by different people. There is therefore 'no such thing as a natural disaster' (Hartman and Squires 2006; Smith 2006). Even though storm surges, tectonic movements, extreme heat and lack of rainfall are the result of natural processes, the consequences of them vary by class, caste, gender, race, occupation, location and so on. Uncertainties are therefore always experienced unevenly.

The 'structural violence' (Galtung 1969) of disasters frequently constructs people as disposable 'victims', simply statistics in disaster assessments and response that only act to reinforce the existing social and political order (Giroux 2006). As discussed in chapter 1, the uncertainties surrounding disasters emerge through long histories of dispossession, exploitation and patterns of colonization that exclude, discriminate and marginalize (Moore 2016; O'Lear et al. 2022). Accepting differential vulnerability in disaster risk reduction and response is important, as it highlights how not everyone is the same and disasters have different consequences. However, 'vulnerability assessments' and 'community resilience' efforts that do not account for the historical patterns that have created such vulnerabilities in the first place can act to silence the discussion of the wider politics of uncertainty that disasters reveal.

In southern Ethiopia, Boru, Qaballe, Jilo, Golicha and other pastoralists across the region suffer the same rainfall declines (or increases) due to climate change, El Niño effects and so on as others, but they are also more affected. This is because of the long-term structural marginalization of pastoralists in the region, with so many 'development' projects failing to support pastoral systems and too often undermining them (Scoones and Nori 2023). In the same way, conflicts that compound drought disasters emerge from failures to address the challenges of borderlands and the inheritance of arbitrary divisions between nation-states. Colonialism in its many forms has much to answer for, as Mike Davis (2002) explains in his devastating book, *Late Victorian Holocausts*, a history of drought responses in India and beyond.

Conclusion

Different types of uncertainty emerge during disasters: a lack of knowledge about the incidence of hazards; not knowing how a particular hazard will interact with others; uncertainties about how hazards will in turn play out on the ground across different social groups of varying vulnerabilities; and not knowing how to act if the disaster is historically unprecedented, where conditions of ignorance prevail.[9] Despite the developments in research on disasters, which emphasize uncertainties and their social dimensions (see Bankoff and Hilhorst 2022), most effort is invested in estimating hazard incidence in the hope of reducing uncertainty and facilitating risk-based responses. But, instead of relying only on assumptions of calculable, single and separate risks as the basis for early warning, insurance schemes, anticipatory action, contingency plans and social assistance programmes, responding to uncertainty requires a more agile, flexible system, which is rooted in local, shared responses and adapted to diverse contexts, centred on collective action and garnering trust through inclusivity (Caravani et al. 2022; Tupper and Fearnley 2023). Such an approach would draw on ways people such as Boru and his pastoralist friends and colleagues actually respond to disasters, located in their own contexts and temporalities. For disasters are always uncertain, part of a complex web of interacting factors that combine and compound – reflecting features of the 'polycrisis' discussed in chapter 1. For many, such as the pastoralists of southern Ethiopia, disasters are part of everyday experience; in some ways, they are also expected and 'normal', even if they are not predictable.

In a reimagined approach to disasters and emergencies, mobilizing networks of practice, knowledge, support and redistribution from within communities is essential. This puts a collective 'moral economy' based on local knowledges and solidarities at the heart of disaster preparedness and response. Of course, this is not an appeal to focus only on the local and vernacular, as such responses must negotiate relationships with scientists, state bureaucracies, NGOs, religious organizations and others, but disaster management and response must always start from people's own experiences and needs.[10]

This suggests a different disaster response politics, informed by a different moral order, with the standard elements of disaster risk reduction and management fundamentally recast. Instead of an external early warning system defining what people should do as part of an intermittent, top-down, event-based emergency response, a permanent, locally networked system of early warning, based on deliberation around uncertainties, can be envisaged. Such systems would be informed by scientific assessments but not be dominated by them, as translating warnings into early action is always social, requiring effective timing, flexibility and transparency in responses.[11] As research in Somalia finds, mobilizing formal and informal networks and galvanizing collective action is also essential.[12] A new approach to early warning and preparedness would therefore make use of diverse sources of knowledge in an equivalent and respectful way, so that practice-based plans emerge that are trusted and implementable. Central to these processes would be the sort of local high-reliability professionals and networks that we met in the context of critical infrastructures in chapter 4. They would be central to building resilience from below, and so would avoid having projects imposed from outside, based on misplaced narratives about what is best.

Whether in pastoral areas of Ethiopia and Kenya confronting drought or flood-prone areas of the United Kingdom, Germany, India or the United States, a reimagined approach to 'civil contingency', early warning and disaster response needs to emerge (Anderson and Adey 2012; Kuklicke and Demeritt 2016), one that is built from below and embedded in the social relationships of moral economies and care. Perhaps now, as the deep uncertainties that influence our turbulent world become more and more evident, is the time for such a fundamental reappraisal (Amin 2013).

As discussed in chapter 1, sometimes it is through the confluence of momentous events and experiences that radical shifts in perspectives can occur. Following the 1755 Lisbon earthquake, the exchanges between Voltaire and Jean-Jacques Rousseau prompted fundamental questions for Enlightenment thinking about ethics, morality and the role of reason in approaching disasters in what was then a new age of modernity and progress (Dynes 2000; see chapter 1 above). Although in a different historical moment around different themes and issues, today such rethinking is needed with equally far-reaching moral, social, political and methodological implications for how disasters are understood and responded to.

As the disaster risk reduction community begins to realize the importance of systemic risk and uncertainty in responding to complex, intersecting and compound hazards, there has been a flourishing of methodological experiments aimed at engaging with local approaches to disaster response. For example, in England approaches to 'community modelling' have been used to explore flood-risk management, bringing scientific and local expertise together in new ways (Landström et al. 2019). Meanwhile, in Brazil, citizen engagement with data collection and analysis, and integration with early warning systems, has reduced flood impacts on riverine communities (de Albuquerque et al. 2021). Such approaches allow for the joint, co-produced navigation of uncertainty in the same way discussed in chapter 5 around epidemic disease. When science is so uncertain, as with volcanology for instance, new approaches to science advice and risk assessment are required (Donovan 2019). These approaches are not antithetical to the use of 'big data', artificial intelligence, mathematical modelling or scenario building but start from a different standpoint, as it is only through local understandings – and cultures, beliefs and practices – that an effective system for disaster preparedness and response can be built.

Reconnecting with local approaches to managing uncertainty would in many ways mean recapturing the origins of insurance approaches and humanitarian and social-protection systems: not as technical-managerial instruments imposed from above, located in an individualized politics of the market or state control but, as discussed further in the concluding chapter, in real, existing processes and practices rooted in vernacular knowledges and collective commitments to solidarity, mutual support and care.

7

Climate Change: Multiple Knowledges, Diverse Actions

Introduction

On 9 August 2021, the International Panel for Climate Change (IPCC) produced its lengthy science report. It was dramatic reading. The Secretary General of the United Nations, António Guterres, pronounced that it was 'code red for humanity'.[1] In subsequent months, further reports from other working groups were produced, which had similarly stark warnings. If humanity did not act now at a global scale, then there was no chance of keeping within the limits for warming set at the United Nations climate summit in Paris in 2015.

The IPCC reports represent a 'scientific consensus' on the scale, intensity and impacts of climate change, with recommendations on what to do about it in respect of both mitigation (reducing global heating) and adaptation (changing practices and technologies to respond). Massive numbers of people are involved. The latest AR6 reports – the sixth global assessment since the IPCC was established in 1988 – involved nearly 800 scientists who review and synthesize the scientific findings from thousands of peer-reviewed academic articles.[2] It is a huge amount of work, and the reports are impressive in their analysis and rigour, although, as many have highlighted over the years, there is a bias towards male scientists and those based in 'northern' institutions (Liverman et al. 2022). The aim, though, is for a global, incontrovertible, evidence-based scientific view, one that is beyond challenge.

Yet inevitably there are many uncertainties: how to achieve a fossil fuel-free, decarbonized future; how to realize an energy transition; how to adapt to now inevitable shifts in climates; how to reshape economies and societies globally to avoid catastrophic climate change. All these present large challenges and many uncertainties. The climate system itself is complex, with multiple variables interacting, and so predictions of what will happen where, when and to whom are always uncertain, as discussed further below. Uncertainties exist around the growing array of climate mitigation options, whether climate geoengineering, bioenergy with carbon capture and storage, alternative wind, solar and hydroelectric energy technologies, modular nuclear power generation and so on. Many applications are new, untested and subject to the same challenges around both safety and efficacy that I discussed in chapter 3. A faith in technological climate 'solutions' can often act to suppress uncertainties and divert attention away from the big question – how to change economic systems and the infrastructures of housing, transport and energy supply in ways that do not in the end destroy the planet.

In the same way, the many elaborate schemes for achieving 'net-zero' emissions – say, for example, through global carbon offsetting schemes under the voluntary carbon market or internationally transferred mitigation outcome (ITMO) bilateral country partnerships under Article 6.2 of the Paris climate agreement – present yet more uncertainties, given the vagaries of the carbon market and the assumptions embedded in carbon offsetting and trading/exchange schemes. Uncertainties arise around the commensurability of carbon as a commodity and whether such marketization efforts genuinely offer both permanence and additionality – and so actually genuinely tackle climate change. As many suspect, such schemes may simply act to salve consciences, tick corporate sustainability boxes and generate profit but fail to address the fundamental challenge of the damaging environmental consequences of capitalism (and of course state socialist) economic activity.

In parallel to mitigation efforts, a focus on facilitating adaptation to a changing climate again provokes many uncertainties: what works in ways that facilitate adaptation while protecting livelihoods? Following a discussion of the modelling that informs both mitigation and adaptation efforts, this chapter focuses on such adaptation responses, leaving aside debates about mitigation options – whether from technological fixes or radical societal transformation. This deserves another book, although there are many overlapping issues around how uncertainties are navigated. Here I concentrate on the urgent challenges of adapting to climate change, with examples from South Asia and Africa. For, in the immediate term, it is these challenges that must be faced, often among highly vulnerable people living in marginal locations. At the regular Conferences of the Parties (COPs) of the United Nations Framework Convention on Climate Change (UNFCCC), the huge adaptation challenge is the focus of much policy debate, many pledges and lots of new funding vehicles.[3] But the question arises: are such initiatives designed with uncertainty in mind, or do they fall into the trap of technology-led climate 'solutionism' that many of the mitigation efforts also suffer from?

In order to answer these questions, we need to travel to where climate change hits hardest, where it is a matter of life and death as global heating affects the very basis of making a living in marginal areas across the world. In this chapter, we hear from Romesh Sarkar from the Sundarbans in West Bengal, India, and Fadzai Mutema from Masvingo province in southern Zimbabwe,[4] along with many of their relatives and friends. They both know that climate change is real. They see it in the increased frequency of flooding events following tropical storms in the Sundarbans delta where Romesh farms and fishes. Houses and fields are washed away and livelihoods for all those in their village are becoming more difficult, encouraging many to leave. In southern Zimbabwe, Fadzai has a small farm, but droughts have ravaged her crops year on year. Making a living from the land has become much harder. However, last year the rains did come, but in huge storms that washed away the soil and destroyed her stand of maize.

Across the world, particularly in poorer, more marginal settings where vulnerabilities are high, people know about climate change but feel powerless to do anything about it. They know that global warming is caused by pollution from faraway factories that their relatives work in and from the planes that they see flying overhead. But, at the same time, their day-to-day practices of farming or fishing and the safety of their homes are becoming more and more precarious. Old systems of responding to variable conditions are often found wanting, as weather events become more extreme and so more damaging. Climate change is perhaps the most challenging source of uncertainty faced by humanity today. It connects with most of the uncertainties generated by different sources of variability discussed in the previous chapters of this book. Climate events can upset stabilized knowledge about economies and financial systems; new technological innovations that facilitate transitions to low-carbon economies carry with them many uncertainties and so regulatory challenges; extreme climate-induced shocks can test any critical infrastructure and those trying to generate a reliable supply of critical services; climate change can result in transformations of environments that entail the emergence of pandemic zoonoses and disasters; and emergencies are frequently made worse by climate change, as droughts or floods for example become more extreme. Climate change therefore impinges on all facets of life, generating new uncertainties, even if we are now certain that change is accelerating. Yet different people – from UN officials to climate modellers to fishers and farmers like Romesh and Fadzai – experience climate change in very different ways. Therefore, in this chapter, I want to ask how can the global science of climate change prediction and scenario development connect with the highly uncertain local conditions that both Romesh and Fadzai face?

Promises of prediction

The modelling efforts at the heart of climate change science and policy offer promises of prediction and guides to global action (Miller 2004; Heymann, Gramelsberger and Mahony 2017). Much of the foundational work of the IPCC and so global climate policy relies on modelling, both in terms of projections of climate change and in relation to scenarios under different options (Guillemot 2022). The core models are global in scope and are hugely complex, with a bewildering number of parameters. Different models inevitably offer different results, which is why, in order to assess the impacts of greenhouse gas emissions, models are combined in 'ensembles', sometimes with weightings for different model types. The World Climate Research Programme's Coupled Model Intercomparison Project (CMIP),[5] for example, offers composite datasets for analysis. This helps to align modelling work, but there are large variations between model outputs and much surrounding uncertainty. In the same way, for the development of scenarios, 'integrated assessment models' have become the standard approach since the 1970s (van Beek et al. 2020), but again these take many forms, making the development of a consensus position always challenging.

Today, thankfully, very few challenge the basic evidence that climate change is occurring with the world getting warmer. The old disputes around the 'hockey stick' model that showed rising global temperatures back in 1998 have largely gone (Mann 2012). However, this does not mean that the predictive science of modelling can anticipate everything, everywhere and at scales that are meaningful for action, as climate scientists of course acknowledge. There remains a lot of uncertainty, even ignorance, about the future climate in particular places and over different timescales. There are similar uncertainties around to what extent extreme events – whether heatwaves, floods or droughts – can be attributed to climate change and what different mitigation and adaptation scenarios might mean for different people (van der Sluijs 2005; Curry and Webster 2011). The focus on global science for global action within a UN framework is of course deliberate, but for those on the front line of climate change, such as Romesh and Fadzai, it raises urgent questions about what to do today as floods arrive, sea levels rise and droughts occur with increasing frequency.

Yet there are many uncertainties inherent in the global models that are central to the IPCC assessments, just as there are in the financial and epidemiological models discussed in earlier chapters. While such models offer indications for global action, they are often of less use to Romesh and Fadzai who are confronting climate change now. Acknowledging the inevitability and unavoidability of such uncertainties is therefore crucial, rather than expecting an assignment of probability to guide climate policy and adaptation action. As Suraje Dessai and Mike Hulme (2004: 107) point out, 'Probability assessment in the context of climate change is always subjective, conditional and provisional.' For many commentators, therefore, it is much better to be roughly right, rather than precisely wrong; to have robust forms of decision making rather than striving for precision and optimality (Dessai, O'Brien and Hulme 2007; Wilby and Dessai 2010).

What uncertainties must be confronted? There are many related to the climate models themselves – with so many parameters, so much complexity and significant non-linearities, this is inevitable. The Global Circulation Models (GCMs) that are central to climate modelling attempt to connect atmospheric patterns with ocean circulation and ice sheet physical processes, taking into account the behaviour of aerosols and cloud formations, to come up with an idea of how changes in the atmosphere due to the increase in 'climate forcing' greenhouse gases affect global surface temperatures. This is not an easy task, to say the least. Add into this the possibility of 'tipping points', such as the thawing of Arctic tundra, sudden changes in ocean currents or major ice sheet collapses, coming up with precise predictions is impossible (Lenton et al. 2019). Relatively small changes to complex 'tele-connected' systems can result in major shifts between what seem to be stable states, meaning that uncertainty and ignorance must be central to understanding earth-system changes (Livina 2023). And there may be blind spots in models themselves when events are synchronized, resulting in major global impacts from climate events (Kornhuber et al. 2023).

Such challenges are well recognized by climate and Earth scientists, even if their aim continues to be to reduce uncertainties, allowing for more effective prediction as part of climate projections and scenarios. A senior scientist based in South Africa commented, 'What we know is that with a forecast . . . you are never going to get an accurate projection . . . [you should] not think that any particular projection is going to give you the exact answers' (quoted by Whitfield 2015: 49). Yet, even so, the ideal is to get to 'the apex of the modelling pyramid' where 'all facets are correctly and adequately incorporated at a high enough resolution', resulting in a model 'presumably identical to the real climate' (quoted by Shackley et al. 1998: 163). In the process of creating models and translating them into policy, uncertainties are translated, condensed and displaced in ways that maintain the dominance of a particular modelling (Shackley and Wynne 1996), even if limitations are recognized.

When models are compared, we can learn if there is a broad convergence, but uncertainties are always present. Combining models to come to a consensus can be tricky as different models have different levels of data and analytical reliability. Weighting between models may not work as it is always a subjective judgement as to what model or scenarios should be most important. As Roger Pielke and Justin Ritchie (2021) point out, the common choice of the IPCC RCP8.5 scenario, first published in 2006 and now superseded by many other scenario analyses, is a political one that needs interrogating. Downplaying other scenarios with less disastrous outcomes is a choice and not one informed only by 'science'. Overemphasizing catastrophic, apocalyptic futures, even if they raise the alarm, may result, at the extreme, in 'despotism and rashness' (Burgess, Pielke and Ritchie 2022: 1) and certainly an unbalanced debate around mitigation and adaptation options. Instead, a more balanced approach is needed that looks at the full range of plausible scenarios (Pielke, Burgess and Ritchie 2022). The climate data driving the models and scenarios of course are embedded in the institutional systems that collect them, reflecting deep-seated biases about what data count and how to interpret complex results (Grossman 2023). As the science becomes more sophisticated, as the data sources expand and the models become more numerous and complex, uncertainties of course increase (Trenberth 2010). As discussed in chapter 1, more knowledge does not mean less uncertainty, in fact the opposite.

There are also inevitable limits to what models can predict for particular places and over different timescales. Romesh and Fadzai want to know what will happen in their area in the next season and across coming years, but we simply do not know. What is called 'downscaling' is very difficult and the models remain imperfect. We (mostly) know how climates will evolve in general but not in particular places for particular times. The promise of precise prediction is therefore some way off. Relying on models for more than a general guide and to provide the much-needed evidence to spur global action is unwise, and there is a need for much more open deliberation about model results and resulting scenarios lest debates about what to do where become narrow and focused on particular solutions. As discussed further below, other complementary approaches are needed to facilitate adaptation to climate change in places like the Sundarbans and dryland southern Zimbabwe, rooted in local contexts and experiences.

In debates about climate policy and the design of different action plans, we also do not know for sure to what extent particular damaging events can be attributed to anthropogenic climate change. Increasingly sophisticated 'attribution science' can use models to tease out different causal factors, but there are many uncertainties that arise as the climate is a highly complex, non-equilibrium system (Stott et al. 2016). In the wider debate about 'loss and damage', therefore, attributing responsibility, liability and compensation levels becomes tricky as so much remains disputed (Tschakert et al. 2017; Boyd et al. 2021). The process by which scientific assessments are used to attribute causality to different factors in the face of diverse uncertainties as a result becomes highly political (Lahsen and Ribot 2022).

Uncertainties are therefore everywhere in climate modelling and scenario development efforts, deeply affecting climate policy and investment choices. As some speculate, perhaps with a different composition of scientists, a more circumspect, reflective, sceptical approach might emerge, going beyond the assertive, northern-dominated, male version of the world. Yet doubt and debate around climate change can provoke mobilization against significant action. Not surprisingly, given the aggressive attacks on climate science (and scientists) by 'climate sceptics', often backed by vested interests in the fossil fuel industry, the scientific ranks have closed down and very often have suppressed healthy scientific doubt and explorations of uncertainty (Hulme 2023). The attacks on Michael Mann and colleagues for their bold claims about global warming trends in the late 1990s, or the 'Climategate' controversy in 2009, where data and informal conversations among scientists at the University of East Anglia in the United Kingdom were exposed, were aimed at sowing the seeds of confusion and the questioning of the science (Pearce 2010). Of course, science should always be questioned, and uncertainty is central to the scientific endeavour, but when the stakes are high and the vested interests so powerful, the politics of climate science becomes rough going (Böhm and Sullivan 2021).

The style of science that has emerged over the last decades has been very much influenced by this context. The aim is to offer a 'scientific' consensus, even if behind the scenes there is much debate about what input data, which modelling results and what projections make sense. The result has been a focus on a particular style of modelling, one focused on global assessments and prescriptions, ending up in an emphasis on generalized targets as the focus for international climate negotiations (Cointe and Guillemot 2023). You can see how concentrating on limiting emissions to a particular level – to avoid exceeding a 1.5°C or 2°C temperature rise, for example – arose. The message was clear, simple and focused the minds of negotiators, but it meant that the science and modelling unduly emphasized a narrow target or a simple deadline, rather than the wider challenge of social and economic transformation addressing underlying causes (Asayama et al. 2019). For some, such as Extinction Rebellion, the pressing urgency requires a declaration of a 'climate emergency' in an attempt to usher in urgent action. For others, such a narrow focus can reduce debate, increase disagreements and ultimately undermine effective action for the long term (Hulme 2009, 2023). In order to define global targets, justify emergency actions and galvanize action, the indeterminacies of system dynamics and the uncertainties that arise may be dismissed or wilfully ignored. As a result, other ways of knowing about climate change that are accepting of uncertainty have been consistently sidelined by what some see as the epistemic hegemony of IPCC-style consensus-based science (Beck and Mahony 2017).

The social and political lives of climate models

Those who study the practices of science have generated important insights into how climate modelling and scenario building works and how this narrowing down occurred. For example, Simon Shackley and Brian Wynne (1995, 1996) highlighted long ago how a global science of the climate was mutually constructed between scientists and policymakers through the development of global circulation models. These acted as powerful 'boundary-ordering devices' in the then emergent field of climate policy, in turn acting to contain uncertainty and sustain the dominance of a particular type of model-based knowledge making. Martin Mahony (2014, 2017) studied the regional climate model, PRECIS, developed by the Hadley Centre in the

United Kingdom,[6] While notionally extending the capacity for 'downscaled' climate analysis to different regions of the global South, a focus on a particular type of model inevitably restricted options for adaptation interventions, relying on a certain 'way of knowing', centred on model-based prediction. Meanwhile, Stephen Whitfield (2015) looked at how climate and crop models are connected in order to predict how climate change might play out in East African farming systems, showing how such connected models have to confront multiple uncertainties when recommending policy options and too often ignore or sideline them.

Various contributions to a fascinating reflection on the role of the IPCC (De Pryck and Hulme 2022) show how modelling practice – whether around climate models or scenarios – shape outcomes and are conditioned by the style of scientific 'evidence'. Explorations of the 'social life' of models illustrate how uncertainties within models can open up or close down debates about climate change (Hastrup and Skrydstrup 2012). The social conditions of doing science, the networks that exist within science and the institutions and funding of science all have deep effects on how climate change is understood and acted upon.

Such a 'constructivist' approach of course does not deny that climate change is real and extremely dangerous – indeed, some studies suggest that modelling practice may underplay the impacts – but the study of science in practice does show how important the social and political contexts for science are. It is these contexts that have for several decades acted to suppress an effective acknowledgement of uncertainty. This distortion is not deliberate, nor part of some hideous conspiracy, but the consequence of how the now deeply embedded, institutionalized practices play out. As Brian Wynne (2010: 289) explains, 'social and technical analysis of climate science is not about denial of the scientific propositional claims at issue, but about understanding the conditional and essentially ambiguous epistemic character of any such knowledge, however technically sophisticated and robust it may be.'

With a greater diversity of scientists involved in assessments and a decline in the organized, well-funded attacks on the basic science, the defensive approach to scientific debate about climate change is hopefully over; although given the way climate debates are being mobilized by reactionary populist politicians and libertarian conspiracy theorists alike, and in turn fuelled by social media misinformation, this may be more hope than reality. Perhaps climate science can return to a more usefully open and deliberative tone, where uncertainties are acknowledged so as to be addressed head-on. Why this is necessary is especially highlighted if we return to the front lines of climate change in the Sundarbans of West Bengal and the drylands of southern Zimbabwe. Here the models show what Romesh and Fadzai already know: while climate change is real, the models cannot suggest what to do and how to adapt to these changing conditions given multiple uncertainties. This requires another focus: the ground-level practices of those confronting the uncertainties of climate change day to day.

Adapting to climate change

With the wide acceptance that climate change is accelerating and that key thresholds will be exceeded no matter what mitigation efforts are put in place, climate adaptation has risen up the agenda within the UNFCCC and across national and city governments (see Adger et al. 2003; Schipper 2006; Eakin, Lemos and Nelson 2014; Inderberg et al. 2014; Eriksen, Nightingale and Eakin 2015). Many of the modelling efforts are focused on estimating what patterns of climate change must be adapted to – increases in heatwaves, droughts, floods, sea-level rise, storm surges, as well as more particular effects such as increasing groundwater-level changes or subsidence. The aim of the modelling is to provide a clear, predictive guide for what to prioritize and where (Dessai et al. 2009).

The result is that a whole array of adaptation efforts has emerged, very often extensions of things that have been part of 'development' efforts everywhere, but now with the 'climate' moniker added. So we get climate-smart, climate-proofed and climate-resilient projects all promoted as ways of addressing the uncertainties of climate change through 'adaptation'. In both the Sundarbans and southern Zimbabwe, there are now numerous 'climate adaptation' projects offered by both the aid agencies and the state. Unfortunately, just like standard, normal 'development', they often involve a lot of labour and don't always make things better.

In Zimbabwe, for example, Fadzai has joined the '*pfumvudza*' programme, which is promoted as a 'climate-smart' solution to farming in dry areas. It involves digging small pits across a plot at specified distances and depths, with seed and fertilizer supplied. The villagers joke that this is the 'dig and die' programme, as it's very hard to dig so many small pits compared to ox-drawn ploughing (Baudron et al. 2012). Some have adapted the system to reduce labour, but they hide it from the extension workers because they will not receive the valuable seed and fertilizer if they don't follow the conservation agriculture guidelines.[7]

In the Sundarbans, Romesh and colleagues complain about the fixed, concrete embankments that have been installed by development projects attempting to control the floods. As they explain, these do not work and often collapse, and the state does not offer compensation for the land lost when they do. The desire to fix and control flexible water flows through infrastructure has been a recurrent theme since colonial times (D'Souza 2006; Dewan 2021). Worse, such interventions remain popular with politicians today, eager to demonstrate that they command resources and have power over nature (Ghosh, Kjosavik and Bose 2022). Only with a sense of climate 'crisis' are the media attracted to showing the 'sinking islands' of the Sundarbans – whether in India or Bangladesh – with visible embankment structures seen as a symbol of development 'saving' people from a climate dystopia (Paprocki 2021). Other NGO projects are also common, with women and youth often mobilized in 'self-help' groups for training in skills for livelihood diversification activities (Ghosh, Kjosavik and Bose 2022). This is constructed as 'adaptation', meaning leaving land-based livelihoods that are being wrecked by climate change.

There has been a huge growth in what are labelled 'community' or 'locally led' adaptation projects in recent years (Rahman et al. 2023),[8] and the Sundarbans and southern Zimbabwe have not missed out. These take some of the ideas from standard development practice – working with local groups, drawing on local knowledge and so on – and translate them into climate-related interventions. Sadly, however, the lessons from past development efforts are not learned. 'Communities' often don't exist, or are highly differentiated by gender, age, caste and class; 'participation' is not a simple quick fix for long-term development in structurally uneven settings; 'localization' is not easy in contexts where institutional and infrastructural capacity is weak; 'indigenous knowledge' cannot be just extracted and distilled for utilitarian purposes; and so on. As discussed in the previous chapter in relation to disasters more generally, 'vulnerability' always emerges from complex underlying structural causes and is not easily addressed by sticking-plaster, project-based solutions (Watts and Bohle 1993; Cannon and Müller-Mahn 2010; Taylor 2014). Even with micro-credit, self-help groups and livelihood diversification projects, the villagers of the Sundarbans, for example, still remain vulnerable to the effects of climate change because they are marginalized and poor.

Of course, local climate adaptation projects can offer some improvements, but the work involved can be considerable, as with the climate-smart conservation agriculture interventions in Zimbabwe or the rehabilitation of mangroves in West Bengal. These can undermine livelihoods in other ways by diverting labour along with institutional and political attention to particular projects (Grove 2014; Brink, Falla and Boyd 2023; Johnson et al. 2023a). Indeed, reviews of climate adaptation interventions generally show that, while some are beneficial, others can hinder or undermine capacities to respond to climate change (Eriksen et al. 2015), resulting in what some have termed 'maladaptation' (Atteridge and Remling 2018; Schipper 2020). Failure to address the wider contextual politics of interventions has repeated the errors of earlier 'hazards' research and policy (Bassett and Fogelman 2013) in a distinct déjà vu.

The problem is that once again such projects aim to 'fix' something through a technical-managerial intervention (Nightingale et al. 2020), aiming to return to stability in the face of variability or reducing 'vulnerability' to climate change (Ribot 2014). Rather, climate adaptation – as the term suggests – is more about living with uncertainties and working with inevitable variability in a warming world, at the same time as transforming the conditions that give rise to vulnerabilities in the first place (Pelling 2010; Leichenko and O'Brien 2019). The trouble is that adaptation for some means isolating yourself from climate change – moving away from a floodplain, buying expensive insurance, installing more air conditioning – while for others it means coping and suffering under increasingly harsh conditions with limited means.

Climate change thus also intersects with wider class, race, gender and other politics. Demands for climate justice of course raise other concerns for the likes of Romesh and Fadzai, as 'climate' cannot be separated off from wider demands for land reclamation, asset redistribution and wider agrarian reform (Borras et al. 2022), alongside addressing questions of 'loss and damage' caused by climate change (Mechler et al. 2020). Articulating climate change debates with wider considerations of justice is therefore essential (Kashwan and Ribot 2021). As discussed many times in this book, not all uncertainties are the same for all people, as they emerge from the particular dynamics of capitalism and its uneven spatial and temporal impacts. Contrasting uncertainties in turn affect the achievement of epistemic, procedural and distributional climate justice for different people in different places (Newell et al. 2021).

Accepting that climate change and capitalism, and so questions of justice and redistribution, are intimately bound up is essential and reminds us that uncertainties are not evenly distributed, and a neoliberal resort to individualized 'flexible coping' through market mechanisms is wholly inadequate (Felli 2021). Addressing the fundamental, underlying causes of climate change remains urgent and must not be lost sight of, but, meanwhile, in particular places such as the Sundarbans and southern Zimbabwe, people must respond to the reality of climate change, right now.

Local responses

As the climate has become more uncertain, Romesh and Fadzai and their families and friends have had to adapt out of necessity. Externally defined 'adaptation' projects are only ever a small part of the story. Local responses involve drawing on local experience to help predict and plan, while also developing new ways of responding through transforming livelihoods (Berrang-Ford et al. 2021).

For Fadzai, adaptation has meant changing her cropping patterns. She has invested in a small pump for irrigated gardening as dryland cropping is now very uncertain. While she insists on planting dryland maize because of its taste and low labour demands, it is very susceptible to mid-season droughts that have become more and more common. She has also experimented with other crops, including returning to small grains such as sorghum, bullrush and finger millet that her parents used to plant. Her cattle herd is now much smaller through mortalities due to drought and disease, but she keeps enough animals to allow her to plough and transport crops from the field. Instead of investing in drought-susceptible cattle, she has encouraged her goat flock to grow and, with advice from her relatives as well as gifts of some kid goats, she has chosen local breeds that she knows can survive if the rains are poor. To ensure nutrition for her family, she has also invested in poultry, including some broilers but also some hardy indigenous chickens. More broadly, her family is involved in other jobs, with her sons now running a minibus from town that was purchased with proceeds from the farm. Together with other neighbours, she sells sweet potatoes at the roadside during the season alongside her vegetables, which provides a decent income. Farming, as she explains, must always change to fit the conditions. These may be changing climatic conditions, with increasing droughts, as well as economic conditions, which in the case of Zimbabwe have been continuously challenging. She explains what farming with variability means: 'My farm is very different to what it was even five years ago. I have to change. I have to adapt by getting help from others to keep going.'[9]

In the Sundarbans, major livelihood changes are occurring in response to flooding, coastal erosion and loss of land. People are no longer able to live with the flows and rhythms of the delta, responding to the volatility of an unpredictable environment through fishing and farming (Krause 2017; Krause and Eriksen 2023; Mukherjee, Lahiri-Dutt and Ghosh 2023). Many men have left the area to work on short-term jobs in Kolkata or beyond, while women remain. Women therefore take on responsibilities for the household, involving care work, farming and a whole host of off-farm activities. The considerable labour required for 'climate adaptation' – whether through externally designed projects or local investments in protecting land – is simply not available. A friend of Romesh, living on the same small delta island, explained how land is being lost, 'I had a plot of land until last year which was very near to the embankment. At the peak of harvesting time, the plot started sliding into the sea.

It happened so rapidly that I could manage to harvest only a few kilos of paddy which was sufficient for household consumption only for a few months' (Ghosh, Kjosavik and Bose 2022: 117). Others are shifting their farming practices. Another villager explained, 'We have now shifted from paddy cultivation to betel leaf cultivation. The continuous intrusion of saline seawater during tidal inundation has reduced the fertility of the land. It can hardly produce paddy and betel once in a year. . . . We are struggling' (Ghosh, Kjosavik and Bose 2022: 117).

Adaptation to variability and responding to uncertainty is not something that is only done as part of projects with a 'climate' label: it is necessarily central to everyday life, as the glimpses into the contexts of Romesh and Fadzai show. It involves experimentation, innovation, sharing and learning – what might be called jointly undertaken improvisation (Roe and Schulman 2023) – along with considerable investments of labour. It also involves working collectively in order to respond and adapt continuously. As we saw in the last chapter, confronting challenges together, never alone, is always important.

That both Romesh and Fadzai have managed to adapt to new patterns of climate vulnerability should not imply any sense of complacency. As Fadzai explains, 'The droughts are becoming worse and worse. I don't know what to do if this carries on. Agriculture will become impossible.' There are serious limitations to the capacity to adapt continuously using local resources, ingenuity and innovation (Adger et al. 2009). This means that working together with those engaged with the science of climate change – the modellers, the scenario builders, the technicians and others – is essential.

Rather than expecting climate science to predict precisely and so recommend what people should do in places like the Sundarbans or southern Zimbabwe, a more modest but nevertheless valuable ambition is required. If uncertainty in the modelling efforts is taken seriously, then a more tentative, collaborative, social process must emerge, whereby the likes of Romesh and Fadzai work together with the modellers of the IPCC. Not to 'extract' local knowledge to make the models 'better', but to test realities together using different insights from multiple knowledges, practices and experiences in a process of joint knowledge making and action.

Co-producing knowledge for action

As we have seen throughout this book – whether around finance, disease, disasters or climate change – predictive models always emerge in social and political contexts. The practices of scientists, the institutional settings within which models are applied, the funding flows and the wider political debates that condition how science is used all affect science, the evidence it generates and the policies that arise. As Brian Wynne explains, 'The intellectual order of climate scientific prediction, and the political order of global management and universal policy control, based as it is on the promise of deterministic processes, smooth changes, long-term prediction, and scientific control, mutually construct and reinforce one another' (Wynne 1996b: 372).

Such a process of 'mutual construction' should not be a surprise. As discussed in chapter 3, science is never independent of society and wider politics. We have already seen how the form of IPCC-led climate science emerged: expert led, consensus based and global in orientation, and dominated by northern, male scientists. This has produced, as discussed earlier, a particular set of responses: limits, targets and top-down, technical responses. The style of the science, focused on global circulation models and scenarios, thus creates a particular type of policy; in this case assertively global in focus and often reinforcing an instrumental view of policy implementation, focused on a self-interested, individual subject (Wynne 2010).

Scientific deliberations therefore – and the associated epistemic knowledge commitments that arise – create a particular social and political order. As noted in earlier chapters, this is what Sheila Jasanoff (2004) terms 'co-production'. Many have taken this term to mean only getting around the table and collaborating through a more participatory approach to knowledge making, but co-production in Jasanoff's sense means more. When different people get together, having different backgrounds, politics and thus framings of problems and solutions, it results in both the science and the proposed policies and practices which emerge changing together. In this way, co-production processes generate new social, political and moral orders.

This is especially important for the challenge of climate change where more fundamental transformations of systems are essential (Pelling 2010; Tschakert et al. 2013; Scoones et al. 2020). As discussed in the next and final chapter, uncertainties can and do open up spaces for change, generating opportunities for transformative action which shifts the power relations that prop up the status quo (Scoones and Stirling 2020). This can be a collaborative exercise, where the considerable expertise of modelling faces the central uncertainties at local level. Moving from abstract disembodied, model scenarios based on prediction and forecasting to a more adaptive process of 'decision-making under deep uncertainty' (Marchau et al. 2019), rooted in engaged, real-time collaborative inquiry, offers much promise, as long as such participatory processes do not just become performative, technical exercises as too often happens. Here, 'models' can take many forms, including stories and narratives or participatory, locally grounded analyses, all helping to elaborate pathways to adaptation (Ayeb-Karlsson, Fox and Kniveton 2019). This must be in the spirit of a 'post-normal' science for the climate that confronts conflicting values, systems complexity and uncertainty head-on (Turnpenny, Jones and Lorenzoni 2011; see chapter 1 above).

Bottom-up adaptation assessments, collaborative modelling approaches, participatory scenario development, plural method-ological approaches, such as combining arts approaches with scientific assessments, and appreciative inquiry of complex problems can therefore all be part of a reimagined science for climate change (Conway et al. 2019; Mehta and Srivastava 2020; Mehta et al. 2021). This requires different types of expertise, including more hybrid, cross-disciplinary capacities, the ability to facilitate and integrate alongside knowledge brokers, and connecting modelling and science 'from above' with the local context (Mehta et al. 2019; Mehta, Adam and Srivastava 2022). This is in addition to more conventional climate science and modelling expertise but it requires such experts to work in new ways with different platforms and institutional settings that reconfigure the power relations of conventional knowledge making for policy.

For some, this may all seem too idealistic and pie in the sky, but an acceptance of the inevitable uncertainties of climate change science requires a new way of doing things to address urgent challenges at the local level. As Geoff Mann (2023) argues in an essay on the limits of probabilistic climate models and the problems of technocratic solutions, 'we are in desperate need of a politics that looks catastrophic uncertainty square in the face.'

Conclusion

Climate change is a global challenge of unparalleled proportions. It requires urgent action in particular places, whether the Sundarbans of West Bengal and Bangladesh or southern Zimbabwe. Translating global knowledge into local action is not straightforward and requires a very different way of linking diverse forms of expertise to local contexts so that existing climate adaptation responses can be enhanced. This must go beyond the project-based, techno-managerial climate solutionism so often seen in both mitigation and adaptation responses to an acceptance that living with climate uncertainty means continuous adaptation, supported by collective experimentation, improvisation innovation and learning. It also means going beyond a focus on presenting evidence, even if translated and transparent, as part of performative consultations with publics. It requires instead encouraging more engaged conversations between scientists and others, so that knowledge making and meaning making in context proceed in tandem (Jasanoff 2010). As Mike Hulme (2012: 33) argues, through processes of 'public witnessing', '[c]limate models need to be "seen" to be performing credibly and reliably. They need to be "made" trustworthy – worthy of the trust of the public. To earn their social authority climate models therefore need to inhabit public venues, displaying to all their epistemic claims of offering credible climate predictions.' In this sense, 'global' climate models are not global at all, nor can they ever be unless they can be translated and domesticated into approaches that work locally on the ground.

Such a transversal process of engagement can of course be enhanced by modelling expertise, but in new ways. As Andrea Saltelli and colleagues argue, 'Mathematical models are a great way to explore questions. They are also a dangerous way to assert answers' (Saltelli 2020: 484). Instead, they argue, modelling needs to be aware of the assumptions that are inbuilt, avoid the hubris of assuming that models are right, be attentive to models' framings, be aware of the unknowns and think about the consequences. There is a need, therefore, to establish 'new social norms such that modellers are not permitted to project more certainty than their models deserve, and politicians are not allowed to offload accountability to models of their choosing' (2020: 483).

The old architecture of reified, expert science generating a 'consensus' view that can be translated into specific policy has been found wanting. But this should not mean despair; instead, the considerable and growing scientific expertise on climate change can be redeployed in new ways in a new style of co-production, generating together with diverse participants the new social and political orders necessary for transformative responses to climate change. In this way, the challenges of mitigation (reducing emissions) and adaptation (shifting practices in the face of climate change) become more firmly linked, whether in particular communities such as those of Romesh and Fadzai, in cities and municipalities or across nations. Reducing emissions through transforming economic and social practices in often radical ways and adapting to climate change now require similar types of engaged debate and action, involving multiple actors.[10] Getting away from quick-fix solutions (which of course often fail) towards a more inclusive, transformational approach is essential if both the causes and consequences of climate change are to be addressed. This means embracing uncertainty through avoiding simple consensus solutions and tech-fix interventions, and instead focusing on experimenting and innovating in ways that can fundamentally change economies and societies, both for immediate adaptation responses and in the longer term. In this vitally important effort, Romesh and Fadzai need to work together with, among many others, climate scientists, agricultural extension workers, investors, infrastructure developers and development practitioners of all stripes. And this is not just a requirement in the Sundarbans and southern Zimbabwe, but everywhere. As Jasanoff argues:

> Living creatively with climate change will require re-linking larger scales of scientific representation with smaller scales of social meaning. How, at the levels of community, polity, space and time, will scientists' impersonal knowledge of the climate be synchronized with the mundane rhythms of lived lives and the specificities of human experience? A global consensus on the meaning and urgency of climate change cannot arise on the basis of expert consensus alone. (Jasanoff 2010: 238)

In other words, addressing global climate change means engaging with how people live with climate-related uncertainties – and that means everyone, the world over. It thus necessitates making responses more real, tangible and urgent than a generic, impersonal risk-based science can ever do. As we have seen throughout this book and as laid out in the final chapter, putting uncertainty front and centre entails a very different set of approaches across policy areas, with some profound and radical implications for the way we conceive science, innovation and development, and hence the far-reaching social and economic transformations required to address the climate challenge.

8

Looking Forward: From Fear to Hope, from Control to Care

> We don't know the future, and what it will bring. Only God can know the future. Our grandfathers made predictions using animal entrails, but we cannot know. Uncertainties are here now; that's our life! We used to have drought every five years, now it's every two. We are being squeezed by outsiders from all sides making things worse.[1]

Halkano Boru, a pastoralist from Isiolo in northern Kenya, highlights many of the aspects of uncertainty discussed throughout this book. The future is unknown. Predictions are possible, but ultimately we cannot know. Drawing on historical knowledge and lived experience can provide important clues. We may rely on others – whether God or science – for guidance but, in the end, we must rely on our own capacities and our own social networks and relations. Uncertain events may be getting worse or more abrupt, often driven by shifts in environmental conditions, resource grabbing and changes in the wider political economy, and this creates new challenges. We must therefore all find ways of living with and responding to uncertainties. Uncertainties, after all, are part of life. This is the message of this book, and that of Halkano.

Living with uncertainty is challenging; it affects how we feel, how we experience the world, whether you are a Boran pastoralist in northern Kenya or a banker in New York, London or

Frankfurt. This book has asked how we can navigate uncertainty in today's turbulent world, whoever we are. This matters because lack of knowledge about future outcomes affects our daily lives and our livelihoods, sometimes as a matter of life and death. But also, uncertainty matters because our responses create a politics that defines how we confront the future. We can 'open up' to the possibilities offered by uncertainty or 'close down' to risk and control. Rather than feeding into a wider politics of despair, where apocalyptic visions dominate and the politics focuses on centralized and authoritarian control with technocratic styles of science in charge, we must ask: can alternative futures be envisaged that take uncertainty seriously?

An uncertain world

As the different chapters have discussed, we must navigate uncertainties in a world that is increasingly fragmented, divided often by populist forms of nationalism and by politicians attempting to 'take back control' from what is perceived to be an elite internationalism. Yet, despite such regressive moves, economic globalization and international connectedness persist. People move through migration; goods are traded globally; finance links multiple centres and information; and knowledge continuously flows across borders, facilitated by new technologies. In an increasingly multipolar world, geopolitical tensions arise between powers, while conflicts erupt within and between nations, challenging stability and unleashing untold suffering, whether in Russia and Ukraine, the Middle East or central Africa. Added to this, climate change, pollution, pandemic threats and other conditions of what some term the 'Anthropocene' can disrupt and challenge any simplistic notion of a stable order amenable to technocratic control.

In today's turbulent world, the likelihood of major shocks to economies and societies is high, but always uncertain. As Christine Lagarde, the president of the European Central Bank, observed at an elite meeting of central bankers at Jackson Hole in August 2023, this requires a radically different approach to economic governance – there is no 'pre-existing playbook', she says, and, in an age of uncertainty, there is a need to 'adjust our analytical frameworks in real time to new developments'.[2] She argues that '[w]e may be entering an age of shifts in economic relationships and breaks in established regularities. For policymakers with a stability mandate, this poses a significant challenge . . . if we are in a new age, past regularities may no longer be a good guide for how the economy works.' In other words, embracing uncertainty is key. As she describes, this must be done with clarity, flexibility and humility, where 'We cannot make policy based on simple rules or intermediate targets in an uncertain economy. And this means that we cannot exclusively rely on models that are estimated with old data, attempting to fine-tune policy around point forecasts.' As she notes, escaping from the strictures of old ideas is especially challenging for institutions and policies forged within a stability and control paradigm. This suggests the urgent need to find new ways of navigating uncertainty across diverse areas of policy and practice, as has been explored throughout the book.

The uncertainties discussed through the different chapters arise, as we have seen, in contexts deeply affected by the far-reaching global changes of concern to Lagarde. These are all of course influenced by the way capitalism – in diverse forms – affects societies and environments, through processes of commoditization, financialization and 'cannibalization' – and therefore the stark creation of unequal relations between and within nations (Patel and Moore 2017; Fraser 2023). Gone are the days when a stable 'world order' could be proclaimed, one that created the twentieth-century institutions such as the United Nations or the post-colonial project of 'development'. No longer will a modernist appeal to science, evidence and technology suffice to address today's challenges. Uncertainties are interwoven with people's identities, sense of belonging and emotional connections to versions of history and place, as populist ideologues know all too well. The old tussles of state versus market or collective versus individual control that characterized earlier debates are much less relevant, as economic and political relations reconfigure. The appeal to a liberal centre ground situated between such extremes will no longer do.[3]

Instead, as this book argues, a new politics of uncertainty must be envisaged that addresses head-on today's challenges where futures are unknown and contested, recasting old, linear notions of innovation, development and public policy in quite fundamental ways. As pointed out in chapter 1, this does not mean rejecting the structural analyses of unequal power relations and political-economic conditions that give rise to uncertainties, nor does it mean dismissing the importance of class and intersecting dynamics of social difference in the ways uncertainties are navigated. Equally, it does not mean a simple universalism that standard solutions must apply everywhere, as contexts, histories, identities and lived experiences matter in how uncertainties are understood and responded to. But it does mean recognizing that many old certainties – often violently imposed through plans, protocols and policies – that informed our thinking and practice and structured our institutions in the past have disappeared; and, of course, this is sometimes for the better. Above all, an appreciation of how uncertainties are continuously emerging from the turbulent dynamics of a complex, fast-changing world is essential, as each of the chapters has vividly shown.

This is therefore not a moment for managed 'transition', one amenable to standard technocratic, expert-led approaches to policy, where the parameters are known and techno-utopian, modernist visions of salvation can be realized. Instead, it is a time of more fundamental 'transformation' or, as in the title of Ulrich Beck's (2016) final book, 'metamorphosis'. The cumulative effects of global challenges and attendant (poly) crises, giving rise to the diverse uncertainties as discussed in this book, provoke the need to reassess, redefine and reimagine. This is when new moral orders, forms of sociality, ways of being and new political responses emerge. These ruptures can, Beck argues, catalyse shifting behaviours and practices, particularly among young people who are living in the world 'risk society' (Mythen 2018). For Beck, this requires taking on new ways of thinking and acting, rejecting standard western knowledge frameworks and imagining new 'cosmopolitan' perspectives. According to Beck, today's seemingly catastrophic context offers the hopeful opportunity for fundamental transformations – metamorphoses – towards more collective commitments and cosmopolitan insti-tutions that are able to address contemporary, trans-boundary challenges. This is the transformatory possibility of embracing uncertainty. However, given uncertainty, the process of transfor-mation cannot be planned; it does not happen in stages towards some defined goal but is more indeterminate and open-ended

– with the possibilities of capture and diversion certainly,
but also with the possibility of progressive change through
navigating diverse, intersecting uncertainties. As discussed throughout the book, a techno-managerial vision
of modernity and progress, a reliance on risk-based policy
and planning and a hubristic overconfidence in our ability to
control the future have often suppressed the 'practical wisdom'
– both knowledges and practices – necessary to live with and
from uncertain conditions. However, despite the many intellectual, practical and political barriers, the chapters have also
shown that there are real possibilities for a more hopeful,
emancipatory, caring alternative if we 'open up' to uncertainty,
rather than 'close down' to risk. Across the chapters, we have
discovered how people are generating new ways of responding
to uncertainty, so generating reliability, linked to alternative
knowledges, embedded cultural practices, social networks and
local institutions. To navigate uncertainty therefore requires
new relationships, retrained professionals and a very different
approach to policy and practice, as this chapter will explore.

Navigating uncertainty

Throughout the book, we have encountered many different ways
people navigate uncertainties. For some, flexible adaptation
to changing, uncertain conditions is feasible and easy, while
for others, options are constrained by a wider structural
political economy that conditions what is possible for whom.
In chapter 2, I discussed responses to volatile markets in an
uncertain economy, with reflections both from bankers at the
core of western capitalist systems and pastoralists responding
to uncertain markets in the Horn of Africa. Both had similar
responses, but it was the bankers who had to re-learn the
importance of social interactions in managing uncertainty in
the aftermath of the financial crash. In chapter 3, I turned
to questions around technology regulation, focusing on crop
biotechnology and moving from the United Kingdom to Brazil,
India and southern Africa. Different perspectives on science
and policy for regulation were seen, reflecting different perspectives on uncertainty associated with contrasting policy cultures.
This resulted in different views on what is safe and useful for

whom. Chapter 4 examined 'critical infrastructures', asking how in California the lights remain on and how a complex electricity supply system is managed when electricity generation is highly variable. This highlighted the importance of 'reliability professionals' at the centre of often informal networks who are highly skilled at managing high levels of uncertainty, a pattern seen also in pastoral settings in northern Kenya when confronting drought or animal diseases. Chapter 5 reflected on the COVID-19 pandemic and how scientists, health professionals and publics responded, both in the United Kingdom and Zimbabwe, with important lessons emerging on pandemic preparedness, the role of epidemiological modelling and the significance of locally rooted, decentralized responses. In chapter 6, I turned to disasters more generally, questioning the standard, top-down, risk management and control approaches usually taken. With examples from southern Ethiopia, as well as New York, Cape Town, Paris, the Gulf of Mexico and beyond, the chapter makes the case for a shift from a calculative, predictive approach to disaster risk management to one more firmly rooted in local contexts and moral economies. Finally, chapter 7 directs attention to the practices of adaptation to climate change and away from the emphasis on models, targets and deadlines, framed by global climate policy. With cases from dryland southern Zimbabwe as well as the Sundarbans in West Bengal, India, the chapter argues that a focus on those living with uncertainty requires learning from their adaptive experiments, improvisations and innovations.

While of course there are many contextual differences across a wide variety of themes and a diversity of cases from different parts of the world, we see some important convergences and common threads. By learning from experiences from the global North as well as the global South, the universality of the challenges, if not the required solutions, is highlighted. Responding to the questions posed at the end of chapter 1, the following sections attempt to summarize – very briefly – key lessons from across the chapters under four headings.

Complex, non-linear systems

- Complex systems of the sort discussed in this book – whether banking and finance, technology systems, critical infrastructures, pandemics, disasters and emergencies or climate change – are always non-linear and rarely at equilibrium. It means that outcomes cannot be predicted, and some may be complete surprises. As a result, standard forms of control-based risk management will not work.

• Complexity, non-linearity and disequilibrium in systems means that responses to uncertainty must avoid thinking that 'optimality' and 'efficiency' are the ideals, but instead 'robustness' and 'reliability' in the face of unknowns are more appropriate goals. This requires systems that are designed with redundancy and modularity embedded. They must involve experienced and skilled 'reliability professionals' who are able to scan horizons and respond in real time to uncertain events, while avoiding the dangers of complete surprises.

• While different sorts of quantitative modelling may be useful in contexts of uncertainty if used to open up debate about possible futures, using models to narrow down to prediction and risk management is foolhardy, even dangerous. As calculative devices they can be misused – which, as we have seen, is quite common. Simplistic models can lead to aggregative responses that miss their mark. Supported by narrow, elite expertise, models exclude other knowledges that are important in addressing uncertain challenges. Self-fulfilling 'conviction narratives' that close down debate can be highly dangerous, diverting attention and resources from foci that matter.

• Quantitative modelling – whether for climate, diseases, disasters, economic policy or any other field – therefore needs to be complemented with other forms of storytelling and narrative construction, involving diverse participants and using processes and practices that are collaborative and inclusive. Extended peer communities can challenge received wisdoms and help co-construct alternatives, making use of multiple, plural knowledges.

• Where the world is uncertain, for some an open-ended future beckons, one that offers multiple opportunities. For others, futures are constrained, with day-to-day survival in the face of intersecting uncertainties the priority. Wealth, age, gender, race, sexuality, (dis)ability, location or occupation all frame how time and the future are understood, in turn affecting how uncertainties are responded to.

Individual and collective capacities for generating reliability

- Reliability professionals and their networks provide a socially embedded basis for transforming high variability inputs into reliable outcomes, while steering organized systems away from ignorance and danger. Whether this is in the context of responding to disasters or in the day-to-day management of critical infrastructures – for example, electricity supply or pastoral systems – such skills and capacities are essential and need recognizing and supporting.
- Responding to uncertainty needs a flexible, adaptive approach, rooted in social learning and deliberation. Being open, aware and responsive is crucial. Making use of diverse sources of information to develop judgements and guide change is vital. Being alert to weak signals and garnering insights from diverse sources is essential. This requires a different sort of institutional context than we often see in mainstream policy-oriented institutions. As we have seen, those that are able to become adaptive learning organizations, whether around technology regulation or emergency disaster response, usually fare better in the face of uncertain knowledge.
- A centring of uncertainty in organizations also requires new forms of leadership that encompass the capacities to listen, learn, consult, convene, collectively imagine, embrace doubt and avoid simplistic 'solutionism'. An array of human talents is needed, often not valued in conventional leadership and standard professional training, including courage, sensitivity, creativity, generosity and commitment to collective approaches.
- This all requires a sense of humility and openness, and the ability to work together on shared problems. If uncertainty is to become an opportunity rather than a threat, offering hope not fear, then the agency of actors in complex systems needs support. At the same time, the institutional and organizational framework needs redefining in order to allow flexibility, adaptability and responsiveness, avoiding capture and closing down. Overall, as discussed further below, a more caring approach needs to be fostered.

Policy and decision-making processes

- When science is uncertain – as it nearly always is – this means that decision making and policy advice should rely on plural and conditional choices. This requires a different style of decision making to one predicated on elite expertise offering definitive options and top-down decision making following a singular science. It requires instead more radical forms of collaboration, linked to deliberation, participation and co-production, with participants offering diverse stories from multiple standpoints, fostering different imaginations and provisional answers. It means moving from following 'the science' to collaborating with multiple forms of science and knowledge in a deliberative mode, where uncertainties are always being negotiated.

- Moving beyond the hubristic, illusory and futile assumptions of control through risk management means a process of navigation that includes improvisation, experimentation and flexible adaptation, making use of windows of opportunity, developing prefigurative experimentation within 'niches' and facilitating processes of structured, deliberative learning. This is challenging, but it is the only approach that allows effective responses to socio-ecological complexity that can respond to uncertainty and build resilience, whether around pandemic responses, in disaster and emergency settings or in response to climate change, as the different chapters have shown.

- An acknowledgement (or not) of uncertainty (and ignorance) in public policy reflects political contexts and cultures. In some settings, accredited scientific expertise is deployed to manage uncertainties; in others, the law and legal processes are used more extensively; while in yet others, civil servants are expected to respond with common sense. Such top-down policy cultures often breed distrust, especially when issues are controversial, poorly understood and deeply uncertain.

- Too infrequently do wider public deliberations occur across diverse groups – creating an 'extended peer community' in the terms of post-normal science. This can allow for a more informed response to emerge, with new ideas and perspectives inevitably arising. Public engagement, both 'upstream' and 'downstream', in science–policy debates is seen to be essential when values are contested, issues are urgent and the stakes are high.

- Forms of policy governance that encourage deliberation, experimentalism and reflexive learning have been proposed. This requires new forms of organization, usually on a decentralized basis, with new hierarchies of expertise involved. But when developed effectively and sustained, the results can be impressive, as we have seen across multiple cases.

Political economy contexts

- Uncertainties, like the intersecting crises that generate them, don't come from nowhere – the conditions that give rise to uncertainties and the impacts that are felt by different people have long histories. Many such conditions arise from the contradictions of contemporary capitalism and the influences on economies, societies and environments. Histories of marginalization, discrimination by race or gender and embedded experiences of colonization all have their imprints on how diverse crises and associated uncertainties are experienced today.
- Risks and uncertainties arise from particular conjunctures and structural conditions in ways that generate highly differentiated vulnerabilities and diverse responses. Individualized, marketized responses to risk and uncertainty – in line with a neoliberal sensibility – are insufficient. Navigating uncertainties means navigating political economies and a wider politics and set of institutions, and so involves contesting power and forms of privileged expertise and control. This requires mobilization for an alternative approach and resistance to impositions of simplistic techno-managerial and market-based solutions.
- Transformational spaces can assist prefiguring changes that allow for uncertainties to become opportunities rather than threats. This means co-developing alternative approaches to managing uncertainty, involving diverse players with multiple forms of expertise. Many such spaces will emerge, not through top-down diktat and macro-design but organically from below, providing demonstrations and examples for others to follow.
- All of these themes – presented here in extremely condensed form – have been explored throughout the book, while reflecting on different issues in different contexts. The evidence for a radical rethinking of approach that facilitates the navigation of uncertainty is incontrovertible, whether in relation to banking and finance, technology regulation, critical infrastructures, pandemics, disasters or climate change.

Together, the four themes laid out above have big implications for how science and legal processes are conducted and articulated with policy; how policy processes are convened for decision making under conditions of uncertainty; whether political conditions allow for an opening up of deliberative debate about alternative futures, while avoiding capture and closing down; and how the skills and capacities of different actors are defined – whether scientific experts, front-line officials, bureaucrats, regulators, judges, policymakers and more – as they work in networks to respond to uncertainty. In sum, as discussed further below and throughout the book, making uncertainty central requires a major paradigm shift in the way we navigate the future.

Ways forward?

So, what are some of the ways forward that have been highlighted by the book? There are basic political questions about whose expertise counts and where epistemic justice lies. There are questions around who is in charge of navigating future pathways and who is responsible for threats and harms and for ensuring safety and reliability. And there are questions around the governance of risk and uncertainty.

In our increasingly uncertain world, should duties and responsibilities be diverted to the state – or even global governance structures – supported by accredited science? Should such roles be devolved to the market, through new market instruments, such as insurance, which address risks through a financialized mechanism? Or instead, should citizens become more involved in collaborative processes of deliberating on alternative futures, assessing risks and uncertainties and defining directions for innovation and development through a more open, inclusive and democratic process?

It will be no surprise to any reader of this book that my preference is for the latter. This is not just because of political-ideological preference, but also because of efficacy and experience. As the cases discussed across the chapters show, in the face of uncertainties and unknowable surprises, a more open, collective approach based on mutual support, equality, solidarity and care is essential. 'Matters of care' focus on neglected and marginalized perspectives, allowing for the imagination of how the world can be different. By rejecting a controlling vision, a perspective centred on 'care' thus encourages openness, humility, flexibility and adaptability as responses to uncertainties, engaging with affective experiences and entanglements between humans and nature (de la Bellacasa 2017). Of course, no single model for such a vision can be offered, and responses must be developed and be appropriate to particular settings. But as an alternative to the techno-managerial, control-oriented vision of modernity and progress so often promoted, an alternative, more humble vision for science, policy and innovation and development more broadly – in whatever field, in any part of the world – has many merits, given the challenges of navigating uncertainty explored across the book.

Getting more tangible, and summarizing some of the discussion above, what then needs to be done? In areas of **governance and policymaking**, whether around technology regulation or disease control, a more decentralized, deliberative, experimental approach is required to open up the debate – allowing for contention, dissensus and multiple voices, rather than closing down to an expert-led or forced consultative consensus. Within **public administration and management**, lessons on 'reliability management' in critical infrastructures can be invaluable. Managing uncertainties, avoiding the dangers of ignorance, error and complete surprise, requires recognizing and rewarding 'reliability professionals' who can respond in real time to uncertainties as they unfold, while being aware of future threats. In matters of **law and legal process**, an excessive reliance on credentialled 'expert' knowledge may narrow the opportunity for deliberation on contested issues when judgements are made around the safety of new technologies, for example. Instead, legal processes can be opened up to provide a space for deliberation on uncertainty. When addressing **environmental and resource management**, an acceptance that such systems are non-linear and complex, potentially with unknown tipping points, is essential and so again requires an approach that avoids top-down imposition, but a style centred on collaborative, adaptive management, involving resource users in navigating uncertainties. The recognition of complexity, non-linearity, lack of equilibrium and thus uncertainty is as relevant to political and economic systems as it is to ecological ones. Therefore, perspectives on **economic decision**

making need to shift from over-reliance on simplistic models or universalization from formulaic experiments to a more adaptive and differentiated style, as highlighted in new approaches such as 'decision making under deep uncertainty' (Marchau et al. 2019). Bringing uncertainty back into economics means reclaiming earlier heterodox traditions that accepted that uncertainty was distinct from risk, with many implications for what can be managed and controlled. In responding to disasters – whether climate change-induced droughts or floods, zoonotic pandemics or other natural hazards – a new culture of **disaster preparedness and response** is required. Rather than relying on predictive models, restricted notions of anticipatory planning and early action or financialized responses such as insurance, a more open approach to developing disaster plans, scenarios and practices is required that includes diverse knowledges and multiple participants in order to co-produce options for the future. This in turn requires contingency plans, advance finance systems and organizational flexibility, with the ability to respond at short notice. Preparedness, like **resilience building**, in the end must be built from below, and this requires rediscovering systems of mutual support and solidarity that help build resilience to uncertain shocks and stresses, as we have seen through experiences of the COVID-19 pandemic and in responses to many other disasters.

Overall, the principles of experimentation, improvisation, incremental learning and local-level adaptation are crucial. This means accepting that under conditions of uncertainty, multiple insights are needed, derived from diverse sources of knowledge, with deliberations on implications for diverse actors. Table 8.1 summarizes the shifts required for moving from a risk-and-control paradigm to one centring uncertainty across the areas of policy and practice highlighted above. These shifts are relevant across policy domains and geographical contexts, although they require adjusting and adapting to particular policy cultures and settings.

A paradigm shift: learning lessons from the margins

The shift from the status quo, mainstream approach based on risk and control to one that truly embraces uncertainty – where

Table 8.1 Shifting to an 'uncertainty paradigm'

	Risk-and-control paradigm	Uncertainty paradigm
Governance and policymaking	Expert-led 'optimization' of policy based on risk-based planning, perhaps supported by performative 'consultation' with publics.	Opening up to wider debate and diverse views, accepting contention and lack of consensus; facilitated policy processes involving diverse participation.
Public administration and management	Following formal protocols, routines and risk assessments; top-down plans and response systems; limited flexibility.	Recognizing and rewarding 'reliability professionals' (and their networks) able to scan horizons for future challenges and help manage uncertainties in real time; a more decentralized and flexible approach.
Law and legal process	Accredited expert, science-based evidence unquestioned; legal judgements purely on process.	Accepting that both science and the law are spaces for deliberation on uncertainty; opening up legal processes to debates about contested evidence from diverse standpoints.
Environmental and resource management	Top-down 'science-based' rules and regulations; assuming ecosystems are stable and that 'balance' has to be restored.	Complex, non-equilibrium socio-ecological systems require open-ended models and management regimes, co-constructed across stakeholders; adaptive management requires recursive learning and flexibility.
Economic decision making	Optimality and efficiency as the criteria for choice; based on equilibrium models and standardized policy experiments; top-down, expert-led process.	Accepting uncertainty (as opposed to risk) means many standard models no longer apply; need for a more open, reflexive approach to experimentation and learning under uncertainty; decision making involving diverse participants testing multiple scenarios.
Disaster preparedness, response and resilience building	Risk models and standardized anticipation and early action responses; rigid financing and standard protocols; governance at a distance through the market, via insurance instruments.	Making use of diverse knowledges and different views and experiences; an adaptive, responsive approach; flexible contingency planning and financing; building resilience from below, nurturing existing systems of mutual support and solidarity.

we don't know the likelihood of outcomes – therefore requires a major transformation in thinking and practice. Rather than a reflex retreat into positivist, deterministic perspectives, as Hannah Arendt (2018) suggests, we need to 'think without a banister', outside conventions and accepting radical unknowability where old models do not apply. While there are perspectives and practices that already exist – under many different labels – the adoption of a new technique or methodology here and there is not enough. A more fundamental shift in paradigm requires a big change in individual mindsets, organizational practices, institutional mandates and policymaking processes, supported by a new politics of uncertainty that encourages a more open, deliberative approach, inclusive of diverse knowledges and experiences.

This means redefining what we mean by innovation, development and public policy, going beyond a view that focuses on linear progress towards a singular outcome to one that embraces multiple, divergent pathways, which are always negotiated in contexts of uncertainty (Leach, Stirling and Scoones 2010; Ang 2018). As discussed in chapter 1, escaping the trap of narrow, disciplining modernist thinking and practice requires drawing on diverse inspirations from different cultures and regions: from art and literature, from interactions with the natural world and from diverse philosophical and spiritual perspectives, for example. Rather than a narrow, abstract, mechanistic view, a more engaged, rooted, affective engagement with a complex world is always required. In uncertain worlds, as pragmatist philosophers suggest,[4] we must grasp what works – creating what is useful and tangible, with imagination, courage and virtue. When standard approaches to risk management fail and uncertainties dominate, engaging with diverse imaginaries, new narratives and even utopian visions can uncover alternative ways of thinking and new practices appropriate to an uncertain world, shaking us from the comfortable complacency of the status quo.[5]

As we saw across the chapters, when we draw on a 'view from somewhere', it is the contextual dimensions of intersecting uncertainties that matter when thinking about policy responses to pandemics, disasters or financial crises, for example. While the detached 'view from nowhere' offered by the abstract mathematical models and generalized policy frameworks may have some use, they are never enough in complex, highly variable systems where uncertainties are everywhere (Jasanoff 2017).

This is why an uncertainty paradigm, as proposed in this book, can help unlock possibilities, offering the foundation for some radical rethinking for our turbulent world.

In the words of Isabelle Stengers (2018), 'another science is possible', one that necessarily works with and through contingency and uncertainty. As Michel Callon and colleagues (2009) describe, 'acting in an uncertain world' requires enlisting knowledges, people and artefacts, whether disaster-response protocols, actuarial tables for insurance or environmental and economic models, in new forms for action under uncertainty. Dealing with 'mess', and so generating reliability in the face of uncertainty, is an active process, as Emery Roe (2013) describes. This means supporting professionals who must operate in real time, making use of often tacit, experiential skills, practices and capacities.

In order to transform uncertainty from a threat to an opportunity requires in turn creating prefigurative, reflexive spaces that generate a sense of hope and the possibilities for emancipatory and transformative action (Scoones and Stirling 2020). Hope emerges from an embrace of 'polyphonic' narratives of uncertainty that celebrate 'mystery, surprise and creativity' (Ezzy 2000: 605), rather than an ambition to return to 'normal' when crises, such as serious illness, are confronted. If crises are unfolding and continuous, then trying to fix them through technocratic, individualized interventions always fails; instead, there is, as Anne-Marie Mol (2008) describes, the need for an affective and collaborative 'logic of care', replacing one of choice and control. Rebecca Solnit puts it well in her inspiring book, *Hope in the Dark*:

> Hope locates itself in the premises that we don't know what will happen and that in the spaciousness of uncertainty is room to act. When you recognize uncertainty, you recognize that you may be able to influence the outcomes – you alone or you in concert with a few dozen or several million others. Hope is an embrace of the unknown and knowable, an alternative to the certainty of both optimists and pessimists. (Solnit 2016: xii)

In *The Way of Ignorance*, Wendell Berry, novelist, poet and farmer, argues:

> The extent of our knowledge will always be . . . the measure of the extent of our ignorance. Because ignorance is thus a part of

our creaturely definition, we need an appropriate way: a way of ignorance, which is the way of neighborly love, kindness, caution, care, appropriate scale, thrift, good work, right livelihood . . . The way of ignorance, therefore, is to be careful, to know the limits and the efficacy of our knowledge. It is to be humble and to work on an appropriate scale. (Berry 2005: ix–x)

In a similar vein, Solnit again makes the argument for a positive, hopeful stance in an uncertain world, one that leads to action rather than following the 'cheerleaders of despair':

What motivates us to act is a sense of possibility within uncertainty – that the outcome is not yet fully determined and our actions may matter in shaping it. This is all that hope is, and we are all teeming with it, all the time, in small ways. . . . If we can recognise that we don't know what will happen, that the future does not yet exist but is being made in the present, then we can be moved to participate in making that future. . . . the future has not yet been decided, because we are deciding it now. (Solnit 2023)[6]

Thus, opening up future imaginaries, allowing ourselves to get lost in exploring diverse alternatives, requires a different mindset to the ones that we are frequently educated into and that define the restrictive institutional parameters of the ways public policies are currently defined, taught and practised.

This in turn requires responses to uncertainty that are translated into action through a new politics. This can provide for the generation of hopeful possibilities and transformations within spaces of change, ones centred on equality, solidarity and mutuality in ways that allow us to navigate uncertainty, both individually and collectively.[7] As we have seen throughout this book, avoiding the dangers of closing down to a control-based form of risk management through individualization, financialization, commodification, bureaucratization and securitization is imperative.

A move from risk to uncertainty, from control to care, from despair to hope, therefore has many implications for the way we see and respond to an uncertain world. As Raymond Williams (1989: 118) famously said, 'To be truly radical is to make hope possible, rather than despair convincing.' As we have seen, such radical rethinking means a new set of practices, policies and politics at the centre of many policy domains – from finance and banking to technology regulation to critical infrastructure to pandemic preparedness to disaster response and climate change. With such a recasting, a new vision of what we mean by modernity, progress and development emerges, one with profound consequences for us all.

If we are to adopt these lessons, individually, institutionally and across societies, we need to seek out those who are already practising such approaches that embrace uncertainty, rather than being constrained by the techno-managerialism of current dominant thinking and practice. These are all people who must, by necessity, live with and from uncertainty. Pastoralists, near-shore fishers, delta dwellers, swidden cultivators, cross-border migrants, inhabitants of urban informal settlements and many, many more have the knowledge and experience that can help us all. For, as the author Elif Shafak describes, we all live in 'liquid lands' these days, as the mirage of the 'solid lands' of stable liberal democracy, reinforced by technocratic designs, is fast disappearing.[8] We have met many such people throughout the book – small-scale farmers in Zimbabwe, farmer-fishers in the Sundarbans in India and pastoralists from the Horn of Africa, for example. All have shown how, around different challenges, uncertainties can be responded to and reliability generated.

As we have seen, their practices are similar to those managing market volatility in banks and financial institutions; those in regulatory agencies responding to uncertain science; doctors, nurses and other health professionals in local hospitals and clinics confronting disease outbreaks on the ground; professionals in disaster management organizations who must respond to a sudden, unexpected event, and indeed many others in the diverse settings encountered in the previous chapters. As discussed, these practices are often under the radar and without recognition, as the people on the front line battle to confront diverse uncertainties, often by opposing or subverting standard approaches.

Of course, as different chapters discuss, such practices for responding to uncertainty don't always work, being constrained and upset by wider structural, political-economic factors. However, learning lessons about opportunities and pitfalls from those with experience and skill – and sharing those lessons – is definitely a good place to start. Uncertainties face us all and are not going away, yet conventional, mainstream institutions and policies are ill-equipped to respond. We therefore urgently need to develop new approaches that help us all navigate uncertainties in new ways. Hopefully, this book has provided some indications of what challenges and opportunities lie ahead.

Notes

Chapter 1 Navigating Uncertainty

1 This chapter sets up the book and locates the idea of 'uncertainty' in diverse literatures. It, however, does not offer a classic 'literature review'. For that you need to look to some of the references offered, along with an earlier paper that I wrote that informs much of what is explored here (Scoones 2019).

2 https://www.themarginalian.org/2015/05/11/richard-feynman -science-religion/

3 https://galileocommission.org/a-very-brief-history-of-certainty-iiya -prigogine/

4 https://www.thebsps.org/reviewofbooks/andy-clark-surfing -uncertainty-prediction-action-and-the-embodied-brain/

5 See, for example, https://www.youtube.com/watch?v=S3CU2kOBt3s and https://www.allthingsrisk.co.uk/books-i-like/

6 'What happened to the risk society?', plenary panel STEPS Centre symposium, 2019, https://www.youtube.com/watch?v=eNt0R8BK8mI

7 https://adamtooze.substack.com/p/chartbook-165-polycrisis -thinking; https://www.ft.com/content/498398e7-11b1-494b-9cd3 -6d669dc3de33

8 See https://cascadeinstitute.org/wp-content/uploads/2022/04/What -is-a-global-polycrisis-version-1.1-27April2022.pdf; Henig and Knight (2023).

9 https://fortune.com/2023/01/11/world-economic-forum-polycrisis -decade-dr-doom-nouriel-roubini-adam-tooze/amp/

10 https://adamtooze.substack.com/p/chartbook-165-polycrisis-thinking; https://m.youtube.com/watch?v=8IB68X0d3Ys
11 https://www.lrb.co.uk/the-paper/v44/n11/william-davies/destination-unknown
12 https://www.greeneuropeanjournal.eu/the-colonial-roots-of-present-crises/
13 https://logicmag.io/nature/a-giant-bumptious-litter/
14 https://www.youtube.com/watch?v=REWeBzGuzCc
15 There are many ways that the contrasts between risk, uncertainty, ambiguity and ignorance are described in the literature, but I have long found this schema especially useful. As argued throughout the book, making clear the key distinction between 'risk' and 'uncertainty' is essential. This is sometimes obscured in discussions of 'risk', which actually may be referring to 'uncertainty'. Others talk of 'radical' or 'deep' uncertainty when they are in fact talking about 'ignorance', which is distinct in the terms here. Still others contrast 'epistemic uncertainty', focusing on disputes about knowledge, and 'variability uncertainty', when referring to underlying dynamics in nature, sometimes referred to as 'aleatory uncertainty' (Walker et al. 2003). In this book, debates about 'incertitude' are all about confidence in *knowledge* of likelihoods and outcomes, and so are always 'epistemic' in character. Variable nature and other conditions of dynamic variability are important, as the chapters show. Such shocks may be constituted as a 'crisis', thus giving rise to the different dimensions of incertitude. Asserting these distinctions and being clear about definitions is, I think, not just semantic nitpicking but is essential for rigorously rethinking how we navigate an uncertain world and the actions, practices and politics that follow. As a reader, I hope you too appreciate the importance of these definitions and distinctions and the value of the schema as the subsequent chapters unfold.
16 https://en.wikipedia.org/wiki/VUCA
17 https://hbr.org/2013/05/living-in-the-futures
18 https://en.wikipedia.org/wiki/The_Age_of_Uncertainty
19 https://psyche.co/ideas/much-ado-about-uncertainty-how-shakespeare-navigates-doubt
20 https://www.bl.uk/romantics-and-victorians/articles/john-keats-and-negative-capability
21 https://aeon.co/essays/when-stoicism-is-a-political-not-just-a-personal-virtue
22 See comments by Dipak Gyawali at STEPS Centre's *The Politics of Uncertainty* symposium, July 2019, www.buff.ly/35D5RSI.

Chapter 2 Finance: Real Markets as Complex Systems

1 https://youtu.be/AVIrUDEw5Gs
2 A repo, or repurchase agreement, is a short-term agreement to sell securities, which are then bought back at a slightly higher price. See https://www.investopedia.com/terms/r/repurchaseagreement.asp
3 https://www.investopedia.com/terms/m/mbs.asp
4 https://amp.theguardian.com/science/2012/feb/12/black-scholes -equation-credit-crunch
5 https://www.federalreserve.gov/newsevents/speech /bernanke20060518a.htm
6 https://www.federalreserve.gov/boarddocs/speeches/2002 /200209253/default.htm
7 https://en.wikipedia.org/wiki/Black%E2%80%93Scholes_model
8 By the end of 2007, the US insurance giant AIG was providing insurance for US$319 billion in assets for European banks, for example (Tooze 2018: 86).
9 https://www.investopedia.com/basel-iv-5218598
10 https://qz.com/africa/1885939/somalias-goats-sheep-wont-be-on -hajj-to-saudi-arabia-on-covid
11 https://www.sparc-knowledge.org/sites/default/files/documents /resources/Livelihoods%2C%20conflict%20and%20mediation %20Somalia.pdf
12 This applies of course to the many informal markets and associated economic relations across Africa (e.g., Roitman 1990; Meagher 2010).

Chapter 3 Technology: What Is Safe and for Whom?

1 http://users.sussex.ac.uk/~prfh0/adams_et_al_briefing_on _uncertainty.pdf
2 A series of reports were published in 2003, including on the findings from the public debate, the GM science review's first report and an economic assessment of costs and benefits of GM crops. https:// webarchive.nationalarchives.gov.uk/ukgwa/20081023141438/http: /www.defra.gov.uk/environment/gm/crops/debate/index.htm
3 https://www.nature.com/articles/4681029a; see the report, http:// users.sussex.ac.uk/~prfh0/stirling_and_mayer_summary_report_on _gm_mcm

4 https://www.youtube.com/watch?v=QobuvWX Grc
5 https://webarchive.nationalarchives.gov.uk/ukgwa/20060525120000/http://www.bseinquiry.gov.uk/report/index.htm
6 https://publications.parliament.uk/pa/ld199900/ldselect/ldsctech/38/3802.htm
7 http://absp2.cornell.edu/
8 http://news.bbc.co.uk/onthisday/hi/dates/stories/february/12/newsid_2541000/2541001.stm; https://www.iatp.org/news/the-great-mexican-maize-scandal
9 https://bch.cbd.int/protocol/
10 https://www.theafricareport.com/311115/blow-to-kenya-us-negotiations-on-gmo-crops-as-court-of-appeal-upholds-ban/
11 See https://www.bailii.org/ew/cases/EWHC/Admin/2023/495.pdf and the response to the decision by the Action Against 5G campaign, https://actionagainst5g.org/case-updates/judgment-received/
12 https://thebadgercrowd.org/wp-content/uploads/2019/09/Langton-v-SSEFRA-FINAL-003.pdf
13 https://www.un.org/en/development/desa/population/migration/generalassembly/docs/globalcompact/A_CONF.151_26_Vol.I_Declaration.pdf
14 https://www.ft.com/content/3f584019-7c51-4c9c-b18f-0e0ac0821bf7 and https://www.bbc.co.uk/news/uk-65746524

Chapter 4 Critical Infrastructures: How to Keep the Lights On and the Animals Alive

1 Quotes in this section are from Roe and Schulman (2008), based on their work between 2001 and 2006 in CAISO. While electricity supply systems have changed since with upgrades in technology and working practices, many of the same challenges apply (see updates in Schulman and Roe 2016; Roe and Schulman 2023).
2 CAISO control room official, 2001 (Roe and Schulman 2008: 135).
3 A 'generation dispatcher' makes economic assessments as to which unit within the wider electricity generation system is brought online to meet demand and increase power output.
4 Gen dispatchers, CAISO, Roe and Schulman (2008: 34).
5 Idem. (2008: 124).
6 Senior Control Room Manager, PG&E Transmission Operations Center (Roe and Schulman 2008: 62).
7 PG&E Shift Supervisor, interviewed in 2001, reflecting on earlier experience, Roe and Schulman (2008: 156).
8 Anonymized interview, Kinna town, Isiolo county, Kenya, February 2023 (for more detail, see https://pastres.org/2023/05/19/building

-resilience-from-below-the-vital-role-of-reliability-professionals-and
-their-networks/).
9 Interview with young pastoralist, North Horr, 2016 (see Tasker and
   Scoones 2022 for details).
10 Idem.
11 Idem.
12 See Nori (2023) for the case of camel milk marketing and Mohamed
   and Scoones (2023), who focus on drought, both using the same
   'high-reliability' framework.

Chapter 5 Pandemics: Building Responses
from Below

1 https://committees.parliament.uk/publications/7496/documents
   /78687/default/ (p. 32).
2 https://www.gov.uk/government/publications/scientific-advisory
   -group-for-emergencies-sage-coronavirus-covid-19-response
   -membership/list-of-participants-of-sage-and-related-sub-groups
   #scientific-advisory-group-for-emergencies-sage
3 https://www.theguardian.com/politics/2020/jul/01/predictive-text
   -why-superforecasting-is-top-of-dominic-cummings-reading-list
4 https://www.buzzfeed.com/alexwickham/10-days-that-changed
   -britains-coronavirus-approach
5 https://www.imperial.ac.uk/media/imperial-college/medicine/sph
   /ide/gida-fellowships/Imperial-College-COVID19-NPI-modelling
   -16-03-2020.pdf
6 https://assets.publishing.service.gov.uk/government/uploads/system
   /uploads/attachment_data/file/1068118/S0384_Sixteenth_SAGE
   _meeting_on_Wuhan_Coronavirus.pdf
7 https://www.gov.uk/government/speeches/pm-address-to-the-nation
   -on-coronavirus-23-march-2020
8 The very generic models that did exist for Africa, even when
   adjusted for different age distributions and contract patterns,
   predicted a fairly similar dynamic to elsewhere, with large numbers
   of cases and high mortalities due to limited mitigation measures and
   poor health services (e.g., van Zandvoort et al. 2020).
9 All quotes from Zimbabwe come from real-time, longitudinal
   research we undertook tracking the pandemic across a number of
   rural sites in different parts of the country between 2020 and 2022.
   More details can be found in Bwerinofa (2022a,b,c). All names are
   anonymized.
10 https://covid19.public-inquiry.uk/
11 https://www.opendemocracy.net/en/oureconomy/complex

-modelling-fuelled-financial-crisis-now-it-has-delayed-action-covid
-19/
12 https://committees.parliament.uk/oralevidence/1323/html/
13 While achieving 'herd immunity' was never official government
policy according to Chris Whitty's evidence (https://twitter.com
/BBCr4today/status/1238390547783528448?s=20), many leading
scientists on SAGE raised the idea at the time. Meanwhile, an influential group released the Great Barrington Declaration in October
2020, which argued against lockdowns informed by a libertarian
approach, actively promoting the idea and gaining surprising access
to media and policy circles (Ball 2021).
14 https://committees.parliament.uk/oralevidence/237/pdf/, Q38 et seq.
15 https://publications.parliament.uk/pa/cm5802/cmselect/cmsctech
/92/9203.htm   and   https://covid19.public-inquiry.uk/modules
/resilience-and-preparedness/   and   https://covid19.public-inquiry
.uk/, notably the 'module 1' hearings on resilience and preparedness.
16 https://www.standard.co.uk/news/uk/david-spiegelhalter-covid19
-statistics-coronavirus-government-a4436471.html
17 https://covid19.public-inquiry.uk/wp-content/uploads/2023/06
/27182201/C-19-Inquiry-27-June-23-Module-1-Day-10.pdf   (pp.
20, 25, 27, 79, 80).
18 https://www.ids.ac.uk/opinions/science-uncertainty-and-the-covid
-19-response/
19 See pp. 29–35, https://covid19.public-inquiry.uk/wp-content
/uploads/2023/11/01181046/Transcript-of-Module-2-Public
-Hearing-on-1-November-2023.pdf
20 The criticisms of the science policy-making approach during the
UK public inquiry into the pandemic have been harsh. A picture
of confusion and incompetence is painted, with scientific advice
being frequently ignored. In his public inquiry evidence, the
Chief Medical Officer Chris Whitty pointed out that 'there was
a complete absence of plans' (https://www.opendemocracy.net/en
/covid-inquiry-chris-whitty-planning-uk-government/). Meanwhile,
the revealing diaries of the then Chief Scientist Patrick Vallance
highlighted the chaos at the heart of the government responses
(https://www.opendemocracy.net/en/boris-johnson-covid-inquiry
-patrick-vallance/), while a former cabinet secretary described
Boris Johnson's premiership as 'brutal and useless' (https://www
.opendemocracy.net/en/covid-inquiry-mark-sedwill-boris-johnson
-sack-matt-hancock/). It's extraordinarily damning stuff – and, on
the themes of decision making and political governance alone, there
are hours and hours of evidence and pages and pages of transcripts
of it (https://covid19.public-inquiry.uk/hearings/core-uk-decision
-making-and-political-governance-module-2-public-hearings/).

21 https://wellcome.org/news/what-we-can-learn-hiv-help-end
   -pandemic?
22 https://www.bmj.com/content/370/bmj.m2814
23 https://www.mirror.co.uk/news/politics/five-garment-factories
   -leicester-forced-22273885
24 https://www.science.org/content/article/mathematics-life-and-death
   -how-disease-models-shape-national-shutdowns-and-other
25 https://www.ghsindex.org/wp-content/uploads/2020/04/2019
   -Global-Health-Security-Index.pdf
26 As recorded on death certificates, https://coronavirus.data.gov.uk
   /details/deaths
27 https://ourworldindata.org/coronavirus/country/zimbabwe
28 https://ourworldindata.org/covid-vaccinations?country=ZWE
   ~GBR
29 https://www.youtube.com/watch?app=desktop&v=e3pFQe8yLNs
30 https://www.who.int/news/item/23-09-2020-managing-the-covid
   -19-infodemic-promoting-healthy-behaviours-and-mitigating-the
   -harm-from-misinformation-and-disinformation
31 https://committees.parliament.uk/publications/7496/documents
   /78687/default/ (p. 15).

Chapter 6 Disasters: Why Prediction and Planning Are Not Enough

1 https://www.preventionweb.net/files/43291
  _sendaiframeworkfordrren.pdf and https://www.preventionweb.net
  /files/46694_readingsendaiframeworkfordisasterri.pdf
2 https://www.undrr.org/media/83749/download?startDownload=
  true (pp. 4–8).
3 https://www.youtube.com/watch?v=7_caijv__Nk
4 https://fews.net/ and https://www.icpac.net/our-projects/forpac/
5 https://pastres.org/2023/05/12/local-early-warning-systems
  -predicting-the-future-when-things-are-so-uncertain/
6 https://fic.tufts.edu/wp-content/uploads/EW-EA-Executive
  -Summary-6-22.pdf
7 https://pastres.org/2023/05/05/the-failure-of-resilience-projects-in
  -northern-kenya-what-can-we-learn/
8 https://foreignpolicy.com/2023/02/10/turkey-earthquake-erdogan
  -government-response-corruption-construction/
9 Thanks to Shilpi Srivastava for suggesting this typology.
10 https://www.thenewhumanitarian.org/opinion/2023/08/02
   /embracing-local-knowledge-key-resilience-northern-kenya-not
   -project-box-ticking

11 https://www.anticipation-hub.org/news/warnings-as-social
   -processes
12 https://www.sparc-knowledge.org/sites/default/files/documents
   /resources/Obstacles%20to%20and%20opportunities%20for
   %20anticipatory%20action%20in%20Somalia%20Final.pdf

Chapter 7 Climate Change: Multiple Knowledges, Diverse Actions

1 https://www.ipcc.ch/report/ar6/wg1/;   https://press.un.org/en/2021
   /sgsm20847.doc.htm
2 https://www.ipcc.ch/report/sixth-assessment-report-cycle/
3 Considerable finance flows towards adaptation, for example via the
   Adaptation Fund (www.adaptation-fund.org/), the Green Climate
   Fund (www.greenclimate.fund/) and the Global Environmental
   Facility's Least Developed Countries Fund (LDCF) and Special
   Climate Change Fund (SCCF). However, according to UNEP, there
   is a huge funding gap, as US$215 billion per year is required to
   address adaptation needs in developing countries (www.unep.org
   /resources/adaptation-gap-report-2023).
4 The discussion of the Sundarbans is based on the work of Upasona
   Ghosh, Shibaji Bose and others under the TAPESTRY project, https://
   tapestry-project.org/ (Ghosh, Kjosavik and Bose 2022; Mehta,
   Adam and Srivastava 2022), while the discussion of southern
   Zimbabwe is based on my own work, together with the team now
   led by Felix Murimbarimba. https://zimbabweland.wordpress.com/.
5 https://www.wcrp-climate.org/wgcm-cmip
6 https://www.metoffice.gov.uk/research/applied/international/precis
   /introduction
7 https://zimbabweland.wordpress.com/2021/04/26/conservation
   -agriculture-latest-experiences-from-zimbabwe/
8 https://www.iied.org/collection/community-based-adaptation
9 https://zimbabweland.wordpress.com/2022/05/23/farming-with
   -variability-mobilising-responses-to-drought-uncertainties-in
   -zimbabwe/
10 For example, processes of deliberative action aimed at sustainably
   transforming local economies have been developed by the 'doughnut
   economics action lab' in a number of cities and regions (https://
   doughnuteconomics.org/themes/1). The principles of inclusion,
   participation and deliberation (Holmes and Scoones 2000) provide
   the basis for 'co-production' in the form discussed here, often
   resulting in the emergence of radical, unexpected, transformative
   responses.

Chapter 8 Looking Forward: From Fear to Hope, from Control to Care

1 Discussion in 2018, Isiolo, Kenya; see Scoones (2019: 31).
2 https://www.ecb.europa.eu/press/key/date/2023/html/ecb.sp230825
   ~77711105fe.en.html
3 https://www.prospectmagazine.co.uk/politics/62813/the-missing
   -centre
4 See, for example, the arguments of those in the US (neo-)pragmatist
   philosophical tradition, such as Richard Rorty and Willard von
   Orman Quine.
5 For example, exploring uncertain futures and imaginaries through
   science fiction writing (Walton and Levontin 2023).
6 https://www.newstatesman.com/environment/2023/07/rebecca
   -solnit-climate-despair-hope
7 For further exploration of these themes – and the shift from
   'control' to 'care', see Arora et al. (2020), Scoones and Stirling
   (2020), Scoones (2023b), Stirling (forthcoming).
8 https://www.dailygood.org/story/1852/the-revolutionary-power-of
   -diverse-thought-elif-shafak/

References

Adam, B. (1996). 'Re-vision: The centrality of time for an ecological social-science perspective', in S. Lash, B. Szerszynski and B. Wynne (eds), *Risk, Environment and Modernity: Towards a New Ecology*. London: Sage.

Adam, B. (2013). *Time and Social Theory*. Chichester: John Wiley & Sons.

Adam, B., Beck, U. and van Loon, J. (eds) (2000). *The Risk Society and Beyond: Critical Issues for Social Theory*. London: Sage.

Adams, S., Rhodes, T. and Lancaster, K. (2022). 'New directions for participatory modelling in health: Redistributing expertise in relation to localised matters of concern'. *Global Public Health* 17(9): 1827–41.

Adey, P., Anderson, B. and Graham, S. (2015). 'Introduction: Governing emergencies: beyond exceptionality'. *Theory, Culture and Society* 32(2): 3–17.

Adger, W. N., Dessai, S., Goulden, M., et al. (2009). 'Are there social limits to adaptation to climate change?' *Climatic Change* 93: 335–54.

Adger, W. N., Huq, S., Brown, K., Conway, D. and Hulme, M. (2003). 'Adaptation to climate change in the developing world'. *Progress in Development Studies* 3(3): 179–95.

Aikman, D., Haldane, A. G., Hinterschweiger, M. and Kapadia, S. (2018). 'Rethinking financial stability'. *Bank of England Staff Working Paper* 712.

Akerlof, G. A. and Shiller, R. J. (2010). *Animal Spirits: How Human Psychology Drives the Economy, and Why It Matters for Global Capitalism*. Princeton: Princeton University Press.

Alborn, T. L. (2009). *Regulated Lives: Life Insurance and British Society, 1800–1914*. Toronto: University of Toronto Press.

Allen, C. and Garmestani, A. (eds) (2015). *Adaptive Management of Socio-Ecological Systems*. New York: Springer.

Amin, A. (2013). 'Surviving the turbulent future'. *Environment and Planning D: Society and Space* 31(1): 140–56.

Amoore, L. (2019). 'Doubt and the algorithm: On the partial accounts of machine learning'. *Theory, Culture and Society* 36(6): 147–69.

Amoore, L. (2023). 'Machine learning political orders'. *Review of International Studies* 49(1): 20–36.

Anand, K., Gai, P. and Marsili, M. (2012). 'Rollover risk, network structure and systemic financial crises'. *Journal of Economic Dynamics and Control* 36(8): 1088–100.

Anderson, B. and Adey, P. (2012). 'Governing events and life: "Emergency" in UK civil contingencies'. *Political Geography* 31(1): 24–33.

Anderson, B., Grove, K., Rickards, L. and Kearnes, M. (2020). 'Slow emergencies: Temporality and the racialized biopolitics of emergency governance'. *Progress in Human Geography* 44(4): 621–39.

Anderson, W. (2021). 'The model crisis, or how to have critical promiscuity in the time of Covid-19'. *Social Studies of Science* 51(2): 167–88.

Ang, Y. Y. (2018). *How China Escaped the Poverty Trap*. Ithaca: Cornell University Press.

Arendt, H. (2018). *Thinking without a Banister: Essays in Understanding, 1953–1975*, ed. J. Kohn. New York: Schocken Books.

Arinaminpathy, N., Kapadia, S. and May, R. M. (2012). 'Size and complexity in model financial systems'. *Proceedings of the National Academy of Sciences* 109(45): 18338–43.

Arora, S., Van Dyck, B., Sharma, D. and Stirling, A. (2020). 'Control, care, and conviviality in the politics of technology for sustainability'. *Sustainability: Science, Practice and Policy* 16(1): 247–62.

Arrighi, G. (1994). *The Long Twentieth Century: Money, Power, and the Origins of Our Times*. New York: Verso.

Asafu-Adjaye, J., Blomquist, L., Brand, S., et al. (2015). *An Ecomodernist Manifesto*. Oakland: Breakthrough Institute.

Asayama, S., Bellamy, R., Geden, O., Pearce, W. and Hulme, M. (2019). 'Why setting a climate deadline is dangerous'. *Nature Climate Change* 9(8): 570–2.

Atteridge, A. and Remling, E. (2018). 'Is adaptation reducing vulnerability or redistributing it?' *Wiley Interdisciplinary Reviews: Climate Change* 9(1): e500.

Ayeb-Karlsson, S., Fox, G. and Kniveton, D. (2019). 'Embracing uncertainty: A discursive approach to understanding pathways for climate adaptation in Senegal'. *Regional Environmental Change* 19: 1585–96.

Bähre, E. (2020). *Ironies of Solidarity: Insurance and Financialization of Kinship in South Africa*. London: Bloomsbury Publishing.

Baker, T. (2002). 'Risk, insurance, and (the social construction of) responsibility', in T. Baker and J. Simon (eds), *Embracing Risk: The Changing Culture of Insurance and Responsibility*. Chicago: University of Chicago Press.

Ball, P. (2021). 'What the COVID-19 pandemic reveals about science, policy and society'. *Interface Focus* 11: 20210022. Available at: https://doi.org/10.1098/rsfs.2021.0022

Ballo, R., Pearce, W., Stilgoe, J. and Wilsdon, J. (2022). 'Socially-distanced science: How British publics were imagined, modelled and marginalised in political and expert responses to the COVID-19 pandemic'. Draft chapter for *Comparative Covid Response: Crisis, Knowledge, Policy* (CompCoRe) project. Available at: https://osf.io/jc82q/download

Bankoff, G. and Hilhorst, D. (eds) (2022). *Why Vulnerability Still Matters: The Politics of Disaster Risk Creation*. Abingdon: Routledge.

Bassett, T. J. and Fogelman, C. (2013). 'Déjà vu or something new? The adaptation concept in the climate change literature'. *Geoforum* 48: 42–53.

Battiston, S., Farmer, J. D., Flache, A., et al. (2016). 'Complexity theory and financial regulation'. *Science* 351(6275): 10031–6.

Baudron, F., Andersson, J. A., Corbeels, M. and Giller, K. E. (2012). 'Failing to yield? Ploughs, conservation agriculture and the problem of agricultural intensification: An example from the Zambezi Valley, Zimbabwe'. *Journal of Development Studies* 48: 393–412.

Bauman, Z. (2013). *Liquid Times: Living in an Age of Uncertainty.* Cambridge: Polity Press.

Beale, N., Rand, D. G., Battey, H., Croxson, K., May, R. M. and Nowak, M. A. (2011). 'Individual versus systemic risk and the regulator's dilemma'. *Proceedings of the National Academy of Sciences* 108(31): 12647–52.

Bear, L. (2016). 'Time as technique'. *Annual Review of Anthropology* 45: 487–502.

Beck, S. and Mahony, M. (2017). 'The IPCC and the politics of anticipation'. *Nature Climate Change* 7(5): 311–13.

Beck, S., Jasanoff, S., Stirling, A. and Polzin, C. (2021). 'The governance of sociotechnical transformations to sustainability'. *Current Opinion in Environmental Sustainability* 49: 143–52.

Beck, U. (1992). *Risk Society: Towards a New Modernity.* London: Sage.

Beck, U. (2016). *The Metamorphosis of the World: How Climate Change is Transforming Our Concept of the World.* Cambridge: Polity Press.

Beck, U. and Levy, D. (2013). 'Cosmopolitanized nations: Re-imagining collectivity in world risk society'. *Theory, Culture and Society* 30(2): 3–31.

Beck, U., Giddens, A. and Lash, S. (1994). *Reflexive Modernization: Politics, Tradition and Aesthetics in the Modern Social Order.* Redwood City: Stanford University Press.

Beckert, J. (2016). *Imagined Futures: Fictional Expectations and Capitalist Dynamics.* Cambridge, MA: Harvard University Press.

Beckert, J. and Bronk, R. (2018). *Uncertain Futures: Imaginaries, Narratives, and Calculation in the Economy.* Oxford: Oxford University Press.

Berrang-Ford, L., Siders, A. R., Lesnikowski, A., et al. (2021). 'A systematic global stocktake of evidence on human adaptation to climate change'. *Nature Climate Change* 11: 989–1000.

Berry, W. (2005). *The Way of Ignorance, and Other Essays.* Berkeley: Counterpoint Press.

Biermann, F. and Möller, I. (2019). 'Rich man's solution? Climate engineering discourses and the marginalization of the Global South'. *International Environmental Agreements: Politics, Law and Economics* 19: 151–67.

Blaikie, P., Cannon, T., Davis, I. and Wisner, B. (2004). *At*

Risk: Natural Hazards, People's Vulnerability and Disasters. Abingdon: Routledge.

Böhm, S. and Sullivan, S. (2021). *Negotiating Climate Change in Crisis*. Cambridge: Open Book Publishers.

Borras, Jr, S. M., Scoones, I., Baviskar, A., Edelman, M., Peluso, N. L. and Wolford, W. (2022). 'Climate change and agrarian struggles'. *Journal of Peasant Studies* 49: 1–28.

Boyd, E., Chaffin, B. C., Dorkenoo, K., et al. (2021). 'Loss and damage from climate change: A new climate justice agenda'. *One Earth* 4: 1365–70.

Braidotti, R. (1994). *Nomadic Subjects: Embodiment and Sexual Difference in Contemporary Feminist Theory*. New York: Columbia University Press.

Braun, B. and McCarthy, J. (2005). 'Hurricane Katrina and abandoned being'. *Environment and Planning D: Society and Space* 23: 802–9.

Brink, E., Falla, A. M. V. and Boyd, E. (2023). 'Weapons of the vulnerable? A review of popular resistance to climate adaptation'. *Global Environmental Change* 80: 102656.

Bronk, R. (2009). *The Romantic Economist: Imagination in Economics*. Cambridge: Cambridge University Press.

Bronk, R. and Jacoby, W. (2016). *Uncertainty and the Dangers of Monocultures in Regulation, Analysis, and Practice*. MPIfG discussion paper.

Brown, K. (2015). *Resilience, Development and Global Change*. Abingdon: Routledge.

Buchanan-Smith, M. and Davies, S. (1995). *Famine Early Warning and Response: The Missing Link*. Rugby: Intermediate Technology Publications.

Burgess, A., Alemanno, A. and Zinn, J. (eds) (2016). *Routledge Handbook of Risk Studies*. Abingdon: Routledge.

Burgess, M. G., Pielke, Jr, R. and Ritchie, J. (2022). 'Catastrophic climate risks should be neither understated nor overstated'. *Proceedings of the National Academy of Sciences* 119(42): e2214347119.

Burton, I., Kates, R. W. and White, G. F. (1978). *The Environment as Hazard*. Oxford: Oxford University Press.

Bwerinofa, I. J., Mahenehene, J., Manaka, M., et al. (2022a). *Learning in a Pandemic: Reflections on COVID-19 in Rural Zimbabwe*. Independent publication, Brighton: Institute of Development Studies.

Bwerinofa, I. J., Mahenehene, J., Manaka, M., et al. (2022b). 'Living through a pandemic: Competing Covid-19 narratives in rural Zimbabwe'. *IDS Working Paper 575*.

Bwerinofa, I. J., Mahenehene, J., Manaka, M., et al. (2022c). 'What is "community resilience"? Responding to COVID-19 in rural Zimbabwe'. *BMJ Global Health* 7(9): e009528.

Cairney, P. (2021). 'The UK government's COVID-19 policy: Assessing evidence-informed policy analysis in real time'. *British Politics* 16(1): 90–116.

Calhoun, C. (2010). 'The idea of emergency: Humanitarian action and global (dis)order', in D. Fassin and M. Pandolfi (eds), *Contemporary States of Emergency: The Politics of Military and Humanitarian Interventions*. New York: Zone Books.

Calhoun, C. and Derluguian, G. M. (2011). *Business as Usual: The Roots of the Global Financial Meltdown*. New York: NYU Press.

Callon, M. and Law, J. (2005). 'On qualculation, agency, and otherness'. *Environment and Planning D: Society and Space* 23(5): 717–33.

Callon, M., Lascoumes, P. and Barthe, Y. (2009). *Acting in an Uncertain World: An Essay on Technical Democracy*. Cambridge, MA: MIT Press.

Caniglia, G., Freeth, R., Luederitz, C., et al. (2023). 'Practical wisdom and virtue ethics for knowledge co-production in sustainability science'. *Nature Sustainability* 6: 493–501.

Cannon, T. (2015). 'Disasters, climate change and the significance of "culture"', in F. Krüger, G. Bankoff, T. Cannon, B. Orlowski and E. Schipper (eds), *Cultures and Disasters: Understanding Cultural Framings in Disaster Risk Reduction*. Abingdon: Routledge.

Cannon, T. and Müller-Mahn, D. (2010). 'Vulnerability, resilience and development discourses in context of climate change'. *Natural Hazards* 55: 621–35.

Caplan, P. (2000). *Risk Revisited*. London: Pluto Press.

Caravani, M., Lind, J., Sabates-Wheeler, R. and Scoones, I. (2022). 'Providing social assistance and humanitarian relief: The case for embracing uncertainty'. *Development Policy Review* 40(5): e12613.

Carter, M., de Janvry, A., Sadoulet, E. and Sarris, A. (2017). 'Index insurance for developing country agriculture: A reassessment'. *Annual Review of Resource Economics* 9: 421–38.

Castells, M. (1996). *The Rise of the Network Society: The Information Age: Economy, Society, and Culture*. Oxford: Blackwell.

Catley, A., Lind, J. and Scoones, I. (eds) (2013). *Pastoralism and Development in Africa: Dynamic Change at the Margins*. Abingdon: Routledge.

Chantarat, S., Mude, A. G., Barrett, C. B. and Carter, M. R. (2013). 'Designing index-based livestock insurance for managing asset risk in northern Kenya'. *Journal of Risk and Insurance* 80(1): 205–37.

Chigudu, S. (2020). *The Political Life of an Epidemic: Cholera, Crisis and Citizenship in Zimbabwe*. Cambridge: Cambridge University Press.

Chilvers, J. and Kearnes, M. (2016). *Remaking Participation: Science, Environment and Emerging Publics*. Abingdon: Routledge.

Christley, R. M., Mort, M., Wynne, B., et al. (2013). '"Wrong, but useful": Negotiating uncertainty in infectious disease modelling'. *PLoS One* 8(10): e76277.

Christophers, B., Bigger, P. and Johnson, L. (2020). 'Stretching scales? Risk and sociality in climate finance'. *Environment and Planning A: Economy and Space* 52(1): 88–110.

Christophers, B., Leyshon, A. and Mann, G. (2017). 'Money and finance after the crisis: Taking critical stock', in B. Christophers, A. Leyshon and G. Mann (eds), *Money and Finance after the Crisis: Critical Thinking for Uncertain Times*. Chichester: John Wiley & Sons.

Clark, A. (2015). *Surfing Uncertainty: Prediction, Action, and the Embodied Mind*. Oxford: Oxford University Press.

Clark, C. (2023). *Revolutionary Spring: Fighting for a New World 1848–1849*. London: Allen Lane.

Clark, G. (2002). *Embracing Fatality through Life Insurance in Eighteenth-Century England*. Chicago: University of Chicago Press.

Clarke, D. and Dercon, S. (2016). *Dull Disasters? How Planning Ahead Will Make a Difference*. Oxford: Oxford University Press.

Cohn, Jr, S. K. (2017). 'Cholera revolts: A class struggle we may not like'. *Social History* 42(2): 162–80.

Cointe, B. and Guillemot, H. (2023). 'A history of the 1.5°C target'. *Wiley Interdisciplinary Reviews: Climate Change* 14(3): e824.

Colander, D. and Freedman, C. (2018). *Where Economics Went Wrong: Chicago's Abandonment of Classical Liberalism.* Princeton: Princeton University Press.

Collier, S. (2009). 'Topologies of power: Foucault's analysis of political government beyond "governmentality"'. *Theory, Culture and Society* 26(6): 78–108.

Collier, S. J. (2008). 'Enacting catastrophe: Preparedness, insurance, budgetary rationalization'. *Economy and Society* 37(2): 224–50.

Collier, S. J. and Lakoff, A. (2021). *The Government of Emergency: Vital Systems, Expertise, and the Politics of Security.* Princeton: Princeton University Press.

Collier, S. J., Elliott, R. and Lehtonen, T. K. (2021). 'Climate change and insurance'. *Economy and Society* 50(2): 158–72.

Conway, D., Nicholls, R. J., Brown, S., et al. (2019). 'The need for bottom-up assessments of climate risks and adaptation in climate-sensitive regions'. *Nature Climate Change* 9(7): 503–11.

Cooper, E. and Pratten, D. (eds) (2014). *Ethnographies of Uncertainty in Africa.* New York: Springer.

Cowen, M. and Shenton, R. W. (1996). *Doctrines of Development.* Abingdon: Routledge.

Coyle, D. (2021). *Cogs and Monsters: What Economics Is, and What It Should Be.* Princeton: Princeton University Press.

Curran, D. (2018). 'Beck's creative challenge to class analysis: From the rejection of class to the discovery of risk-class'. *Journal of Risk Research* 21(1): 29–40.

Curry, J. A. and Webster, P. J. (2011). 'Climate science and the uncertainty monster'. *Bulletin of the American Meteorological Society* 92(12): 1667–82.

da Col, G. and Humphrey, C. (2012). 'Introduction: Subjects of luck – contingency, morality, and the anticipation of everyday life'. *Social Analysis* 56(2): 1–18.

Damasio, A. (2006). *Descartes' Error.* London: Vintage.

Daston, L. (1988). *Classical Probability in the Enlightenment.* Princeton: Princeton University Press.

Davidson, P. (1982). 'Rational expectations: A fallacious foundation for studying crucial decision-making processes'. *Journal of Post Keynesian Economics* 5(2): 182–98.

Davis, M. (2002). *Late Victorian Holocausts: El Niño Famines and the Making of the Third World.* London: Verso.

de Albuquerque, J. P., Anderson, L., Calvillo, N., Coaffee, J., et al. (2021). 'The role of data in transformations to sustainability: A critical research agenda'. *Current Opinion in Environmental Sustainability* 49: 153–63.

De Alcantara, C. H. (1992). *Real Markets: Social and Political Issues of Food Policy Reform*. Abingdon: Routledge.

de Graaff, B., Huizenga, S., van de Bovenkamp, H. and Bal, R. (2023). 'Framing the pandemic: Multiplying "crises" in Dutch healthcare governance during the emerging COVID-19 pandemic'. *Social Science and Medicine* 328: 115998.

De la Bellacasa, M. P. (2017). *Matters of Care: Speculative Ethics in More than Human Worlds*. Minneapolis: University of Minnesota Press.

De Pryck, K and Hulme, M. (eds) (2022). *A Critical Assessment of the Intergovernmental Panel on Climate Change*. Cambridge: Cambridge University Press.

De Waal, A. (2021). *New Pandemics, Old Politics: Two Hundred Years of War on Disease and Its Alternatives*. Chichester: John Wiley & Sons.

Deleuze, G. and Guattari, F. (1988). *A Thousand Plateaus: Capitalism and Schizophrenia*. London: Bloomsbury Publishing.

DeMartino, G., Grabel, I. and Scoones, I. (2024). 'Economics for an uncertain world'. *World Development* 173: 106426.

Dessai, S. and Hulme, M. (2004). 'Does climate adaptation policy need probabilities?' *Climate Policy* 4(2): 107–28.

Dessai, S., Hulme, M., Lempert, R. and Pielke, Jr, R. (2009). 'Climate prediction: A limit to adaptation', in N. Adger, I. Lorenzoni and K. O'Brien (eds), *Adapting to Climate Change: Thresholds, Values, Governance*. Cambridge: Cambridge University Press.

Dessai, S., O'Brien, K. and Hulme, M. (2007). 'On uncertainty and climate change'. *Global Environmental Change* 1(17): 1–3.

Dewan, C. (2021). *Misreading the Bengal Delta: Climate Change, Development, and Livelihoods in Coastal Bangladesh*. Seattle: University of Washington Press.

Dewey, J. (1988 [1929]). 'The quest for certainty', in J. Boydston (ed.), *John Dewey: The Later Works, 1925–1953 (Vol. 4)*. Carbondale: Southern Illinois University Press.

Dillon, M. (2007). 'Governing through contingency: The security of biopolitical governance'. *Political Geography* 26(1): 41–7.

Donovan, A. (2019). 'Critical volcanology? Thinking holistically about risk and uncertainty'. *Bulletin of Volcanology* 81(4): 20.

Doran, N. (1994). 'Risky business: Codifying embodied experience in the Manchester Unity of Oddfellows'. *Journal of Historical Sociology* 7(2): 131–54.

Dotson, T. (2021). *The Divide: How Fanatical Certitude is Destroying Democracy.* Cambridge, MA: MIT Press.

Douglas, M. (1966). *Purity and Danger: An Analysis of Concepts of Pollution and Taboo.* Abingdon: Routledge and Kegan Paul.

Douglas, M. (1986). *Risk Acceptability According to the Social Sciences.* New York: Russell Sage.

Douglas, M. (1992). *Risk and Blame: Essays in Cultural Theory.* Abingdon: Routledge.

Douglas, M. and Wildavsky, A. (1983). *Risk and Culture: An Essay on the Selection of Technological and Environmental Dangers.* Oakland: University of California Press.

Dowd-Uribe, B. (2023). 'Just agricultural science: The green revolution, biotechnologies, and marginalized farmers in Africa'. *Elementa: Science of the Anthropocene* 11(1): 00144.

Dryzek, J. S. (2002). *Deliberative Democracy and Beyond: Liberals, Critics, Contestations.* Oxford: Oxford University Press.

D'Souza, R. (2006). 'Water in British India: The making of a "colonial hydrology"'. *History Compass* 4(4): 621–8.

Dynes, R. R. (2000). 'The dialogue between Voltaire and Rousseau on the Lisbon earthquake: The emergence of a social science view'. *International Journal of Mass Emergencies & Disasters* 18(1): 97–115.

Eakin, H. C., Lemos, M. C. and Nelson, D. R. (2014). 'Differentiating capacities as a means to sustainable climate change adaptation'. *Global Environmental Change* 27: 1–8.

Eggert, K. (2008). 'The great collapse: How securitization caused the subprime meltdown'. *Connecticut Law Review* 41: 1257–308.

Elliott, R. (2021). *Underwater: Loss, Flood Insurance, and the Moral Economy of Climate Change in the United States.* New York: Columbia University Press.

Ely, A., Friedrich, B., Glover, D., et al. (2022). 'Governing agricultural biotechnologies in the United States, the United

Kingdom, and Germany: A trans-decadal study of regulatory cultures'. *Science, Technology, and Human Values* 48(6): 1292–328.

Eriksen, S. H., Nightingale, A. J. and Eakin, H. (2015). 'Reframing adaptation: The political nature of climate change adaptation'. *Global Environmental Change* 35: 523–33.

Ewald, F. (1991). 'Insurance and risk', in G. Burchell, C. Gordon and P. Miller (eds), *The Foucault Effect: Studies in Governmentality: With Two Lectures by and an Interview with Michel Foucault*. Chicago: University of Chicago Press.

Ewald, F. (2020). *The Birth of Solidarity: The History of the French Welfare State*. Durham, NC: Duke University Press.

Ezzy, D. (2000). 'Illness narratives: Time, hope and HIV'. *Social Science and Medicine* 50(5): 605–17.

Farmer, P. (2001). *Infections and Inequalities: The Modern Plagues*. Berkeley: University of California Press.

Farrar, J. and Ahuja, A. (2021). *Spike: The Virus vs. the People – The Inside Story*. London: Profile Books.

Fearnley, C. J. (2013). 'Assigning a volcano alert level: Negotiating uncertainty, risk, and complexity in decision-making processes'. *Environment and Planning A* 45(8): 1891–911.

Felli, R. (2021). *The Great Adaptation: Climate, Capitalism and Catastrophe*. London: Verso Books.

Feynman, R. P. (2001 [1956]). *The Pleasure of Finding Things Out: The Best Short Works of Richard P. Feynman*. New York: Basic Books.

Firestein, S. (2012). *Ignorance: How It Drives Science*. Oxford: Oxford University Press.

Foucault, M. (2008). *The Birth of Biopolitics: Lectures at the Collège de France, 1978–1979*, ed. Michel Senellart. New York: Springer.

Fraser, N. (2023). *Cannibal Capitalism: How Our System is Devouring Democracy, Care, and the Planet and What We Can Do about It*. London: Verso Books.

Friedman, M. (1953). *Essays in Positive Economics*. Chicago: University of Chicago Press.

Fuller, S. (2020). *A Player's Guide to the Post-Truth Condition: The Name of the Game*. London: Anthem Press.

Funk, C., Harrison, L., Segele, Z., Rosenstock, T., et al. (2023). 'Tailored forecasts can predict extreme climate informing proactive interventions in East Africa'. *Earth's Future* 11(7): e2023EF003524.

Funtowicz, S. O. and Ravetz, J. R. (1990). *Uncertainty and Quality in Science for Policy*. New York: Springer.

Funtowicz, S. O. and Ravetz, J. R. (1993). 'Science for the post-normal age'. *Futures* 25(7): 739–55.

Funtowicz, S. O. and Ravetz, J. R. (1994). 'The worth of a songbird: Ecological economics as a post-normal science'. *Ecological Economics* 10(3): 197–207.

Gabor, D. (2021). 'The Wall Street consensus'. *Development and Change* 52(3): 429–59.

Gai, P., Haldane, A. and Kapadia, S. (2011). 'Complexity, concentration and contagion'. *Journal of Monetary Economics* 58(5): 453–70.

Galtung, J. (1969). 'Violence, peace, and peace research'. *Journal of Peace Research* 6(3): 167–91.

Geschiere, P. (1997). *The Modernity of Witchcraft: Politics and the Occult in Post-Colonial Africa*. Charlottesville: University of Virginia Press.

Ghosh, A. (2021). *The Nutmeg's Curse*. Chicago: University of Chicago Press.

Ghosh, U., Kjosavik, D. J. and Bose, S. (2022). 'The certainty of uncertainty: Climate change realities of the Indian Sundarbans', in L. Mehta, H. N. Adam and S. Srivastava (eds), *The Politics of Climate Change and Uncertainty in India*. Abingdon: Routledge.

Gibson-Graham, J. K. (2008). 'Diverse economies: Performative practices for other worlds'. *Progress in Human Geography* 32(5): 613–32.

Giddens, A. (1999). 'Risk and responsibility'. *Modern Law Review* 62(1): 3–10.

Giroux, H. A. (2006). 'Reading Hurricane Katrina: Race, class, and the biopolitics of disposability'. *College Literature* 33: 171–96.

Glover, D. (2010). 'The corporate shaping of GM crops as a technology for the poor'. *Journal of Peasant Studies* 37(1): 67–90.

Grabel, I. (2017). *When Things Don't Fall Apart: Global Financial Governance and Developmental Finance in an Age of Productive Incoherence*. Cambridge, MA: MIT Press.

Graeber, D. (2012). 'The sword, the sponge, and the paradox

of performativity: Some observations on fate, luck, financial chicanery, and the limits of human knowledge'. *Social Analysis* 56: 25–42.

Gramsci, A. (1971). *Selections from the Prison Notebooks of Antonio Gramsci*. London: International Publication Company.

Greenwood, R., Landier, A. and Thesmar, D. (2015). 'Vulnerable banks'. *Journal of Financial Economics* 115(3): 471–85.

Grossman, S. J. (2023). *Immeasurable Weather: Meteorological Data and Settler Colonialism from 1820 to Hurricane Sandy*. Durham, NC: Duke University Press.

Grove, K. (2012). 'Preempting the next disaster: Catastrophe insurance and the financialization of disaster management'. *Security Dialogue* 43(2): 139–55.

Grove, K. (2014). 'Biopolitics and adaptation: Governing socio-ecological contingency through climate change and disaster studies'. *Geography Compass* 8(3): 198–210.

Grove, K. (2017). 'Disaster biopolitics and the crisis economy', in J. Lawrence and S. Wiebe (eds), *Biopolitical Disaster*. Abingdon: Routledge.

Grove, K., Rickards, L., Anderson, B. and Kearnes, M. (2022). 'The uneven distribution of futurity: Slow emergencies and the event of COVID-19'. *Geographical Research* 60(1): 6–17.

Grove-White, R. (2006). 'Britain's genetically modified crop controversies: The Agriculture and Environment Biotechnology Commission and the negotiation of "uncertainty"'. *Public Health Genomics* 9(3): 170–7.

Guillemot, H. (2022). 'Climate models', in K. De Pryck and M. Hulme (eds), *A Critical Assessment of the Intergovernmental Panel on Climate Change*. Cambridge: Cambridge University Press.

Guston, D. H. (2014). 'Understanding "anticipatory governance"'. *Social Studies of Science* 44(2): 218–42.

Guston, D. H. and Sarewitz, D. (2002). 'Real-time technology assessment'. *Technology in Society* 24(1–2): 93–109.

Guyer, J. (2002). 'Contemplating uncertainty'. *Public Culture* 14(3): 599–602.

Guyer, J. (2007). 'Prophecy and the near future: Thoughts on macroeconomic, evangelical, and punctuated time'. *American Ethnologist* 34(3): 409–21.

Hacking, I. (1975). *The Emergence of Probability: A Philosophical Study of Early Ideas about Probability, Induction and Statistical Inference*. Cambridge: Cambridge University Press.

Hacking, I. (1990). *The Taming of Chance*. Cambridge: Cambridge University Press.

Hagmann, T. and Stepputat, F. (eds) (2023). *Trade Makes States: Governing the Greater Somali Economy*. London: Hurst Publishers.

Hajer, M., Nilsson, M., Raworth, K., et al. (2015). 'Beyond cockpit-ism: Four insights to enhance the transformative potential of the sustainable development goals'. *Sustainability* 7(2): 1651–60.

Hajer, M. A. and Wagenaar, H. (2003). *Deliberative Policy Analysis: Understanding Governance in the Network Society*. Cambridge: Cambridge University Press.

Haldane, A. (2009a). *Rethinking the Financial Network*. BIS Review 53/2009. Available at: https://www.bis.org/review/r090505e.pdf

Haldane, A. (2009b). *Why Banks Failed the Stress Test*. BIS Review 18/2009. Available at: https://www.bis.org/review/r090219d.pdf

Haldane, A. (2009c). 'Why banks failed the stress test'. Speech given at the Marcus-Evans Conference on Stress-Testing. Available at: https://www.bankofengland.co.uk/-/media/boe/files/speech/2009/why-banks-failed-the-stress-test.pdf

Haldane, A. (2010). *The $100 Billion Question*. BIS Review 40/2010. Available at: https://www.bis.org/review/r100406d.pdf

Haldane, A. (2012). 'The Dog and the Frisbee. BIS central bankers' speeches'. Available at: https://www.bis.org/review/r120905a.pdf

Haraway, D. (1988). 'Situated knowledges: The science question in feminism and the privilege of partial perspective'. *Feminist Studies* 14(3): 575–99.

Harding, S. (1991). *Whose Science? Whose Knowledge? Thinking from Women's Lives*. New York: Cornell University Press.

Harremoës, P., Gee, D., MacGarvin, M., et al. (2001). *Late Lessons from Early Warnings: The Precautionary Principle 1896–2000*. Luxembourg: Office for Official Publications of the European Communities.

Hartman, C. W. and Squires, G. D. (2006). *There Is No Such*

Thing as a Natural Disaster: Race, Class, and Hurricane Katrina. Abingdon: Routledge.

Harvey, D. (2007). *A Brief History of Neoliberalism*. Oxford: Oxford University Press.

Hastrup, K. and Skrydstrup, M. (2012). *The Social Life of Climate Change Models: Anticipating Nature*. Abingdon: Routledge.

Hayek, F. A. von (1945). 'The use of knowledge in society'. *American Economic Review* 35(4): 519–30.

Hayek, F. A. von (1975). 'The pretence of knowledge'. *Swedish Journal of Economics* 77(4): 433–42.

Heffernan, M. (2021). *Uncharted: How Uncertainty Can Power Change*. London: Simon and Schuster.

Henig, D. and Knight, D. M. (2023). 'Polycrisis: Prompts for an emerging worldview'. *Anthropology Today* 39(2): 3–6.

Heymann, M., Gramelsberger, G. and Mahony, M. (eds) (2017). *Cultures of Prediction in Atmospheric and Climate Science: Epistemic and Cultural Shifts in Computer-based Modelling and Simulation*. Abingdon: Routledge.

Hinchliffe, S. (2020). 'Model evidence – the COVID-19 case'. *Somatosphere*. Available at: http://somatosphere.net/forumpost/model-evidence-covid-19/

Hirschman, A. O. (2013 [1970]). 'The search for paradigms as a hindrance to understanding', in J. Adelman (ed.), *The Essential Hirschman*. Princeton: Princeton University Press, pp. 137–54.

Ho, K. (2009). *Liquidated: An Ethnography of Wall Street*. Durham, NC: Duke University Press.

Holmes, D. R. (2013). *Economy of Words: Communicative Imperatives in Central Banks*. Chicago: University of Chicago Press.

Holmes, T. and Scoones, I. (2000). 'Participatory environmental policy processes: Experiences from North and South'. *IDS Working Paper* 113. Brighton: Institute of Development Studies.

Hough, S. E. (2002). *Earthshaking Science: What We Know (and Don't Know) about Earthquakes*. Princeton: Princeton University Press.

Hoydis, J. (2019). *Risk and the English Novel: From Defoe to McEwan*. Berlin: Walter de Gruyter GmbH & Co KG.

Hulme, M. (2009). *Why We Disagree about Climate Change:*

Understanding Controversy, Inaction and Opportunity. Cambridge: Cambridge University Press.

Hulme, M. (2012). 'How climate models gain and exercise authority', in K. Hastrup and M. Skrydstrup (eds), *The Social Life of Climate Change Models.* Abingdon: Routledge.

Hulme, M. (2023). *Climate Change isn't Everything: Liberating Climate Politics from Alarmism.* Cambridge: Polity Press.

IDS (2023). *Pandemic Preparedness for the Real World: Why We Must Invest in Equitable, Ethical and Effective Approaches to Help Prepare for the Next Pandemic.* Brighton: Institute of Development Studies.

Inderberg, T. H., Eriksen, S., O'Brien, K. and Sygna, L. (2014). *Climate Change Adaptation and Development: Transforming Paradigms and Practices.* Abingdon: Routledge.

Innes, A. (2023). *Late Soviet Britain: Why Materialist Utopias Fail.* Cambridge: Cambridge University Press.

Irwin, A. (2001). 'Constructing the scientific citizen: Science and democracy in the biosciences'. *Public Understanding of Science* 10(1): 1–18.

Isakson, S. R. (2015). 'Derivatives for development? Small-farmer vulnerability and the financialization of climate risk management'. *Journal of Agrarian Change* 15(4): 569–80.

Jasanoff, S. (1997). *Science at the Bar: Law, Science, and Technology in America.* Cambridge, MA: Harvard University Press.

Jasanoff, S. (ed.) (2004). *States of Knowledge: The Co-Production of Science and the Social Order.* Abingdon: Routledge.

Jasanoff, S. (2005a). *Designs on Nature: Science and Democracy in Europe and the United States.* Princeton: Princeton University Press.

Jasanoff, S. (2005b). 'Law's knowledge: Science for justice in legal settings'. *American Journal of Public Health* 95(S1): S49–S58.

Jasanoff, S. (2005c). *Technologies of Humility: Citizen Participation in Governing Science.* New York: Springer.

Jasanoff, S. (2010). 'A new climate for society'. *Theory, Culture and Society* 27(2–3): 233–53.

Jasanoff, S. (2017). 'Virtual, visible, and actionable: Data assemblages and the sightlines of justice'. *Big Data and Society* 4(2): 2053951717724477.

Jasanoff, S. (2021). 'Humility in pandemic times', in J. Cohen and D. Chasman (eds), *Uncertainty: Boston Review Forum 20*. Cambridge, MA: MIT Press.

Jasanoff, S. and Wynne, B. (1998). 'Science and decision making', in S. Rayner and E. Malone (eds), *Human Choices and Climate Change*. Columbus: Battelle Press.

Jensen, N. D., Barrett, C. B. and Mude, A. G. (2015). 'The favourable impacts of index-based livestock insurance: Evaluation results from Ethiopia and Kenya'. *ILRI Research Brief*. Nairobi: International Livestock Research Institute.

Jensen, N. D., Barrett, C. B. and Mude, A. G. (2016). 'Index insurance quality and basis risk: Evidence from northern Kenya'. *American Journal of Agricultural Economics* 98(5): 1450–69.

Johnson, L. (2021). 'Rescaling index insurance for climate and development in Africa'. *Economy and Society* 50(2): 248–74.

Johnson, L., Mikulewicz, M., Bigger, P., et al. (2023a). 'Intervention: The invisible labor of climate change adaptation'. *Global Environmental Change* 83: 102769.

Johnson, L., Mohamed, T., Scoones, I. and Taye, M. (2023b). 'Uncertainty in the drylands: Rethinking in/formal insurance from pastoral East Africa'. *Environment and Planning A: Economy and Space* 55(8). doi.org/10.1177/0308518X231168396

Johnson-Hanks, J. (2002). 'On the limits of life stages in ethnography: Toward a theory of vital conjunctures'. *American Anthropologist* 104(3): 865–80.

Jonik, M. (2014). '"The péripéties of the contest": Risk, love, and anarchism in James's *The Princess Casamassima* and Conrad's *The Secret Agent*'. *English Academy Review* 31(2): 20–34.

Joseph, J. (2018). *Varieties of Resilience: Studies in Governmentality*. Cambridge: Cambridge University Press.

Kahneman, D., Slovic, P. and Tversky, A. (1982). *Judgment under Uncertainty: Heuristics and Biases*. Cambridge: Cambridge University Press.

Kashwan, P. and Ribot, J. (2021). 'Violent silence: The erasure of history and justice in global climate policy'. *Current History* 120(829): 326–31.

Katzenstein, P. J. and Seybert, L. A. (2018). *Protean Power: Exploring the Uncertain and Unexpected in World Politics*. Cambridge: Cambridge University Press.

Kay, J. and King, M. (2020). *Radical Uncertainty: Decision-Making for an Unknowable Future*. London: Hachette.

Keller, R. C. (2019). *Fatal Isolation: The Devastating Paris Heat Wave of 2003*. Chicago: University of Chicago Press.

Keynes, J. M. (1937). 'The general theory of employment'. *Quarterly Journal of Economics* 51(2): 209–23.

Kirby, P. and Webb, R. (2023). *Creating with Uncertainty: Sustainability Education Resources for a Changing World*. [ebook] Falmer: University of Sussex Open Press. Available at: https://openpress.sussex.ac.uk/creatingwithuncertainty/

Klein, N. (2007). *The Shock Doctrine: The Rise of Disaster Capitalism*. London: Macmillan.

Knight, F. H. (1921). *Risk, Uncertainty and Profit*. Boston, MA: Houghton Mifflin.

Könings, M. (2015). *The Emotional Logic of Capitalism: What Progressives Have Missed*. Redwood City: Stanford University Press.

Kornhuber, K., Lesk, C., Schleussner, C. F., Jägermeyr, J., Pfleiderer, P. and Horton, R. M. (2023). 'Risks of synchronized low yields are underestimated in climate and crop model projections'. *Nature Communications* 14(1): 3528.

Koselleck, R. (2000). *Critique and Crisis: Enlightenment and the Pathogenesis of Modern Society*. Cambridge, MA: MIT Press.

Kothari, A., Salleh, A., Escobar, A., Demaria, F. and Acosta Espinosa, A. (2019). *Pluriverse: A Post-Development Dictionary*. Chennai: Tulika Books.

Krätli, S. and Schareika, N. (2010). 'Living off uncertainty: The intelligent animal production of dryland pastoralists'. *European Journal of Development Research* 22: 605–22.

Krause, F. (2017). 'Towards an amphibious anthropology of delta life'. *Human Ecology* 45(3): 403–8.

Krause, F. and Eriksen, T. H. (2023). 'Inhabiting volatile worlds'. *Social Anthropology/Anthropologie Sociale* 1: 1–13. Available at: https://doi.org/10.3167/saas.2023.04132300

Krüger, F., Bankoff, G., Cannon, T., Orlowski, B. and Schipper, E. L. F. (eds) (2015). *Cultures and Disasters: Understanding Cultural Framings in Disaster Risk Reduction*. Abingdon: Routledge.

Kuklicke, C. and Demeritt, D. (2016). 'Adaptive and risk-based approaches to climate change and the management of uncertainty and institutional risk: The case of future flooding in England'. *Global Environmental Change* 37: 56–68.

La Porte, T. R. (1996). 'High reliability organizations: Unlikely, demanding and at risk'. *Journal of Contingencies and Crisis Management* 4(2): 60–71.

Lahsen, M. and Ribot, J. (2022). 'Politics of attributing extreme events and disasters to climate change'. *Wiley Interdisciplinary Reviews: Climate Change* 13(1): e750.

Lakoff, A. (2017). *Unprepared: Global Health in a Time of Emergency*. Berkeley: University of California Press.

Lam, R., Sanchez-Gonzalez, A., Willson, M., Wirnsberger, P., et al. (2023). 'Learning skilful medium-range global weather forecasting'. *Science*: eadi2336.

Lancaster, K., Rhodes, T. and Rosengarten, M. (2020). 'Making evidence and policy in public health emergencies: Lessons from COVID-19 for adaptive evidence-making and intervention'. *Evidence and Policy* 16(3): 477–90.

Landström, C., Becker, M., Odoni, N. and Whatmore, S. J. (2019). 'Community modelling: A technique for enhancing local capacity to engage with flood risk management'. *Environmental Science and Policy* 92: 255–61.

Latour, B. (1987). *Science in Action: How to Follow Scientists and Engineers through Society*. Cambridge, MA: Harvard University Press.

Latour, B. (2007). *Reassembling the Social: An Introduction to Actor-Network-Theory*. Oxford: Oxford University Press.

Law, J. (2004). *After Method: Mess in Social Science Research*. Abingdon: Routledge.

Lawrence, J. L. and Wiebe, S. M. (2017). *Biopolitical Disaster*. Abingdon: Routledge.

Leach, M. and Scoones, I. (2006). *The Slow Race: Making Science and Technology Work for the Poor*. New York: Demos.

Leach, M. and Scoones, I. (2013). 'The social and political lives of zoonotic disease models: Narratives, science and policy'. *Social Science and Medicine* 88: 10–17.

Leach, M., Scoones, I. and Thompson, L. (2002). 'Citizenship, science and risk: Conceptualising relationships across issues and settings'. *IDS Bulletin* 33: 1–12.

Leach, M., Scoones, I. and Wynne, B. (eds) (2005). *Science and Citizens: Globalization and the Challenge of Engagement*. London: Zed Books.

Leach, M., Stirling, A. C. and Scoones, I. (2010). *Dynamic Sustainabilities: Technology, Environment, Social Justice.* Abingdon: Routledge.

Leach, M., MacGregor, H., Ripoll, S., Scoones, I. and Wilkinson, A. (2022). 'Rethinking disease preparedness: Incertitude and the politics of knowledge'. *Critical Public Health* 32(1): 82–96.

Leach, M., MacGregor, H., Scoones, I. and Taylor, P. (2024). 'Post-pandemic transformations and the recasting of development – A comment and further reflections'. *Development and Change*. Available at: https://doi.org/10.1111/dech.12811

Leach, M., MacGregor, H., Scoones, I. and Wilkinson, A. (2021). 'Post-pandemic transformations: How and why COVID-19 requires us to rethink development'. *World Development* 138: 105233.

Le Billon, P., Suji, M., Baniya, J., et al. (2020). 'Disaster financialization: Earthquakes, cashflows and shifting household economies in Nepal'. *Development and Change* 51(4): 939–69.

Lees, E. (2020). '*Langton v Secretary of State for Environment, Food and Rural Affairs*: Badger cull in the Court of Appeal'. *Environmental Law Review* 22(1): 43–8.

Leichenko, R. and O'Brien, K. (2019). *Climate and Society: Transforming the Future.* Abingdon: Routledge.

Leins, S. (2018). *Stories of Capitalism: Inside the Role of Financial Analysts.* Chicago: University of Chicago Press.

Lennard, N. (2022). 'Certainty in uncertain times'. *Verso blog.* Available at: https://www.versobooks.com/en-gb/blogs/news/5455-certainty-in-uncertain-times

Lenton, T. M., Rockström, J., Gaffney, O., et al. (2019). 'Climate tipping points – too risky to bet against'. *Nature* 575(7784): 592–5.

Lépinay, V. A. (2015). *Codes of Finance: Engineering Derivatives in a Global Bank.* Princeton: Princeton University Press.

Lerner, A. P. (1944). *The Economics of Control: Principles of Welfare Economics.* New York: Macmillan.

Li, T. M. (2007). *The Will to Improve: Governmentality, Development, and the Practice of Politics.* Durham, NC: Duke University Press.

Little, P. D., Tiki, W. and Debsu, D. N. (2015). 'Formal or informal, legal or illegal: The ambiguous nature of cross-border livestock trade in the Horn of Africa'. *Journal of Borderlands Studies* 30(3): 405–21.

Liverman, D., von Hedemann, N., Nying'uro, P., et al. (2022). 'Survey of gender bias in the IPCC'. *Nature* 602(7895): 30–2.

Livina, V. N. (2023). 'Connected climate tipping elements'. *Nature Climate Change* 13(1): 15–16.

Luhmann, N. (1993). *Risk: A Sociological Theory*, trans. R. Barrett. Berlin: A. de Gruyter.

MacGregor, H., Ripoll, S. and Leach, M. (2020). 'Disease outbreaks: Navigating uncertainties in preparedness and response', in I. Scoones and A. Stirling (eds), *The Politics of Uncertainty: Challenges of Transformation*. Abingdon: Routledge.

MacKenzie, D. (1998). 'The certainty trough', in R. Williams, W. Faulkner and J. Fleck (eds), *Exploring Expertise: Issues and Perspectives*. New York: Macmillan.

MacKenzie, D. and Spears, T. (2014). '"The formula that killed Wall Street": The Gaussian copula and modelling practices in investment banking'. *Social Studies of Science* 44(3): 393–417.

Macnaghten, P. (2020). *The Making of Responsible Innovation*. Cambridge: Cambridge University Press.

Mahmoud, H. A. (2008). 'Risky trade, resilient traders: Trust and livestock marketing in northern Kenya'. *Africa* 78(4): 561–81.

Mahony, M. (2014). 'The predictive state: Science, territory and the future of the Indian climate'. *Social Studies of Science* 44(1): 109–33.

Mahony, M. (2017). 'The (re)emergence of regional climate: Mobile models, regional visions and the government of climate change', in M. Heymann, G. Gramelsberger and M. Mahony (eds), *Cultures of Prediction in Atmospheric and Climate Science*. Abingdon: Routledge.

Mann, G. (2023). 'Treading thin air'. *London Review of Books* 45(17), 7 September.

Mann, M. E. (2012). *The Hockey Stick and the Climate Wars: Dispatches from the Front Lines*. New York: Columbia University Press.

Marchau, V. A., Walker, W. E., Bloemen, P. J. and Popper, S. W. (2019). *Decision Making under Deep Uncertainty: From Theory to Practice*. London: Springer Nature.

Maru, N. (2020). 'A relational view of pastoral (im)mobilities'. *Nomadic Peoples* 24(2): 209–27.

Mawere, M. and Mubaya, T. (2016). *African Philosophy and*

Thought Systems: A Search for a Culture and Philosophy of Belonging. Bamenda: Langaa.

May, R. (1973). *Stability and Complexity in Model Ecosystems*. Princeton: Princeton University Press.

May, R. M., Levin, S. A. and Sugihara, G. (2008). 'Ecology for bankers'. *Nature* 451(7181): 893–4.

Maynard, A. and Stilgoe, J. (2020). *The Ethics of Nanotechnology, Geoengineering, and Clean Energy*. Abingdon: Routledge.

Mbembe, J. A. and Nuttall, S. (2004). 'Writing the world from an African metropolis'. *Public Culture* 16(3): 347–72.

McMillan, J. (2003). *Reinventing the Bazaar: A Natural History of Markets*. New York: W. W. Norton and Company.

McPeak, J. G. and Little, P. D. (eds) (2006). *Pastoral Livestock Marketing in Eastern Africa: Research and Policy Challenges*. Rugby: Intermediate Technology Publications.

Meagher, K. (2010). *Identity Economics: Social Networks and the Informal Economy in Nigeria*. Woodbridge: Boydell and Brewer.

Mechler, R., Singh, C., Ebi, K., et al. (2020). 'Loss and damage and limits to adaptation: Recent IPCC insights and implications for climate science and policy'. *Sustainability Science* 15: 1245–51.

Mehta, L. and Srivastava, S. (2020). 'Uncertainty in modelling climate change', in I. Scoones and A. Stirling (eds), *Politics of Uncertainty: Challenges for Transformation*. Abingdon: Routledge.

Mehta, L., Adam, H. N. and Srivastava, S. (eds) (2022). *The Politics of Climate Change and Uncertainty in India*. Abingdon: Routledge.

Mehta, L., Srivastava, S., Adam, H. N., et al. (2019). 'Climate change and uncertainty from "above" and "below": Perspectives from India'. *Regional Environmental Change* 19: 1533–47.

Mehta, L., Srivastava, S., Movik, S., et al. (2021). 'Transformation as praxis: Responding to climate change uncertainties in marginal environments in South Asia'. *Current Opinion in Environmental Sustainability* 49: 110–17.

Merton, R. K. (1973). *The Sociology of Science: Theoretical and Empirical Investigations*. Chicago: University of Chicago Press.

Michie, S., Ball, P., Wilsdon, J. and West, R. (2022). 'Lessons from the UK's handling of Covid-19 for the future of scientific advice to government: A contribution to the UK Covid-19 public inquiry'. *Contemporary Social Science* 17(5): 418–33.

Miller, C. A. (2004). 'Climate science and the making of a global political order', in S. Jasanoff (ed.), *States of Knowledge*. Abingdon: Routledge.

Millo, Y. and MacKenzie, D. (2009). 'The usefulness of inaccurate models: Towards an understanding of the emergence of financial risk management'. *Accounting, Organizations and Society* 34(5): 638–53.

Millstone, E. (2007). 'Can food safety policy-making be both scientifically and democratically legitimated? If so, how?' *Journal of Agricultural and Environmental Ethics* 20: 483–508.

Millstone, E. (2009). 'Science, risk and governance: Radical rhetorics and the realities of reform in food safety governance'. *Research Policy* 38(4): 624–36.

Millstone, E., Brunner, E. and Mayer, S. (1999). 'Beyond "substantial equivalence"'. *Nature* 401(6753): 525–6.

Mohamed, T. (2023). 'Responding to uncertainties in pastoral northern Kenya: The role of moral economies', in I. Scoones (ed.), *Pastoralism, Uncertainty and Development*. Rugby: Practical Action Publishing.

Mohamed, T. and Scoones, I. (2023). 'Embracing local knowledge is the key to resilience in northern Kenya, not project box-ticking'. *New Humanitarian* (August).

Mohmand, S. K., Loureiro, M. and Sida, L. (2023). 'What lies beneath Pakistan's disastrous floods'. *Current History* 122: 149–54.

Mol, A.-M. (2008). *The Logic of Care: Health and the Problem of Patient Choice*. Abingdon: Routledge.

Molesworth, J. (2010). *Chance and the Eighteenth-Century Novel: Realism, Probability, Magic*. Cambridge: Cambridge University Press.

Moore, J. W. (ed.) (2016). *Anthropocene or Capitalocene? Nature, History, and the Crisis of Capitalism*. New York: PM Press.

Mukherjee, J., Lahiri-Dutt, K. and Ghosh, R. (2023). 'Beyond (un)stable: Chars as dynamic destabilisers of problematic binaries'. *Social Anthropology/Anthropologie Sociale* 1: 1–18.

6662

Mythen, G. (2018). 'The metamorphosis of the world: Society in pupation?' *Theory, Culture and Society* 35(7–8): 189–204.

Mythen, G., Burgess, A. and Wardman, J. K. (2018). 'The prophecy of Ulrich Beck: Signposts for the social sciences'. *Journal of Risk Research* 21(1): 96–100.

Negri, A. (2008). *Reflections on Empire*. Cambridge: Polity Press.

Newell, P., Srivastava, S., Naess, L. O., Torres Contreras, G. A. and Price, R. (2021). 'Toward transformative climate justice: An emerging research agenda'. *Wiley Interdisciplinary Reviews: Climate Change* 12(6): e733.

Newhouse, L. S. (2017). 'Uncertain futures and everyday hedging in a humanitarian city'. *Transactions of the Institute of British Geographers* 42(4): 503–15.

Ng'asike, O. P., Hagmann, T. and Wasonga, O. V. (2021). 'Brokerage in the borderlands: The political economy of livestock intermediaries in northern Kenya'. *Journal of Eastern African Studies* 15(1): 168–88.

Nightingale, A. J., Eriksen, S., Taylor, M., et al. (2020). 'Beyond technical fixes: Climate solutions and the great derangement'. *Climate and Development* 12(4): 343–52.

Nixon, R. (2011). *Slow Violence and the Environmentalism of the Poor*. Cambridge, MA: Harvard University Press.

Nori, M. (2023). 'High quality, high reliability: The dynamics of camel milk marketing in northern Kenya'. *Pastoralism* 13(1): 9.

North, D. C. (1999). 'Dealing with a non-ergodic world: Institutional economics, property rights, and the global environment'. *Duke Environmental Law and Policy Forum* 10: 1–12.

Nowotny, H. (2015). *The Cunning of Uncertainty*. Cambridge: Polity Press.

NRC (1983). *Risk Assessment in the Federal Government: Managing the Process*. Washington, DC: US National Academies Press.

O'Keefe, P., Westgate, K. and Wisner, B. (1976). 'Taking the naturalness out of natural disasters'. *Nature* 260(5552): 566–7.

O'Lear, S., Masse, F., Dickinson, H. and Duffy, R. (2022). 'Disaster making in the Capitalocene'. *Global Environmental Politics* 22(3): 2–11.

O'Mahony, T., Luukkanen, J., Vehmas, J. and Kaivo-oja, J. R. T. (2023). 'Time to build a new practice of foresight for national economies? Ireland, and uncertain futures in forecasts and scenarios'. *Foresight*. Available at: https://doi.org/10.1108/FS-10-2021-0191

O'Malley, P. (1996). 'Risk and responsibility', in A. Barry, T. Osborne and N. Rose (eds), *Foucault and Political Reason: Liberalism, Neo-liberalism and Rationalities of Government*. Abingdon: Routledge.

O'Malley, P. (2002). *Imagining Insurance: Risk, Thrift, and Life Insurance in Britain*. Chicago: University of Chicago Press.

Oxley, N. (2020). 'Unsettling the apocalypse: Uncertainty in spirituality and religion', in I. Scoones and A. Stirling (eds), *The Politics of Uncertainty: Challenges of Transformation*. Abingdon: Routledge.

Pan, D., Martin, C. A., Nazareth, J., et al. (2021). 'Ethnic disparities in COVID-19: Increased risk of infection or severe disease?' *The Lancet* 398(10298): 389–90.

Paprocki, K. (2021). *Threatening Dystopias: The Global Politics of Climate Change Adaptation in Bangladesh*. New York: Cornell University Press.

Paprocki, K. (2022). 'Anticipatory ruination'. *Journal of Peasant Studies* 49(7): 1399–408.

Pareek, M., Bangash, M. N., Pareek, N., et al. (2020). 'Ethnicity and COVID-19: An urgent public health research priority'. *The Lancet* 395(10234): 1421–2.

Parker, M., MacGregor, H. and Akello, G. (2020). 'COVID-19, public authority and enforcement'. *Medical Anthropology* 39(8): 666–70.

Patel, R. and Moore, J. W. (2017). *A History of the World in Seven Cheap Things: A Guide to Capitalism, Nature, and the Future of the Planet*. Berkeley: University of California Press.

Pearce, F. (2010). *The Climate Files: The Battle for the Truth about Global Warming*. London: Guardian Faber Publishing.

Pearce, W. (2020). 'Trouble in the trough: How uncertainties were downplayed in the UK's science advice on Covid-19'. *Humanities and Social Sciences Communications* 7: 122.

Pelling, M. (2003). 'Paradigms of risk', in M. Pelling (ed.), *Natural Disasters and Development in a Globalizing World*. Abingdon: Routledge.

Pelling, M. (2010). *Adaptation to Climate Change: From Resilience to Transformation.* Abingdon: Routledge.

Perrow, C. (1999). *Normal Accidents: Living with High Risk Technologies.* Princeton: Princeton University Press.

Peters, O. (2019). 'The ergodicity problem in economics'. *Nature Physics* 15(12): 1216–21.

Pidgeon, N. (2011). 'In retrospect: *Normal Accidents'. Nature* 477: 404–5.

Pidgeon, N. and Beattie, J. (1998). 'The psychology of risk and uncertainty', in P. Callow (ed.), *Handbook of Environmental Risk Assessment and Management.* Hoboken: John Wiley & Sons.

Pielke, Jr, R. A. (2007). *The Honest Broker: Making Sense of Science in Policy and Politics.* Cambridge: Cambridge University Press.

Pielke, Jr, R. and Ritchie, J. (2021). 'Distorting the view of our climate future: The misuse and abuse of climate pathways and scenarios'. *Energy Research and Social Science* 72: 101890.

Pielke, Jr, R., Burgess, M. G. and Ritchie, J. (2022). 'Plausible 2005–2050 emissions scenarios project between 2°C and 3°C of warming by 2100'. *Environmental Research Letters* 17(2).

Polanyi, K. (1944). *The Great Transformation: The Political and Economic Origins of Our Time.* Boston, MA: Beacon Press.

Porter, T. M. (1996). *Trust in Numbers: The Pursuit of Objectivity in Science and Public Life.* Princeton: Princeton University Press.

Power, M. (2004). 'The risk management of everything'. *Journal of Risk Finance* 5(3): 58–65.

Price, S. and Harbisher, B. (2021). *Power, Media and the COVID-19 Pandemic: Framing Public Discourse.* Abingdon: Routledge.

Prigogine, I. (1989). 'The philosophy of instability'. *Futures* 21(4): 396–400.

Prigogine, I. and Stengers, I. (1997). *The End of Certainty: Time, Chaos, and the New Laws of Nature.* New York: Simon and Schuster.

Rahman, M. F., Falzon, D., Robinson, S., et al. (2023). 'Locally led adaptation: Promise, pitfalls, and possibilities'. *Ambio*: 1–15.

Ramalingam, B. (2013). *Aid on the Edge of Chaos: Rethinking International Cooperation in a Complex World.* Oxford: Oxford University Press.

Ramalingam, B., Wild, L. and Ferrari, M. (2020). 'Adaptive leadership in the coronavirus response'. *Coronavirus Briefing Note*. London: Overseas Development Institute.

Rammel, C., Stagl, S. and Wilfing, H. (2007). 'Managing complex adaptive systems – A co-evolutionary perspective on natural resource management'. *Ecological Economics* 63(1): 9–21.

Rees, M. (2021). *On the Future: Prospects for Humanity*. Princeton: Princeton University Press.

Renn, O. (2008). *Risk Governance: Coping with Uncertainty in a Complex World*. Abingdon: Routledge-Earthscan.

Reyers, B., Moore, M.-L., Haider, L. J. and Schlüter, M. (2022). 'The contributions of resilience to reshaping sustainable development'. *Nature Sustainability* 5(8): 657–64.

Rhodes, T. and Lancaster, K. (2020). 'Mathematical models as public troubles in COVID-19 infection control: Following the numbers'. *Health Sociology Review* 29(2): 177–94.

Rhodes, T. and Lancaster, K. (2022a). 'Making pandemics big: On the situational performance of Covid-19 mathematical models'. *Social Science and Medicine* 301: 114907.

Rhodes, T. and Lancaster, K. (2022b). 'Uncomfortable science: How mathematical models, and consensus, come to be in public policy'. *Sociology of Health and Illness* 44(9): 1461–80.

Ribot, J. (2014). 'Cause and response: Vulnerability and climate in the Anthropocene'. *Journal of Peasant Studies* 41(5): 667–705.

Richards, P. (2016). *Ebola: How a People's Science Helped End an Epidemic*. London: Zed Press.

Rip, A., Schot, J. and Misa, T. J. (1995). 'Constructive technology assessment: A new paradigm for managing technology in society', in A. Rip, T. Misa and J. Schot (eds), *Managing Technology in Society: The Approach of Constructive Technology Assessment*. London: Pinter Publishers.

Roba, G. M. (2020). 'Winners and losers in livestock commercialisation in northern Kenya'. *Future Agricultures Consortium Working Paper*. Brighton: Institute of Development Studies.

Roba, G. M., Lelea, M. A. and Kaufmann, B. (2017). 'Manoeuvring through difficult terrain: How local traders link pastoralists to markets'. *Journal of Rural Studies* 54: 85–97.

Rochlin, G. I. (1993). 'Defining "high reliability" organizations in practice: A taxonomic prologue', in K. Roberts (ed.),

New Challenges to Understanding Organizations. New York: Macmillan.

Rock, J. S., Schnurr, M. A., Kingiri, A., et al. (2023). 'Beyond the genome: Genetically modified crops in Africa and the implications for genome editing'. *Development and Change* 54(1): 117–42.

Rockström, J., Steffen, W., Noone, K., et al. (2009). 'Planetary boundaries: Exploring the safe operating space for humanity'. *Ecology and Society* 14(2).

Roe, E. (2013). *Making the Most of Mess: Reliability and Policy in Today's Management Challenges*. Durham, NC: Duke University Press.

Roe, E. (2016). 'Policy messes and their management'. *Policy Sciences* 49: 351–72.

Roe, E. (2020). 'A new policy narrative for pastoralism? Pastoralists as reliability professionals and pastoralist systems as infrastructure'. *STEPS Centre Working Paper* 113. Brighton: STEPS Centre.

Roe, E. and Schulman, P. R. (2008). *High Reliability Management: Operating on the Edge*. Redwood City: Stanford University Press.

Roe, E. and Schulman, P. (2023). 'An interconnectivity framework for analyzing and demarcating real-time operations across critical infrastructures and over time'. *Safety Science* 168: 106308.

Roe, E., Huntsinger, L. and Labnow, K. (1998). 'High reliability pastoralism'. *Journal of Arid Environments* 39(1): 39–55.

Roitman, J. L. (1990). 'The politics of informal markets in sub-Saharan Africa'. *Journal of Modern African Studies* 28(4): 671–96.

Roitman, J. (2013). *Anti-Crisis*. Durham, NC: Duke University Press.

Saltelli, A., Bammer, G., Bruno, I., et al. (2020). 'Five ways to ensure that models serve society: A manifesto'. *Nature* 582: 482–84.

Sarewitz, D. (2004). 'How science makes environmental controversies worse'. *Environmental Science and Policy* 7(5): 385–403.

Savage, M. (2021). *The Return of Inequality: Social Change and the Weight of the Past*. Cambridge, MA: Harvard University Press.

Schipper, E. L. F. (2006). 'Conceptual history of adaptation in the UNFCCC process'. *Review of European Community and International Environmental Law* 15(1): 82–92.

Schipper, E. L. F. (2020). 'Maladaptation: When adaptation to climate change goes very wrong'. *One Earth* 3(4): 409–14.

Schulman, P. R. (1996). 'Heroes, organizations and high reliability'. *Journal of Contingencies and Crisis Management* 4(2): 72–82.

Schulman, P. and Roe, E. (2016). *Reliability and Risk: The Challenge of Managing Interconnected Infrastructures.* Redwood City: Stanford University Press.

Schulman, P., Roe, E., Van Eeten, M. and De Bruijne, M. (2004). 'High reliability and the management of critical infrastructures'. *Journal of Contingencies and Crisis Management* 12(1): 14–28.

Scoones, I. (ed.) (1994). *Living with Uncertainty: New Directions in Pastoral Development in Africa.* Rugby: Intermediate Technology Publications.

Scoones, I. (2002). 'Science, policy and regulation: Challenges for agricultural biotechnology in developing countries'. *IDS Working Paper* 147.

Scoones, I. (2006). *Science, Agriculture and the Politics of Policy: The Case of Biotechnology in India.* Hyderabad: Orient Black Swan.

Scoones, I. (2008). 'Mobilizing against GM crops in India, South Africa and Brazil'. *Journal of Agrarian Change* 8(2–3): 315–44.

Scoones, I. (2019). 'What is uncertainty and why does it matter?' *STEPS Centre Working Paper* 105. Brighton: STEPS Centre/ PASTRES.

Scoones, I. (2021a). 'Pastoralists and peasants: Perspectives on agrarian change'. *Journal of Peasant Studies* 48(1): 1–47.

Scoones, I. (2021b). 'What pastoralists know'. *Aeon.* Available at: https://aeon.co/essays/what-bankers-should-learn-from-the -traditions-of-pastoralism

Scoones, I. (ed.) (2023a). *Pastoralism, Uncertainty and Development.* Rugby: Practical Action Publishing.

Scoones, I. (2023b). 'Confronting uncertainties in pastoral areas: Transforming development from control to care'. *Social Anthropology/Anthropologie Sociale* 1: 1–19.

Scoones, I. and Glover, D. (2009). 'Africa's biotechnology battle'. *Nature* 460: 797–8.

Scoones, I. and Nori, M. (2023). 'Pastoralism, uncertainty, and development: Perspectives from the rangelands', in I. Scoones (ed.), *Pastoralism, Uncertainty and Development*. Rugby: Practical Action Publishing.

Scoones, I. and Stirling, A. (eds) (2020). *The Politics of Uncertainty: Challenges of Transformation*. Abingdon: Routledge.

Scoones, I., Edelman, M., Borras, Jr, S. M., Forero, L. F., et al. (eds) (2022). *Authoritarian Populism and the Rural World*. Abingdon: Routledge.

Scoones, I., Jones, K., Lo Iacono, G., Redding, D. W., et al. (2017). 'Integrative modelling for One Health: Pattern, process and participation'. *Philosophical Transactions of the Royal Society B: Biological Sciences* 372(1725): 20160164.

Scoones, I., Marongwe, N., Mavedzenge, B., et al. (2010). *Zimbabwe's Land Reform: Myths and Realities*. Woodbridge: James Currey.

Scoones, I., Mohamed, T. and Taye, M. (forthcoming). 'The politics of anticipation in East Africa's rangelands', in D. Müller-Mahn and M. Bollig (eds), *Future Rural Africa: Shaping Social-Ecological Transformation in a World of Changing Aspirations*. Woodbridge: James Currey.

Scoones, I., Stirling, A., Abrol, D., et al. (2020). 'Transformations to sustainability: Combining structural, systemic and enabling approaches'. *Current Opinion in Environmental Sustainability* 42: 65–75.

Scott, J. C. (1998). *Seeing Like a State: How Certain Schemes to Improve the Human Condition Have Failed*. New Haven: Yale University Press.

Scott, J. C. (2017). *Against the Grain: A Deep History of the Earliest States*. New Haven: Yale University Press.

Shackle, G. L. S. (1992 [1972]). *Epistemics and Economics: A Critique of Economic Doctrines*. Abingdon: Routledge.

Shackley, S. and Wynne, B. (1995). 'Global climate change: The mutual construction of an emergent science-policy domain'. *Science and Public Policy* 22(4): 218–30.

Shackley, S. and Wynne, B. (1996). 'Representing uncertainty in global climate change science and policy: Boundary-ordering devices and authority'. *Science, Technology, and Human Values* 21(3): 275–302.

Shackley, S., Young, P., Parkinson, S. and Wynne, B. (1998). 'Uncertainty, complexity and concepts of good science in climate change modelling: Are GCMs the best tools?' *Climatic Change* 38: 159–205.

Sharpe, C. (2016). *In the Wake: On Blackness and Being*. Durham, NC: Duke University Press.

Shen, C., Taleb, N. N. and Bar-Yam, Y. (2020). 'Review of Ferguson et al., "Impact of Non-pharmaceutical Interventions"'. *New England Complex Systems Institute*, 17 March.

Simula, G. (2023). 'Uncertainty, markets, and pastoralism in Sardinia, Italy', in I. Scoones (ed.), *Pastoralism, Uncertainty and Development*. Rugby: Practical Action Publishing.

Sinozic-Martinez, T., Weinberger, N. and Hahn, J. (2023). 'Post-normal crises and technology assessment'. *TATuP-Zeitschrift für Technikfolgenabschätzung in Theorie und Praxis* 32(2): 11–16.

Skidelsky, R. (2011). 'The relevance of Keynes'. *Cambridge Journal of Economics* 35(1): 1–13.

Skrimshire, S. (2014). 'Climate change and apocalyptic faith'. *Wiley Interdisciplinary Reviews: Climate Change* 5(2): 233–46.

Smith, A. and Stirling, A. (2016). 'Grassroots innovation and innovation democracy'. *STEPS Working Paper* 89. Brighton: STEPS Centre.

Smith, N. (2006). 'There's no such thing as a natural disaster', in Social Science Research Council, *Understanding Katrina: Perspectives from the Social Sciences*. Available at: https://items.ssrc.org/understanding-katrina/theres-no-such-thing-as-a-natural-disaster/

Solnit, R. (2016). *Hope in the Dark: Untold Histories, Wild Possibilities*. Chicago: Haymarket Books.

Solnit, R. (2023). 'Why climate despair is a luxury'. *New Statesman*, 17 July. Available at: https://www.newstatesman.com/environment/2023/07/rebecca-solnit-climate-despair-hope

Sorkin, A. R. (2010). *Too Big to Fail: The Inside Story of How Wall Street and Washington Fought to Save the Financial System – and Themselves*. London: Penguin.

Sovacool, B. (2021). 'Reckless or righteous? Reviewing the sociotechnical benefits and risks of climate change geoengineering'. *Energy Strategy Reviews* 35: 100656.

Sridhar, D. (2022). *Preventable: How a Pandemic Changed the World and How to Stop the Next One*. London: Penguin.

Star, L. S. (2010). 'This is not a boundary object: Reflections on the origin of a concept'. *Science, Technology, and Human Values* 35(5): 601–17.

Steigerwald, B., Weibezahn, J., Slowik, M. and Von Hirschhausen, C. (2023). 'Uncertainties in estimating production costs of future nuclear technologies: A model-based analysis of small modular reactors'. *Energy* 281: 128204.

Stengers, I. (2018). *Another Science is Possible: A Manifesto for Slow Science*. Chichester: John Wiley & Sons.

Stewart, I. (2012). *In Pursuit of the Unknown: 17 Equations that Changed the World*. New York: Hachette.

Stigler, S. M. (1986). *The History of Statistics: The Measurement of Uncertainty before 1900*. Cambridge, MA: Harvard University Press.

Stilgoe, J. (2007). 'The (co-)production of public uncertainty: UK scientific advice on mobile phone health risks'. *Public Understanding of Science* 16(1): 45–61.

Stilgoe, J. (2021). 'How can we know a self-driving car is safe?' *Ethics and Information Technology* 23(4): 635–47.

Stilgoe, J., Irwin, A. and Jones, K. (2006). *The Received Wisdom: Opening Up Expert Advice*. London: Demos.

Stirling, A. (1999). 'On "precautionary" and "science-based" approaches to risk assessment and environmental appraisal', in A. Klinke, O. Renn, A. Rip, A. Salo and A. Stirling (eds), *On Science and Precaution in the Management of Technological Risk, Vol. II, Case Studies*. Brussels: European Commission Joint Research Centre.

Stirling, A. (2008). '"Opening up" and "closing down" power, participation, and pluralism in the social appraisal of technology'. *Science, Technology, and Human Values* 33(2): 262–94.

Stirling, A. (2009). 'Direction, distribution and diversity! Pluralising progress in innovation, sustainability and development'. *STEPS Working Paper* 32. Brighton: STEPS Centre.

Stirling, A. (2010). 'Keep it complex'. *Nature* 468(7327): 1029–31.

Stirling, A. (forthcoming). 'From controlling global mean temperature to caring for a flourishing climate', in Z. Baker, T. Law, M. Vardy and S. Zehr (eds), *Climate, Science and Society: A Primer*. Abingdon: Routledge.

Stirling, A. and Mayer, S. (2001). 'A novel approach to the

appraisal of technological risk: A multicriteria mapping study of a genetically modified crop'. *Environment and Planning C: Government and Policy* 19(4): 529–55.

Stirling, A. and Scoones, I. (2020). 'COVID-19 and the futility of control in the modern world'. *Issues in Science and Technology* 36(4): 25–7.

Stirling, A., Leach, M., Mehta, L., Scoones, I., et al. (2007). 'Empowering designs: Towards more progressive social appraisal of sustainability'. *STEPS Centre Working Paper 3*. Brighton: STEPS Centre.

Stoler, A. L. (2013). *Imperial Debris: On Ruins and Ruination.* Durham, NC: Duke University Press.

Stone, D. A. (2002). 'Beyond moral hazard: Insurance as moral opportunity', in T. Baker and J. Simon (eds), *Embracing Risk: The Changing Culture of Insurance and Responsibility.* Chicago: University of Chicago Press.

Stone, G. D. (2022). *The Agricultural Dilemma: How Not to Feed the World.* Abingdon: Routledge.

Stott, P., Christidis, N., Otto, F., et al. (2016). 'Attribution of extreme weather and climate-related events'. *Wiley Interdisciplinary Reviews: Climate Change* 7(1): 23–41.

Sultana, F. (2022). 'The unbearable heaviness of climate coloniality'. *Political Geography* 99: 102638.

Sutoris, P., Murphy, S., Borges, A. and Nehushtan, Y. (2022). *Pandemic Response and the Cost of Lockdowns: Global Debates from Humanities and Social Sciences.* Abingdon: Routledge.

Taleb, N. N. (2007). *The Black Swan: The Impact of the Highly Improbable.* New York: Random House.

Tasker, A. and Scoones, I. (2022). 'High reliability knowledge networks: Responding to animal diseases in a pastoral area of northern Kenya'. *Journal of Development Studies* 58(5): 968–88.

Taye, M. T. (2022). *Financialisation of Risk among the Borana Pastoralists of Ethiopia: Practices of Integrating Livestock Insurance in Responding to Risk.* PhD thesis. Brighton: University of Sussex.

Taye, M. T. (2023). 'Livestock insurance in southern Ethiopia: Calculating risks, responding to uncertainties', in I. Scoones (ed.), *Pastoralism, Uncertainty and Development.* Rugby: Practical Action Publishing.

Taylor, M. (2014). *The Political Ecology of Climate Change Adaptation: Livelihoods, Agrarian Change and the Conflicts of Development*. Abingdon: Routledge.

Tett, G. (2009). *Fool's Gold: How Unrestrained Greed Corrupted a Dream, Shattered Global Markets and Unleashed a Catastrophe*. New York: Hachette.

Tett, G. (2019). 'Faith-based finance: How Wall Street became a cult of risk'. *Foreign Affairs* 98: 34.

Tett, G. (2021). *Anthro-vision: How Anthropology Can Explain Business and Life*. New York: Random House.

Tilley, H. (2016). 'Medicine, empires, and ethics in colonial Africa'. *AMA Journal of Ethics* 18(7): 743–53.

Tooze, A. (2014). *The Deluge: The Great War and the Remaking of the Global Order, 1916–1931*. London: Penguin Allen Lane.

Tooze, A. (2018). *Crashed: How a Decade of Financial Crises Changed the World*. London: Penguin.

Trenberth, K. (2010). 'More knowledge, less certainty'. *Nature Climate Change* 1(1002): 20–1.

Tschakert, P., Barnett, J., Ellis, N., et al. (2017). 'Climate change and loss, as if people mattered: values, places, and experiences'. *Wiley Interdisciplinary Reviews: Climate Change* 8(5): e476.

Tschakert, P., Van Oort, B., St Clair, A. L. and LaMadrid, A. (2013). 'Inequality and transformation analyses: A complementary lens for addressing vulnerability to climate change'. *Climate and Development* 5(4): 340–50.

Tsering, P. (2023). 'Hybrid rangeland governance: Ways of living with and from uncertainty in pastoral Amdo Tibet, China', in I. Scoones (ed.), *Pastoralism, Uncertainty and Development*. Rugby: Practical Action Publishing.

Tuckett, D. (2011). *Minding the Markets: An Emotional Finance View of Financial Instability*. New York: Springer.

Tuckett, D. and Nikolic, M. (2017). 'The role of conviction and narrative in decision-making under radical uncertainty'. *Theory and Psychology* 27(4): 501–23.

Tupper, A. C. and Fearnley, C. J. (2023). 'Disaster early-warning systems are "doomed to fail" – only collective action can plug the gaps'. *Nature* 623(7987): 478–82.

Turnpenny, J., Jones, M. and Lorenzoni, I. (2011). 'Where now for post-normal science? A critical review of its development, definitions, and uses'. *Science, Technology, and Human Values* 36(3): 287–306.

UNDRR (United Nations Office for Disaster Risk Reduction) (2022). *Global Assessment Report on Disaster Risk Reduction 2022: Our World at Risk: Transforming Governance for a Resilient Future*. Geneva: UNDRR.

van Asselt, M. B. and Renn, O. (2011). 'Risk governance'. *Journal of Risk Research* 14(4): 431–49.

van Beek, L., Hajer, M., Pelzer, P., van Vuuren, D. and Cassen, C. (2020). 'Anticipating futures through models: The rise of integrated assessment modelling in the climate science–policy interface since 1970'. *Global Environmental Change* 65: 102191.

van der Sluijs, J. (2005). 'Uncertainty as a monster in the science–policy interface: Four coping strategies'. *Water Science and Technology* 52(6): 87–92.

van Zandvoort, K., Jarvis, C., Pearson, C., et al. (2020). 'Response strategies for COVID-19 epidemics in African settings: A mathematical modelling study'. *BMC Med* 18: 324.

van Zwanenberg, P. and Millstone, E. (2005). *BSE: Risk, Science and Governance*. Oxford: Oxford University Press.

Velásquez, T. (2022). *Pachamama Politics: Campesino Water Defenders and the Anti-Mining Movement in Andean Ecuador*. Tucson: University of Arizona Press.

Vigh, H. (2008). 'Crisis and chronicity: Anthropological perspectives on continuous conflict and decline'. *Ethnos* 73(1): 5–24.

Visvanathan, S. (2005). 'Knowledge, justice and democracy', in M. Leach, I. Scoones and B. Wynne (eds), *Science and Citizens: Globalization and the Challenge of Engagement*. London: Zed Books.

Wagner, A. (2022). *Emergency State: How We Lost Our Freedoms in the Pandemic and Why It Matters*. London: Bodley Head.

Walker, B. and Salt, D. (2012). *Resilience Thinking: Sustaining Ecosystems and People in a Changing World*. Washington, DC: Island Press.

Walker, W., Harremoës, P., Rotmans, J., van der Sluijs, J., et al. (2003). 'Defining uncertainty: A conceptual basis for uncertainty management in model-based decision support'. *Integrated Assessment* 4(1): 5–17.

Wallace, R. (2020). *Dead Epidemiologists: On the Origins of COVID-19*. New York: Monthly Review Press.

Walter, T. and Wansleben, L. (2020). 'The assault of financial futures on the rest of time', in I. Scoones and A. Stirling (eds), *The Politics of Uncertainty: Challenges of Transformation*. Abingdon: Routledge.

Walton, J. and Levontin, P. (2023). 'Torque control: Apply science fiction here'. *Vector* 297: 3–7.

Wandji, D., Allouche, J. and Marchais, G. (2021). 'Vernacular resilience: An approach to studying long-term social practices and cultural repertoires of resilience in Côte d'Ivoire and the Democratic Republic of Congo'. *STEPS Working Paper* 113. Brighton: STEPS Centre.

Wansleben, L. (2012). 'Financial analysts', in K. Knorr Cetina and A. Preda (eds), *Handbook of the Sociology of Finance*. Oxford: Oxford University Press.

Wansleben, L. (2023). *The Rise of Central Banks: State Power in Financial Capitalism*. Cambridge, MA: Harvard University Press.

Watts, D. J. and Strogatz, S. H. (1998). 'Collective dynamics of "small-world" networks'. *Nature* 393(6684): 440–2.

Watts, M. (2016). 'Accumulating insecurity and manufacturing risk along the energy frontier', in S. Soederberg (ed.), *Risking Capitalism* (Research in Political Economy) 31. Bingley: Emerald Group Publishing.

Watts, M. J. and Bohle, H. G. (1993). 'The space of vulnerability: The causal structure of hunger and famine'. *Progress in Human Geography* 17(1): 43–67.

Weick, K. E. and Roberts, K. H. (1993). 'Collective mind in organizations: Heedful interrelating on flight decks'. *Administrative Science Quarterly* 38: 357–81.

West, S., Haider, L. J., Stålhammar, S. and Woroniecki, S. (2020). 'A relational turn for sustainability science? Relational thinking, leverage points and transformations'. *Ecosystems and People* 16(1): 304–25.

Whitfield, S. (2015). *Adapting to Climate Uncertainty in African Agriculture: Narratives and Knowledge Politics*. Abingdon: Routledge.

Whyte, S. R. (1997). *Questioning Misfortune: The Pragmatics of Uncertainty in Eastern Uganda*. Cambridge: Cambridge University Press.

Wilby, R. L. and Dessai, S. (2010). 'Robust adaptation to climate change'. *Weather* 65: 180–5.

Williams, R. (1989). *Resources of Hope: Culture, Democracy, Socialism*. London: Verso Books.

Wilsdon, J. and Willis, R. (2004). *See-through Science: Why Public Engagement Needs to Move Upstream*. London: Demos.

Woods, N. (2023). 'Multilateralism in the twenty-first century'. *Global Perspectives* 4(1): 68310.

Wynne, B. (1992). 'Uncertainty and environmental learning: Reconceiving science and policy in the preventive paradigm'. *Global Environmental Change* 2(2): 111–27.

Wynne, B. (1993). 'Public uptake of science: A case for institutional reflexivity'. *Public Understanding of Science* 2(4): 321–37.

Wynne, B. (1996a). 'May the sheep safely graze? A reflexive view of the expert–lay knowledge divide', in S. Lash, B. Szerszynski and B. Wynne (eds), *Risk, Environment and Modernity: Towards a New Ecology*. London: Sage.

Wynne, B. (1996b). 'SSK's identity parade: Signing-up, off-and-on'. *Social Studies of Science* 26: 357–91.

Wynne, B. (2010). 'Strange weather, again'. *Theory, Culture and Society* 27(2–3): 289–305.

Wynne, B. (2016). 'Misunderstood misunderstanding: Social identities and public uptake of science'. *Public Understanding of Science* 1: 281–304.

Yates, K. (2023). *How to Expect the Unexpected: The Science of Making Predictions and the Art of Knowing When Not to*. London: Quercus.

Zaloom, C. (2006). *Out of the Pits: Traders and Technology from Chicago to London*. Chicago: University of Chicago Press.

Zinn, J. (2016). '"In-between" and other reasonable ways to deal with risk and uncertainty: A review article'. *Health, Risk and Society* 18(7–8): 348–66.

Zinn, J. and Brown, P. (2022). 'COVID-19 risks: Dynamics of culture and inequality across six continents', in J. Zinn and P. Brown (eds), *Covid-19 and the Sociology of Risk and Uncertainty: Studies of Social Phenomena and Social Theory across Six Continents*. Cham: Springer International Publishing.

Zuboff, S. (2019). *The Age of Surveillance Capitalism: The Fight for a Human Future at the New Frontier of Power*. London: Profile Books.

Index